电·影

ELECTRIC SHADOWS

A Century of Chinese Cinema

Edited by
James Bell

A BFI Compendium

BFI
21 Stephen Street
London W1T 1LN

www.bfi.org.uk
First published 2014

© 2014 BFI

ISBN 978-1-84457-849-8

A CIP catalogue record for this book
is available from the British Library

Typeset in Caecilia, Fedra Sans
and Benton Sans
Designed by chrisbrawndesign.com
Printed in England by Colt Press
Image retouching by DawkinsColour

Front cover:
Gong Li in 'Farewell My Concubine' (1993)

Back cover:
Tony Leung in 'In the Mood For Love'
(2000)

Inside front cover:
Jackie Chan in 'Drunken Master' (1978)

Inside back cover:
Zhang Ziyi in 'House of Flying Daggers'
(2004)

This page:
Maggie Cheung in 'Hero' (2002)

CONTENTS

PREFACE
BY HEATHER STEWART, CREATIVE DIRECTOR, BFI

We at the BFI are thrilled to publish this introduction to the history of Chinese cinema in a year in which we celebrate Chinese film both past and present with a series of film programmes and cultural exchange events.

China is one of the great filmmaking nations, with a rich tradition of cinema that stretches back to the silent era. It's an astonishingly diverse tradition, when you consider the classic Shanghai filmmaking of the 1930s and 40s, the bold and captivating films of the 'Fifth Generation', the many thrilling *wuxia* and action films, the innovative visions of Hong Kong's Wong Kar Wai, as well as contemporary work as varied as the vital films of Jia Zhangke, the popular blockbusters of Feng Xiaogang and Jackie Chan's exhilarating martial-arts spectacles.

The BFI has presented a range of Chinese cinema for many years, but has not shone such a light on Chinese filmmaking since the 1980s, when we hosted two pioneering programmes of Chinese films. Through our partnership with Toronto's TIFF Bell Lightbox we have once again been able to bring many of the greatest films in Chinese cinema history to UK screens – and several of the titles in our season have very rarely been screened in the UK, if at all. But our celebration doesn't stop there: in addition to the film season we have a programme of education events, nationwide theatrical releases, new DVD editions and – drawn from the BFI's own National Film Archive and available to view online on the BFI Player – a fascinating collection of rare archival documentary films shot in China between 1901-49.

The glories of Chinese cinema are many, and are waiting to be explored. We hope that this book helps you to navigate them.

INTRODUCTION

BY JAMES BELL

China's history over the past century is one of extraordinary, tumultuous change and of clearly distinguishable epochs, and the same is true of its cinema. Each of the formative ruptures of recent Chinese history, from the fall of the Qing dynasty through to the Japanese occupation of 1937-45, the Cultural Revolution of the late 1960s and 70s and the booming 'state capitalism' of the new millennium, profoundly marked the cinema of their time.

The chapters that follow offer an introduction to these cinematic epochs, as well as the continuities that span them. They explore the specific cinemas of Hong Kong and Taiwan, Chinese documentary filmmaking, the unique role played by women in Chinese cinema and, of course, the singular glories of China's genre cinema, from Bruce Lee's kung fu flicks to King Hu's spectacular *wuxia* epics.

In truth, we should really speak of the *long* century of Chinese cinema, for film first came to China in 1896, when the Lumière brothers exhibited their *cinématographe* in Shanghai, and China's first film, *The Battle of Dingjunshan*, was made in 1905. Precious little Chinese cinema of the silent era survives, but the *dianying*, or 'electric shadows', gradually took hold of the Chinese imagination, flowering into the great 'Second Generation' of leftist Chinese directors in Shanghai in the 1930s. This golden age saw the emergence of key film studios, and of grand stars like Ruan Lingyu and Li Lili, whose glamour and fame rivalled that of anyone in Hollywood. It also produced a number of classic films, culminating in Fei Mu's 1948 postwar masterpiece *Spring in a Small Town*, released on the eve of the founding of the People's Republic of China in 1949.

In the 'Seventeen Years' period of 1949-66 that followed the Communist Party's victory, the film industry was nationalised and films from the Mainland – among them the stirring dramas of director Xie Jin – became increasingly subject to Communist Party strictures. Meanwhile, parallel industries developed in Hong Kong and Taiwan, with a Cantonese-language cinema and the dominance of prolific studios like Shaw Brothers. As Hong Kong cinema expanded, Mainland cinema entered the dark days of the Cultural Revolution decade of 1966-76, when the production of films was drastically limited.

The arrival of the 1980s saw a grand renaissance of Chinese-language cinema, as the Hong Kong New Wave, the New Taiwan Cinema and the 'Fifth Generation' on the Mainland all emerged, bringing with them radical ideas and exhilarating new forms, and attracting acclaim and audiences around the world.

Electric Shadows examines that renaissance and all that led to it. It also explores the vibrant independent cinema that grew through the 1990s via directors such as Jia Zhangke, and considers the popular Chinese 'multiplex' cinema of the present, when the Chinese film industry rivals Hollywood for box office and influence. The century of Chinese cinema is truly a garden of forking paths, with little-explored nooks and hidden glories sitting alongside renowned masterworks. *Electric Shadows* takes a tour through its many treasures.

Lastly, a note on the Romanisation system used throughout for original Chinese film titles and names. Names of directors and actors are given in their established form (ie, Mandarin, Cantonese or Anglo-Cantonese where appropriate), but for consistency all original Chinese-language film titles are given in their Mandarin *pinyin* form, following their English-language title.

When the Lumière brothers' *cinématographe* was shown for the first time in China on 11 August 1896 in Xu Garden, Shanghai, it was initially greeted as just one of many new mechanical devices that came and went amid the era's stage entertainment. This new European machine was but one attraction within a variety show, seen as a novelty by many Shanghai spectators, just as its American version, the Vitascope, had been for their New York counterparts during the previous theatrical season. But for many Chinese playwrights, novelists and intellectuals, the potential of the *cinématographe* as a new creative and educational medium was clear.

The formative years of Chinese cinema, which span roughly 1896-1930, are best understood as a period of negotiation between the stage and the screen, with the full potential of cinema as an independent artform only truly recognised and developed in the latter half of the 1920s. In Shanghai, this period transitioned into the 'golden age' of Chinese cinema in the 1930s, when a new generation of politically conscious filmmakers and critics began to view the cinema as a medium independent of the theatre.

The Chinese theatre was a highly organised popular entertainment in major urban centres by the end of the 19th century. In the north, the Jingju (the Peking [Beijing] opera, which had been formalised in 1790) dominated Beijing and Shanghai; while in the south, the Yueju (the Cantonese theatre, which emerged around the mid-16th century) occupied the Canton-Hong Kong region. Both traditions were made up of smaller troupes and productions, and larger, more commercialised operations. Within this system, top theatres – sponsored by wealthy patrons – would compete for the most reputed stars and spectacular troupes, and would hire their own playwrights to tailor new acts and musical numbers for their contracted players.

With the arrival of cinema at the turn of the century, such top theatres started to incorporate Lumière and Edison films into their programmes. Audiences for these screenings seem to have greeted the films primarily as visual spectacles, as opposed to stories driven by narratives. This is borne out by one of the surviving critical responses to these early films, written by a Chinese spectator:

"After the house light was dimmed, we suddenly saw a shadow. Two Western women appeared to be dancing. Their golden hair was so fluffy and silly that you couldn't help but wish to reach out and touch it. Then, we saw two Westerners wrestling. After that, two Russian princesses danced together with music accompaniment. A sight of a woman bathing herself in a bathtub then followed…. [Towards the end,] we saw the streets in America. These streets were brightly lit. Cars passed through them like a swimming dragon. Crowds of people walked around like layers of colourful flags waving on their own. As viewers, we felt like we had entered the picture itself…. Yet, once the house light was turned on again, the image immediately turned into ashes…. Isn't life, like the cinema, a transient image that appears and disappears in an unpredictable manner?"

The shadow play

The new technology of the cinema soon became known in China as *yingxi* (shadow play), a name popularly used until the early 1930s. In 1920, the Chinese film producer Gu Kenfu suggested that by naming this new technology 'shadow play' – a theatrical form that could be traced back to the 10th century – early Chinese film spectators were encouraged to consider the cinema not as a new art, but as a new mechanical device that rebooted an existing theatrical tradition.

However the connection between theatre and early Chinese cinema

resided in more than simply its name. In 1906, a group of Chinese students in Tokyo, inspired by the Japanese *shingeki* (the Japanese 'New Drama' form that developed at the end of the 19th century, and which involved Japanese retellings of realist European and American plays by playwrights such as Ibsen, Chekhov, Gorky and O'Neill) established the *Chunliushe* ('Spring Willow Society') theatre company. These students incorporated two modern technologies, *guangxue* (light) and *dianxue* (electricity) to stage their plays.

The resulting *xinju* (new theatre), was a new theatrical form that deliberately aspired to be 'cinematic', and its popularity spread back to China itself. Many early Chinese films made in the 1900s and 1910s were dramatic or comic acts taken from this new theatre; in many ways, the shadow play and the new theatre became co-dependent artforms.

It wasn't long before showmen working for Lumière brothers or Edison rented their cameras to local Chinese new theatre artists, educators and still photographers. The earliest known film made by a Chinese photographer, probably produced under such an arrangement, was a filmed Beijing opera act *The Battle of Dingjunshan* (*Dingjun Shan*, Fengtai Photo Studio, Beijing, 1905). Meanwhile, Cantonese film historians have claimed that a new theatre performance titled *The Haunted Pot* (*Wapen Shenyuan*) was filmed in Hong Kong in or before 1909.

Film companies in the early years of Chinese cinema were often foreign-owned. A crucial figure was the Russian-American Benjamin Brodsky, who travelled to East Asia in the early 1900s. In 1909, Brodsky was associated with the San Francisco-registered but Hong Kong-based film company Yaxiya (Asia), and also established the Xinmin Film Company, hiring the new theatre artists Zhang Shichuan (1890-1954) and Zheng Zhengqiu (1889-1935) in Shanghai, and Lai Man-Wai (Li Minwei, 1893-1953) and Lai Buk-Hoi (Li Beihai, 1889-1955) in Hong Kong.

Lai Man-Wai used the opportunity to produce his first new theatre play *Stealing a Roast Duck* (*Tou Shaoya*) in 1909. Around 1912 or 1913, Brodsky moved back to San Francisco, leaving Xinmin to be run by Zhang Shichuan and Zheng Zhengqiu, and the Hua-Mei (China-America) Motion Picture Co. to be run by Lai Man-Wai and Lai Buk-Hoi in Hong Kong.

In 1913, Lai Man-Wai filmed another new theatre act, *Zhuangzi Tests His Wife* (*Zhuangzi Shi Qi*), generally known as the first multi-reel fiction film made in Hong Kong. Three years later, he bought the equipment and studio facilities from Brodsky and established the Huanxian Motion Picture Company. Huanxian made probably the first multi-reel film in China, *Lost Souls on the Black [Opium] Register* (*Heiji Yuanhun*, 1916), a new theatre piece that responded to the increased opium production and consumption in rural areas following the 1911 Revolution.

Film production in Shanghai and Hong Kong could hardly be called industrial during the 1910s, but film exhibition was already well established. The number of *daxiyuan* (grand theatres) increased dramatically in Beijing, Shanghai and Hong Kong in these years. Many of these would themselves commission films to be made of the signature performances of their top-billed stars. These films would sometimes serve as previews of upcoming bills, or they might be played with musical accompaniment or gramophone recordings as *intermezzi* entertainments between other stage performances. By the early 1920s, some grand theatres had become institutions akin to Hollywood studios, with the theatre owners overseeing their stars' stage and screen programmes, gramophone recordings, press coverage and overseas tours.

Meanwhile, smaller troupes continued to perform in playhouses, gardens, teahouses and amusement parks, or in Shanghai department

stores. Like the American nickelodeons and vaudeville theatres, these smaller establishments would sometimes run film programmes between theatrical acts. Department stores set up motion picture departments where customers could purchase camera equipment and projectors, or buy short films for domestic consumption.

The 1910s: industrialisation and nationalisation

During the 1910s, the grand theatres became prestigious social institutions in which Chinese audiences could see the new narrative fiction films that had become dominant in America and Europe. Regulations in Shanghai stipulated that intertitles could not be added to European or American productions, and consequently grand theatres often published gazettes supplying the films' plots. In addition, film distributors would commission intellectuals to write reviews. Many of these intellectuals were in fact popular writers belonging to a school of melodramatic writing called the *Yuanyang Hudie Pai* (Mandarin Ducks and Butterfly School). They included such figures as Zhang Henshui (1897-1967), Bao Tianxiao (1876-1973) and Xu Zhuodai (1881-1958), all of whose work would later be adapted by Chinese filmmakers, particularly at the Mingxing (Star) Motion Picture Co.

By the mid-to-late-1910s, Shanghai and Hong Kong had become the distribution centre of American films in China, Japan and South-east Asia. Discourses on Hollywood's representation of Chinese in European and American films soon emerged in film magazines and newspapers, particularly following the exhibition of Cecil B. De Mille's *The Cheat* (1915), which starred Japanese-American actor Sessue Hayakawa. Many Shanghai critics considered the production a *ru Hua pian* (a 'film that humiliates China'). Issues about onscreen representation became a hot topic: film magazines and newspapers started to offer 'humiliation film alerts' in their columns, and in 1917 the *Shangwu Yingshuguan* (Commercial Press) in Beijing established the Motion Picture Department, which produced educational films, travelogues, newsreels, new theatre acts and period dramas with the intention of letting the audience see 'China' from a 'Chinese' perspective. In 1920, producer Gu Kenfu founded the magazine *Yingxi Zazhi* (*Motion Picture Review*), which advocated the use of film criticism to raise awareness among Shanghai spectators of Hollywood representation of Chinese characters, and also to push for the active development of domestic film production. A few years later, in 1926, film director Hou Yao (1903-42) published a screenwriting manual, *Yingxi Juben Zuofa* (*Methods of Writing a Shadow Play*), in which he urged Chinese screenwriters to master their techniques in order to better represent the reality of Chinese life.

Chinese cinema's industrial reorganisation and ideological transformation went hand-in-hand with the political turmoil during these years. Since its founding in 1912, the newly established Republic had multiple political centres. The Beijing or Beiyang government inherited the state authority handed over by the Qing imperial court, while local warlords became de facto rulers of individual regions. In 1921, the revolutionary leader Sun Yat-sen (Sun Yixian, 1866-1925) and his faction of the Guomindang (Kuomintang, KMT or the Nationalist Party) established a government in Guangzhou, with the ambition of launching a northern expedition to unify China.

Cinema was increasingly seen as a potentially powerful political tool. In 1922, Lai Man-Wai and Lai Buk-Hoi established the Minxin (China Sun) Motion Picture Company, with Sun's personal blessing, to act as the KMT's official documentarian. In 1924, the KMT established the *Zhongyang Xuanchuan Bu* (Central Ministry of Propaganda), and

(Top)
'Yan Ruisheng' (1921) was based on the real-life case of the murder of a prostitute.

(Middle)
The wuxia film 'Burning of the Red Lotus Temple' (1928) was so successful that it ran to an 18-part serial.

(Bottom)
'Love's Labours' (aka 'Labourer's Love', 1922), the earliest known surviving Chinese fiction film.

in 1925, it hired an advisor from the recently established L' Unione Cinematographica Educativa (LUCE) in Italy, which proposed plans to consolidate and nationalise the Chinese film industry after the Northern Expedition (1926-28) military campaign.

But state organisation of the cinema would only be possible once the private infrastructure was installed, and by the 1920s this started to develop in earnest, with the founding or expansion of an increasing number of Chinese-owned film companies. In 1922, Zhang Shichuan and Zheng Zhengqiu bought Brodsky's Xinmin and turned it into the Mingxing (Star) Motion Picture Co., which would become Shanghai's largest studio in the 1930s. In 1924, the Da Zhonghua (Great China) Film Company of Feng Zhen'ou and the Baihe (Lilium) Film Company of Zhu Souju and Wu Xingzai merged into the Great China Lilium Film Company. And in 1925, Shao Renje (Runje Shaw, one of the famous four Shaw brothers who would go on to dominate film production in China and then Hong Kong for decades) established the Tianyi (Unique) Film Company.

During the first half of the 1920s, most of these studios made short films and comic skits. China Sun made a Cantonese feature film called *Rouge* (*Yanzhi*, 1925); but despite its relative box-office success (it made HK$6,000), it only recovered two-thirds of its production budget. As a result, the film bankrupted China Sun's yet-to-be-formed feature department. Another early multi-reel film is *Yan Ruisheng* (1921). Based on a real criminal case, *Yan* tells the story of a college student, Yan Ruisheng, who falls in love with a Shanghai sex worker, and eventually murders her. The onscreen display of murder made the film an instant sensation. The first financially successful feature film in Shanghai was Star's *Kong Gulan* (1926), an adaptation of a Japanese translation of Henry Wood's *East Lynne* by Zhang Shichuan, based on a script by Bao Tianxiao. However the first real box-office sensation in Shanghai was Star's *Burning of the Red Lotus Temple* (*Huoshao Honglian Si*, 1928), a martial-arts gods-and-demons extravaganza based on the *wuxia* novel *Tales of Spectacular Warriors Among Rivers and Lakes* (*Jianghu Qixia Zhuan*) by author Pingjiang Buxiaosheng. The film was so successful that within one year Star turned *Burning* into a ten-part serial, and then an 18-part serial up to 1931.

Many intellectuals at the time considered such 'gods and demons' films as legacies of Chinese feudalism and superstition. However *Burning of the Red Lotus Temple* was a key film for demonstrating the potential of the new medium. Cinematographer Dong Keyi uses sophisticated techniques such as superimposition and complex double exposure to create phantasmagorical effects, and hand-drawn graphics to enhance the spectacular fight scenes.

Today, only a tiny handful of the many films made during this 1920s period are accessible. Some of these early prints were destroyed during the Japanese invasion between January and March, 1932, and the Sino-Japanese War (1937-45), while others might have been brought to Hong Kong and North America, and could still be in the hands of the progeny of the studio owners.

One of the few that has survived is Zhang Shichuan's *Love's Labours* aka *Labourer's Love* (*Lao Gong de Aiqing*, 1922), a short comic skit about a carpenter using his wit and technical talent to win the trust of his fiancée's father. Though shot entirely in a series of tableaux, *Love's Labours* shows Zhang's astute use of optical tricks such as superimposition and multiple exposure, as well as match cutting to convey subjective perspectives.

Less than an hour survives of Hou Yao's 1927 film *Romance of the Western Chamber* (*Xi Xiang Ji*, China Sun Shanghai), a lavish adaptation of a literary and theatrical classic that charts a love affair between a young scholar and a courtier's daughter, and boasts spectacular on-location scenic photography, sophisticatedly orchestrated parallel editing, hand-tinted sequences and humour.

The most popular genre during the 1920s, the gods-and-demons films, unfortunately only survives in fragments, many of which have yet to be restored. Until recently, the most complete was Wen Yimen's *Red Heroine* (*Hong Xia*, Youlian Film Company, 1929), an adaptation of a *wuxia* fiction from the Tang dynasty (618-907). The film tells the story of an orphaned heroine, Yungu, who is abducted by a bandit and then rescued by an old Taoist priest, the White Ape (*Baiyuan Laoren*).

More recently, in 2011 the National Library in Norway discovered in their archives a print of *Cave of the Silken Web* (*Pansi Dong*, 1927), an adaptation of the 16th-century novel *Journey to the West* (*Xi Youji*) that was long presumed lost. In 1921, the film's director Dan Duyu met Shanghai socialite Yin Mingzhu (Pearl Ing), who had grown up in a wealthy intellectual family, and graduated from an English school. In the film, Pearl stars as a spider-turned-seductress, who captures Buddhist monk Xuanzang as he is on his way to India in search of Buddhist scriptures. Like other gods-and-demons films, *Cave* combines eroticism and martial-arts spectacle. Even though the film is set in medieval China, Pearl Ing's presence and the film's overall eroticism constantly remind viewers of its modernity.

The end of the formative era

With the increasing fascination among Chinese filmmakers and critics with the 'cinematic', and the state's interest in turning the cinema into a tool for national education, Shanghai cinema had, by the second half of the 1920s, departed from the 'theatrical'. In 1930, Shanghai saw the emergence of Marxist film criticism on the one hand, and film phenomenology on the other. With these theoretical frameworks in mind, filmmakers began to look to the unique potentials of the cinema, as distinct from the theatre.

The year 1930 also saw the Hong Kong-born and Beijing-based theatre-chain owner Luo Mingyou (Lo Ming-yau) join forces with Lai Man-Wai in Hong Kong to establish the Lianhua Film Company (United Photoplay Service) in Shanghai, under the auspices of the KMT as part of its nationalising effort. Meanwhile, between 1927-29, Shanghai and Hong Kong film theatres had begun installing equipment for showing Hollywood sound films. In 1931, Zhang Shichuan made the musical *Sing-Song Girl Red Peony* (*Genü Hong Müdan*, Star and Pathé), starring Cantonese actress Hu Die (Butterfly Wu), the first 'sound-on-disc' film in Chinese cinema.

Meanwhile, filmmakers in Xiamen, Guangzhou and Hong Kong also made sound films, and in 1933, Runje Shaw produced the first Cantonese-theatre sound film, *White Gold Dragon* (*Bai Jinlong*), starring young Cantonese theatre artist Xue Juexian, thus renewing the bond between the theatre and cinema in the Canton-Hong Kong region.

With the end of the formative era, the shadow play also gradually became known as the *dianying* (which translates literally as 'electric shadow' or 'electric image'), a change that signalled a shift of focus from the theatrical to the photographic. The *cinématographe* might well have come and gone in the Shanghai theatrical scene in 1896 as a passing fancy, but the shadow play took root and became an integral part of the urban Chinese cultural and political imagination, helping China to negotiate a turbulent era in which colonial influences from Europe and America interacted with Shanghai and Hong Kong's home-grown mode of urban and intellectual modernity. ◑

BOXERS AND BARBERS: FILM IN THE LATE QING DYNASTY

By Edward Anderson
and Robin Baker

Shanghai's Nanjing Road, 1901. European women riding bicycles jostle for space on the busy street with Chinese passengers carried in rickshaws, palanquins and sedan chairs. A detachment of the Sikh branch of the Shanghai Municipal Police marches by closely followed by two German soldiers in Pickelhaube helmets. One soldier lights a cigarette and looks up at the camera.

It's a startling moment: the soldier's glance reaches out across more than a century and yanks us back to late Qing dynasty China. This short actuality film (*Nankin Road*, 1901), taken from a single, fixed position, resonantly captures the collision and cohabitation of nations and races in one of the world's most cosmopolitan cities at the dawn of the 20th century.

Cinema was fast to China. Just eight months after the Lumière brothers' first public demonstration in Paris, 'Western shadow plays' (*xiyang yingxi*) were exhibited before an audience at Shanghai's Xu Gardens on 11 August 1896. And yet not a single film by a native Chinese filmmaker is known to survive from China's imperial period (which ended with the foundation of the Republic in 1912).

Among the missing is Zhu Liankui's *The War of Wuhan* (*Wuhan Zhanzheng*, 1911), a reconstruction of the bloody Wuchang Uprising – catalyst of the Xinhai Revolution. Also missing is any of the footage that may have been shot by Li Hongzhang, one of China's most prominent politicians. Li was filmed being presented with a Mutoscope camera by Biograph's visiting cameraman, Fred Ackerman, in Beijing in 1900. We don't know if he ever used it.

But a remarkable, if disparate, film record of the end of China's imperial period does survive, preserved in the BFI National Archive and other film archives across Europe and America. For this we can thank the enterprising foreign filmmakers who ventured to China in search of scenes of the exotic Far East to peddle to audiences back home.

In 1900 Britain's Warwick Trading Company sent its war correspondent Joseph Rosenthal to China to capture scenes of the Boxer Rebellion, the anti-foreign, anti-Christian uprising that gripped and outraged the public imagination. But by the time Rosenthal arrived in China the rebellion was past its peak. He struggled to catch up with any front-line fighting – or any military action at all. Despite this, Warwick's 1901 film catalogue boasted "the only animated pictures taken in China since the trouble began". The tantalising footage of Nanjing Road is the miraculous sole survivor of the 38 "genuine Chinese films" – some 40 minutes in total – that Rosenthal brought home.

The appetite for images of the Boxer uprising was so ardent that newsworthy events were staged and reconstructed. James Williamson's Hove-filmed *Attack*

Modern China (aka In Quaint Pekin, 1910)

Modern China (aka In Quaint Pekin, 1910)

Nankin Road (1901)

on a China Mission (1900) and Mitchell and Kenyon's *Beheading a Chinese Boxer* (1900) – shot near Blackburn – both sought to profit from the Boxer frenzy, much to the annoyance of Warwick, which pleaded with filmgoers: "BEWARE of so-called sensational war films of the Chinese crisis… Don't be misled into the belief that they are genuine".

Even before Rosenthal, a succession of pioneering film cameramen had journeyed east to shoot and exhibit films. Among the first were representatives of two American companies. For Edison, James White and Frederick Blechynden made a series of 14 films of Hong Kong, Macau and Shanghai in 1898. The same subjects – via a detour to Guangzhou – were captured between 1897 and 1898 by James Ricalton for Underwood and Underwood. French and Spanish filmmakers joined in too: Lumière's Francis Doublier and Gabriel Veyre filmed in China in 1899, arriving at much the same time as exhibitor Antonio Ramos. Another camera-toting Brit also beat Rosenthal to China. Conservative MP Ernest F.G. Hatch shot some 20 scenes of everyday life in China (all lost) around 1899 or 1900. Back at home, the films were distributed to a public newly eager for any images of China, rebellion or no rebellion.

Probably the most potent record of the period is contained within the 40-odd minutes of surviving film shot between 1901 and 1904 by French consul and part-time photographer and filmmaker Auguste François. Known as

'the White Mandarin', François had a deeper understanding of the country than most visiting cameramen and a series of connections that gave him the kind of access that would have eluded others. He left behind a series of films showing life in and around Guangxi and Yunnan provinces that are by turns epic, shocking and intimate: from public processions to graphic animal slaughter and even the smoking of opium.

As China continued to open up to Western interests in the later 1900s, filmmakers switched their focus to making travelogues. The new audience for the *cinématograph* craved novelty, and China delivered exoticism in spades.

Given the available technology and the wariness of the ruling classes, much of what was recorded by filmmakers of the period were street scenes and attractions, with a focus necessarily on the lives of the poor and the easily accessible: open-air kitchens, beggars, funeral processions, craftsmen at work and imposing architecture. A recurring image across the films shows barbers styling the 'Manchu queue'. Until the fall of the Qing dynasty, the Manchu hairstyle – with the front of the head shaved and a long pigtail-style plait – was imposed on all Chinese men. These images now serve to illustrate the Qing domination of the Han majority. To the original cameramen, though, they were more likely just food for audiences' appetite for otherness.

Charles Urban's *Modern China,* aka *In Quaint Pekin* (1910), a vivid collage of

scenes shot in and around Beijing, is a great example of this kind of travelogue. The film's very existence is a triumph over adversity. During a 12-month tour Urban's cameraman accumulated over 7,000 feet of film. Through bad luck, incompetence or both (Urban subsequently sacked his photographer), more than 90 per cent was lost or unusable. In spite of this, the assembly of the remaining footage is remarkable. Ambitious, too: Urban's film was marketed as offering "unusual geographical, political and anthropological value". The BFI's 2014 digital restoration has reintroduced the film's brilliantly coloured tints, enhancing the magical otherworldliness of "this country strange to Western eyes".

For all their pursuit of exoticism and spectacle, these disparate records of early 20th century China offer us something truly unexpected – and not just the very fact of their survival. Shot for commercial reasons to satisfy the demands of audiences with only the sketchiest of cultural understanding, they stand as the only moving image records of a lost China.

It's a small miracle, too, that these filmmakers, who arrived in China shouldering Western suspicion and hostility, took away images of China and its people that are not just authentic but frequently sensitive and generous. These fragments of China – lost, re-discovered, broken, restored – preserve some of the life and landscape of a country that has feverously reinvented itself over the last century. ☢

The notion that Chinese film history could be written across five distinct 'generations' of filmmakers took hold only in the late 1980s. It was adapted from an academic study of the way that leftist ideologies in China have developed across generational shifts and disruptions, so we should certainly treat it with caution. But if we accept that Chinese film has gone through a succession of formative periods, the 'generation' schema provides a handy way of defining them.

The 'First Generation' were the pioneers of the 1910s and 1920s; nearly all of their work is lost, so we'll never know exactly if or how they got past their reliance on foreign models of storytelling, staging and editing, always assuming they wanted to. The 'Second Generation' were the heroes and heroines who created a distinctively Chinese cinema in the 1930s and 1940s, despite the depredations of the invading Japanese army and the near-continuous conflicts between Chiang Kaishek's nationalists and Mao Zedong's communists; the Communist Party's official history of Chinese cinema (edited by Cheng Jihua and published in 1963) offers a comprehensive but politically biased account of this generation, praising Party-liners and dissing almost everyone else.

The 'Third Generation' were the communist filmmakers who began directing after the establishment of the PRC in 1949 and tried to create a 'model' communist cinema; some of them were sent to Moscow for training. There were rumbling tensions throughout the 1950s and early 1960s between these hard-line Stalinist-Maoists and the 'old-school' leftists who came from or were formed by Shanghai's less doctrinaire pre-PRC film industry. The 'Fourth Generation' were the unfortunates who graduated from the Beijing Film Academy in the early 1960s but then had their careers derailed by the Cultural Revolution; a few of them managed to make interesting films in the late 1970s and 1980s, but they were all swept aside in the film industry's subsequent transition from the state sector to the private sector.

The 'Fifth Generation' were, of course, the group who graduated from the Film Academy in 1982, the first since the school's re-opening after the Cultural Revolution; many of them had been rebellious Red Guards between 1966-68, and the way the Party had brought them back under control galvanised the films they made in the mid-1980s. The protest-occupation of Tiananmen Square in the spring of 1989 and the Party's use of military force to end it similarly marked the next generation of young people, but those of them who went on to make films uniformly reject the 'Sixth Generation' label, no doubt largely because it's so deeply rooted in a communist way of thinking.

Leaving the question of ideological taints to one side, it's the 'Second Generation' which stands out as the group of highest achievers. Of course the Shanghai film industry was built from the 1920s onwards on the efforts of entrepreneurs and would-be moguls, some of them hand-in-glove with Chiang Kaishek's push to unify the country under his nationalist KMT government. But the lasting qualities of the best Chinese films of the 1930s and 1940s are down to the talent, energy, imagination and ingenuity of the people who actually made the films, many of them younger and more inventive than their 'Fifth Generation' successors. We'll use the corporate structure of the industry to frame this short essay, but when the full story of Chinese cinema's 'Golden Era' is told it will need to pay heavy dues to the many individual artists who created a modern and distinctive national cinema. Nearly all of them met miserable ends in the first two decades of the PRC – either running headlong into Party dogmatism or driven to suicide (or persecuted to

The Goddess

Wu Yonggang, 1934

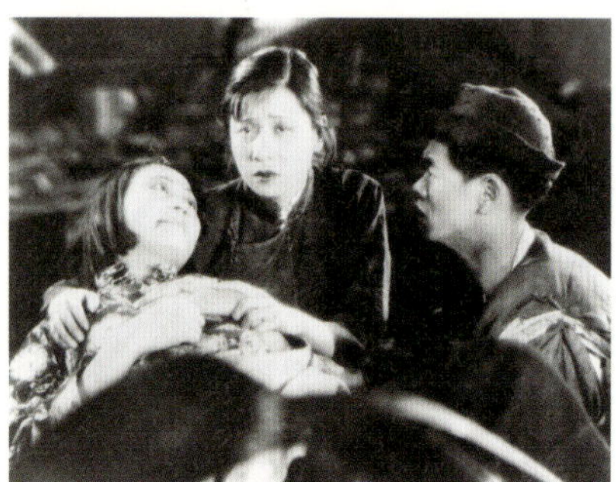

Chinese film history was more or less unknown in the Hong Kong of my childhood. I grew up watching Hong Kong films, and some from Taiwan, but almost nothing from China. So when I had the chance to look at some Shanghai classics in the early 1980s, it was a bit of a bombshell. The film that really hit me was *The Goddess* (*Shennü*), starring the Cantonese actress Lily Yuen (aka Ruan Lingyu, pictured above in *Little Toys*, 1933). I was just stunned by her performance, which was subtle but at the same time powerful and rich – an emotional *tour de force*. It was amazing to me that such a thing could be achieved in silent cinema. It was seeing *The Goddess* that inspired me to make *Centre Stage* (below) the film in which I tried to use the history of Shanghai filmmaking in the 1930s to pay tribute to the 'Golden Age' of Chinese cinema – and to pay tribute to one great artist who was gone too soon.

death) in the 'anti-rightist purge' of 1957 or the Cultural Revolution. Some paid the highest price simply for having known Mao Zedong's last wife, Jiang Qing, during her time as the movie actress 'Lan Ping' in the 1930s.

Before we turn to the outputs of the various production companies, we need to establish a few basic points about the city of Shanghai and the young filmmakers who flocked to it. The city was by far the most modern and sophisticated urban development in China, most of it comprising the 'International Settlement' established in the 1860s and administered by five foreign powers. Shanghai was home to countless expats (traders, diplomats, refugees from Soviet Russia and Nazi Germany, etc) as well as the vast Chinese population, but the majority of the Chinese were crammed into the roughly 20 square miles of the 'Chinese city', much of it the sprawling labyrinth of alleyways and tenement slums seen in movies like Yuan Muzhi's *Street Angel* (*Malu Tianshi*, 1937). Cinemas in the International Settlement played the latest Hollywood movies – and occasionally European hits too – but not the Chinese movies produced by Shanghai companies. These were seen in local cinemas, in China's relatively few other cinemas (no accurate data is available, but it's estimated that there were not many more than 100 screens for Chinese movies, most of them in the 'Treaty Ports' of the East Coast) and, from the late 1920s onwards, in South-east Asian countries with substantial Chinese communities.

The individuals who wrote and directed films for the Shanghai companies were a motley crew: a few were foreign-educated, some came from backgrounds in theatre or music, and others were 'movie brats' in the Western sense, drawn to the medium by their love of watching films. What they all had in common was their formation in the 'May Fourth Movement', sparked by a 1919 demonstration in Beijing against the terms of the Treaty of Versailles, which had ceded German colonial territory in Shandong Province to Japan rather than returning it to China. The May Fourth Movement turned into a huge and often contradictory campaign, arguing from a position of national pride for a strong and independent China capable of standing up for itself, but also stressing the need for Chinese culture to modernise by studying and implementing ideas from abroad. Virtually all educated young Chinese of the 1920s were in some sense products of the Movement, and the major Shanghai films of the 1930s embody its aspirations (and contradictions) with remarkable precision.

Two brief notes before we proceed. The vast bulk of 'Second Generation' cinema is believed lost; scripts and stills survive for some titles. The following notes deal mostly with films that can still be seen. And, for more on the city of Shanghai in the 1920s and 1930s, for gossip about its Babylonian decadence (including some from Auden and Isherwood) and for sketches of the careers of director-actor Yuan Muzhi and 'the Chinese Garbo' Lily Yuen (Ruan Lingyu), please see my essay 'Labyrinth of chances' in the July 2001 issue of *Sight & Sound*.

The Star Film Company (Mingxing Yingpian Gongsi)

Our sketches of some leading Shanghai film companies must start here. Star was the oldest and largest film company in the city, founded in 1922 by producer-director Zhang Shichuan (1889-1953), who had begun writing scripts for Chinese movies ten years earlier. It remained active until the Chinese part of Shanghai fell to the Japanese in 1937, weathering several financial crises along the way; Zhang himself was the company's most prolific director, but Star hired most of the industry's top talents at one time or another. In its 15-year lifespan, Star produced around 200 fiction features (three inaugural productions were shorts) and a large number of newsreels.

The Japanese first shelled Shanghai in January 1932, causing casualties and incidentally reducing nearly half of the city's 39 cinemas to rubble. The Japanese army's brief invasion of the city (troops withdrew on 6 May) had a useful side-effect on the film industry by activating – or reinforcing – its sense of the need for patriotic resistance. Film companies responded to the loss of their cinemas by stepping up production and hiring new personnel. Some of the new writers who came into the industry were secretly members of the Communist Party, and their routine reports to Party cells inspired the Party plan to infiltrate the film industry in a more systematic way. Star was a prime target for infiltration because of its size and stature, but it already had a left-leaning intellectual on its books in the person of the writer-educator Hong Shen (1894-1955), who had an MA from Harvard. Hong's connections with the Pathé Gramophone Company had made possible Star's production of China's first sound-on-disc talkie *Sing-Song Girl Red Peony* (*Genü Hong Müdan*, directed by Zhang Shichuan and Cheng Bugao, 1931).

A substantial part of Star's fortunes had been built on Zhang Shichuan's *Burning of the Red Lotus Temple* series (*Huoshao Honglian Si*), a martial arts/special effects extravaganza which ran to 18 feature-length episodes between 1928 and 1931; the city's smaller companies rushed to produce imitations, and the *wuxia* genre was briefly as dominant as it became again in Hong Kong in the late 1960s and early 1970s. Ironically, it seems to have been the *wuxia* movies (rather than any Hays-Code-type moral concerns) which prompted the KMT government to rein in the industry. Production of *wuxia* films was banned in 1931, for fear that they would stimulate social and political unrest, along with any

film which directly criticised or attacked the government. Explicit attacks on Japanese militarist incursions were similarly prohibited for running counter to Chiang Kaishek's initial policy of appeasement.

Around the same time, the authorities began pressuring company bosses to include pro-KMT propaganda in their films. The best example of this interference is Star's portmanteau epic *A Bible for Girls* (*Nü'er Jing*, 1934), which opens with the caption: "This film employs the talents of 56 actors and of nine directors, each responsible for one episode. It is a great achievement for contemporary Chinese cinema." The film shows a reunion of former high-school classmates, each of whom tells the story of what has befallen her since they last met; the improbably wide range of class backgrounds yields several tales of suffering and near-destitution. Despite the involvement of numerous underground communists and sympathisers – the directors included Xu Xinfu, Cheng Bugao and Shen Xiling, and the writing team included Hong Shen, A Ying and the leader of the Party's covert operations in the industry, Xia Yan – Zhang Shichuan caved in to government demands that the film should be given a pro-KMT spin. And so the climactic story (told by the hostess Hu Ying, played by top star Butterfly Wu) ends with its 'revolutionary' protagonist joining the KMT; in a wrap-up, all the women watch a lantern parade for the 'New Life Movement,' a Confucian-Christian campaign launched by the KMT to counter the growing influence of communism. The film was none the less considered subversive enough for Xia Yan to be fired from Star.

We don't have the time or space to enumerate all the highlights of Star's output, which include Cheng Bugao's extraordinary social-realist *Spring Silkworms* (*Chun Can*, 1933), adapted from Mao Dun's story, and Shen Xiling's brilliant social comedy *Crossroads* (*Shizi Jietou*, 1937), the film which Tsui Hark sort-of remade as *Shanghai Blues* (*Shanghai zhi Ye*, 1984). So let's just note that Star became the last refuge before the Japanese occupation of the Chinese city for several key covert communists. The team responsible for the seminal *Plunder of Peach and Plum* (*Tao Li Jie*, 1934, made at the small leftist company Denton) – that is, director Ying Yunwei and star Yuan Muzhi – regrouped at Star to make the masterly *Unchanged Heart in Life and Death* (*Sheng Si Tong Xin*, 1936), a 'revolutionary' entertainment with a great debt to *The Prisoner of Zenda*. And Yuan Muzhi went on to write and direct (but not star in) the classic *Street Angel*, released shortly before Shanghai fell.

The United Photoplay Service (Lianhua Yingye Gongsi)

If Star was Shanghai's MGM, then the United Photoplay Service – abbreviated to 'UPS' on the fuselage of an animated airplane in the opening credits of some early productions – was its Warner Brothers. The company was founded in 1930 through a string of mergers by theatre-owner Luo Mingyou, who was close to the KMT and had strong right-wing convictions. So it was obviously embarrassing for Luo that the first directors he hired swung sharply to the left soon after joining the company: Sun Yu, Shi Dongshan and Richard Poh (Bu Wancang) had all made sentimental melodramas and/or *wuxia* movies before coming to UPS, but they were happy to work with underground communists like script-writers Xia Yan and Tian Han after the Japanese raids of 1932. From 1934 UPS's 'second studio' became a base for covert leftist operations, controlled and protected by Wu Xingcai, one of Luo's main financiers. As Jay Leyda noted in his pioneering English-language account of Chinese film history (*Dianying – Electric Shadows*, published in 1972), the company paradoxically ended up producing both the most right-wing *and* the most left-wing films in China.

UPS rarely aspired to the glitz of Star productions, even in a relatively

(Top)
*China's Dietrich, Li Lili (centre),
in the climactic scene of
Sun Yu's 'Daybreak' (1933).*

(Middle)
Sun Yu's 'The Highway' (1934).

(Bottom)
*Zheng Junli (right) with Ruan
Lingyu (left) in Ruan's penultimate
film, 'New Women' (1934).*

lavish dynastic melodrama like *Filial Piety* (*Tianlun*, 1935, directed by Fei Mu under Luo Mingyou's supervision), which survives in two shortened versions as *Song of China*, shown in Britain and the US in support of the anti-Japanese war effort. UPS films did tend to resemble Warner Brothers movies in their grittiness and social engagement, but their more immediate debts were to Paramount and Fox.

The American-educated Sun Yu had already worked with the conspicuously unsubmissive woman star Wang Renmei when he began a series of movies with the young Li Lili, modelled on the von Sternberg films with Dietrich at Paramount and clearly intent on turning Ms Li into China's answer to Marlene. There was only one overt filch from Sternberg – the climax of *Daybreak* (*Tianming*, 1933) is lifted wholesale from the final reel of *Dishonored* (1931) – but the overall aim of the series was to showcase Li Lili in a range of archetypal female roles, usually with a patriotic, anti-Japanese edge. The series included *Little Toys* (*Xiao Wanyi*, 1933), which also stars the 23-year-old Lily Yuen – better known nowadays as Ruan Lingyu – as Li Lili's mother (!) and ends with a classic May Fourth Movement denunciation of Japanese aggression and the ruinous effect of cheap imports on the Chinese economy, and *The Highway* (*Da Lu*, 1934), in which the construction of the titular road becomes symbolic of China's need for improved national defences. The famous scene in *The Highway* in which Li Lili as waitress Moli brazenly dares a gang of naked, bathing road-workers to come out of the water and show themselves was evidently inspired by a scene in Frank Borzage's *The River* (1927), with Mary Duncan brooding on the bank and Charles Farrell swimming naked nearby. Borzage's late silents at Fox were probably the most influential of all Hollywood imports on the romantic young leftists of the 'Second Generation'.

Between joining UPS in 1930 and her suicide in 1935, Ruan Lingyu not only established herself as one of the screen's greatest actresses – somewhere between the ageless modernity of Louise Brooks and the interiority of Garbo – but also became an icon of Chinese female emancipation. All of her surviving work was done at UPS, and it adds up to a surprisingly cohesive picture of the options and pitfalls facing women in republican China. The earliest survivors are three silent melodramas, all made in 1931 and all directed by Richard Poh, which come from the 'right-wing' side of UPS: in the very ambitious, 152-minute *Love and Duty* (*Lian'ai yu Yiwu*), for example, she plays a wife who leaves her middle-class husband and children for her impoverished graduate lover – and pays a high price for her rebellion against the social order.

Three years later she starred in the 26-year-old Wu Yonggang's debut feature *The Goddess* (*Shennü*, 1934) as a woman who prostitutes herself to support her young son, evidently the first film anywhere not to equate prostitution with moral degradation and a film that would definitely have had global impact if it had been seen outside China at the time. (Wu, incidentally, is credited as writer, director *and* art director; none of his later films achieves the perfection of this debut, but several are excellent by any measure.) The two films that Ruan made with Fei Mu in 1934 are both considered lost, leaving the triumphs of *Little Toys* and *The Goddess* as her best surviving work – although they're rivalled by her penultimate film, Cai Chusheng's overtly feminist *New Women* (*Xin Nüxing*, 1934), in which she plays an artist defeated by sexism and social constraints. This Party-guided film makes exceptionally vivid use of Shanghai locations. Sadly her swansong came from the reactionary side of UPS: Luo Mingyou's *Soul of the Nation* (*Guo Feng*, 1935, co-directed by Zhu Shilin), turns the story of two contrasted sisters in

Shanghai – Li Lili plays the younger one – into an extended promo for the KMT. The film opens with a caption dedicating it to her memory.

United Photoplay Service, too, closed down in 1937. It began and ended its final year of operation with terrific portmanteau films. The first release of the year was *UPS Symphony* (*Lianhua Jiaoxiangqu*, 1937), with eight episodes, containing first-rate work from Fei Mu, Shen Fu and Sun Yu. And the last was the three-parter *Vistas of Art* (*Yihai Fengguang*, 1937), in which Zhu Shilin's opening episode *Film City* (*Dianying Cheng*) offers fascinating 'backstage' glimpses of the UPS studio. In its eight years of activity, the company had produced 85 features. Some of its key leftist personnel regrouped in Shanghai after the war to relaunch the company as The Peak Film Industries Corporation.

Unique Film Company (Tianyi Yingpian Gongsi)

Not one film from Unique is known to survive, but there are two reasons for noting the company's existence here. First, it inaugurated the Shao family's involvement in production, distribution and exhibition. The family westernised its name to 'Shaw' and became known internationally when the youngest of four brothers, Run Run Shaw (Shao Renleng, later changed to Shao Yifu), founded Shaw Brothers in Hong Kong in 1958. Unique was launched in 1923 when the eldest brother Shao Renje (Runje Shaw) took over a bankrupted theatre in Shanghai (some say he got it in settlement of a gambling debt) and converted it to show films. He began producing films himself a couple of years later.

Second, Unique's rapid rise and aggressively populist output alarmed Star and other companies like China Sun (Minxin Yingpian Gongsi) sufficiently to prompt Zhang Shichuan to convene a cartel of six companies to fight the upstart. In 1928 the cartel threatened to withhold its productions from theatres which screened Unique productions. Unique carried on regardless; it responded by expanding its own theatre-chain and by starting to explore the possibility of exporting its films to South-east Asian countries with large émigré Chinese populations. This laid the foundations for the post-war Shaw regional 'empire,' forced other Shanghai companies to scramble to catch up, and prompted ethnic Chinese in Manila, Kuala Lumpur, Bangkok and Jakarta to start film companies of their own.

Unique made films in many genres but specialised in versions of 'mythological' tales such as *Madame White-Snake* and *Journey to the West* (aka *Monkey*). Between 1925 and its shut-down in 1937, the company made over 100 features.

Denton (Diantong Gongsi Zhipianchang)

Denton was founded in 1934 by three men: sound technician Situ Huimin (a Cantonese who had studied art in Japan), his American cousin Situ Yimin (a Harvard graduate in wireless technology) and their friend Ma Dejian (a tech graduate from Washington University). Its *raison d'être* was to supply new sound-recording technology to other film companies to help them make sound-on-film talkies – which provided a useful front for its production of uncompromisingly left-wing movies. Denton made only four films before the KMT forced the company to close at the end of 1935; the three that are fairly readily viewable today are all excellent, and one is arguably one of the greatest Chinese films ever.

The first Denton production was China's first sound-on-film talkie: *Plunder of Peach and Plum* (*Tao Li Jie*, 1934), directed by the 30-year-old Ying Yunwei (a former female impersonator in leftist stage operas) and starring its writer, the debuting 25-year-old Yuan Muzhi, alongside his wife-to-be

(*Above*)
An advertisement produced to promote the release of Yuan Muzhi's masterly 'Scenes of City Life' (1935).

Chen Bo'er. The film mounts a lacerating critique of Chinese society across the story of a promising graduate who is eventually forced into destitution and crime because he has challenged corruption and injustice. The company's follow-up, *Children of Troubled Times* (*Fengyun Ernü*, 1935, directed by Xu Xinfu from a script by Tian Han and Xia Yan) centres on northern Chinese driven out of Manchuria by the Japanese; it's the least politically evasive of all anti-Japanese films of the period. It's notable for containing the song by Nie Er which was later adopted as China's national anthem. The third production was *Statue of Liberty* (*Ziyou Shen*, 1935, directed by Situ Huimin from a Xia Yan script), which reputedly survives – Jay Leyda says he saw it – but hasn't been let out recently by the Beijing Film Archive.

The last Denton film was an unequivocal masterpiece: Yuan Muzhi's first film as writer *and* director *Scenes of City Life* (*Dushi Fengguang*, 1935). As overexcited provincials clamour at a railway station for tickets to Shanghai, a peepshow showman (played by Yuan himself in a way that suggests he had seen Brecht's *The Threepenny Opera*) reveals what they can expect to find in the big city in a series of comic/dramatic/musical vignettes. Yuan even brought in China's pioneering animators the Wan brothers to contribute a parody of Disney cartoons. The level of visual and aural invention throughout is off the scale.

The KMT took action against 'leftist subversion' in 1935, and Denton was one of a dozen or so small companies forced to close. Some leftist filmmakers were arrested; others dispersed to major companies like Star and UPS.

1938-1945: 'Orphan Island', inland and occupied Shanghai

Between the fall of Shanghai's Chinese city in 1937 and the bombing of Pearl Harbor in 1941, the International Settlement became a haven of tenuous security, analogous to West Berlin in the days of East Germany. It was known as the 'Orphan Island', and various filmmakers who had chosen not to flee inland stayed there to make entertainments. A handful of surviving films suggest the dominant flavours of the period. For Hwa Cheng Studio, Richard Poh made *Mulan Joins the Army* (*Mulan Cong Jun*, 1939, written by the great Ouyang Yuqian), a spirited musical version of the old story of a tomboy daughter who replaces her wounded father in battle; its depiction of patriotic Chinese fighting off barbarian invaders made it popular wherever Chinese films could be shown. A much less frisky version of the patriotic imperative was offered in Fei Mu's *Confucius* (*Kongfuzi*, 1940) for Ming Hwa Motion Picture company, a daringly stylised account of its hero's failure to impose his vision of morality and social ethics on a nation constantly at war. Fei Mu may well have intended the film as a rebuke to the first self-styled 'super-production' of 'Orphan Island' cinema, Fang Peilin's *Empress Wu* (*Wu Zetian*, 1939), made for United China (Xinhua Zhipianchang), which set the imperial-soap-opera pattern for many later movies and TV serials.

The most off-the-wall 'Orphan Island' productions were the films made by James Whale fan Ma-Xu Weibang, who had acted and directed at UPS in the mid-1930s before making the ineffably turgid *Song at Midnight* (*Yeban Gesheng*, 1937) for the previous incarnation of United China (Xinhua Yingye Gongsi). That was a laborious remake of *Phantom of the Opera* with a vaguely leftist spin, much helped by Jin Shan's performance in the lead. For the producers of *Empress Wu*, Ma-Xu delivered *Song at Midnight 2* (*Yeban Gesheng Xuji*, 1941) and this time hit his stride with a very raunchy conflation of *Frankenstein* and *The Island of Doctor Moreau* starring director-to-be Liu Qiong. This is one of the most startling Chinese films ever made, with the phantom morphing into Frankenstein's monster and seeking

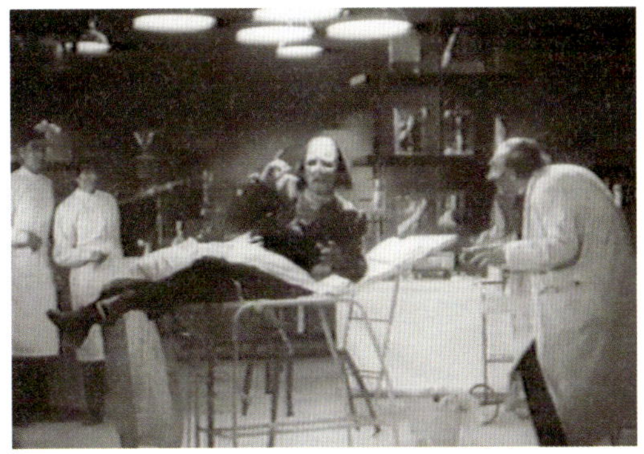

remedial surgery from a mad doctor who has nude women posing as statues in his quarters but keeps a female mannequin in his bed.

Meanwhile much of the old Shanghai film industry had uprooted and moved up-river along the Yangtze, first to Wuhan and Hankou, then to Chongqing. Compounding the constant threat of Japanese shelling, the KMT tried to organise film production in these temporary bases, imposing its lumbering bureaucracy on predominantly leftist filmmakers who were fired up to help the resistance. Little is now viewable from this chaotic period, but an incomplete copy of a short from the four-film series *Popular Chinese War Songs* (*Kangzhan Geji*, 1938) is preserved in the National Film Archive – it contains a wonderful animated sequence from the Wan brothers, who later returned to 'Orphan Island' Shanghai to finish their feature *Princess Iron-Fan* (*Tieshan Gongzhu*, 1940) – and Ying Yunwei's magnificent *800 Heroes* (*Babai Zhuangshi*, 1938), which stars Yuan Muzhi as a KMT army officer sacrificing himself and his men to defend a warehouse in the Shanghai docks, has been rescued by the Hong Kong Film Archive.

Some directors went further afield to make contributions to the war effort. Cai Chusheng decamped to Hong Kong to make, among other things, the ludicrous spy melodrama *Orphan Island Paradise* (*Gudao Tiantang*, 1939, starring Li Lili). Ying Yunwei went north from Chongqing to Inner Mongolia to shoot the rousing *Storm on the Border* (*Sai Shang Fengyun*, 1940), in effect the first Chinese western. Yuan Muzhi and a few others made their way to the Communist Party base in Yan'an and shot documentary footage there, using a camera donated by Joris Ivens.

As readers of J.G. Ballard and viewers of Spielberg know, the Japanese seized control of Shanghai's International Settlement immediately after the bombing of Pearl Harbor. What's less well known is that filmmaking continued in Shanghai under Japanese supervision. (Cheng Jihua omits this entire period from his official history, "on principle".) The Japanese army persuaded the boss of Towa (a Tokyo-based distributor of European art films), Kawakita Nagamasa, to move to Shanghai and run the industry. As he explains in his brief memoir *My Recollections* (first published in the newspaper *Nippon Keizai Shinbun* in 1980; an English translation was published by the Kawakita Memorial Film Institute in 1988), Kawakita was an enlightened and covertly anti-militarist boss. He worked with Zhang Shankun, the head of United China, to make notionally apolitical entertainments. The only accessible production from the period is Ma-Xu Weibang's bizarre *Autumn Begonia* (*Qiu Haitang*, 1943), with Lü Yukun as a female impersonator in Peking Opera who gives his virginity to a lustful warlord to protect an innocent girl. The latter is played by Li Lihua, later a big star in Hong Kong movies by such directors as Li Hanxiang and King Hu. It must be said that this mournful film was unlikely to have boosted anyone's morale in 1943.

The post-war revival: The Peak Film Industries Corp (Kunlun Yingye Gongsi), Wenhua Yingye Gongsi, et al

The first area of China liberated from the Japanese was Manchuria in the north-east, and the first communist-produced films were made there in 1949. Their harbinger was the excellent *Along the Sungari River* (*Songhuajiang Shang*, 1947), written and directed by Jin Shan for Changchun Film Productions. The film summarises Japan's occupation of the region, from 1931 to the successful fight-back in 1945, across the story of one young couple. Jin, a theatre activist who had starred in the original *Song at Midnight*, went on to have a particularly difficult relationship with the Party's Film Bureau in the 1950s, in part because

his debut feature proposed a Dovzhenko-like aesthetic for China's new cinema and not the Stalinist model favoured by the bureaucrats.

Back in Shanghai, the KMT's Zhongdian Film Company was struggling to reactivate a film industry while its masters waged civil war on Mao's communists elsewhere in China. As usual, KMT bureaucracy and censorship got in the way of most production; ironically, most of the films that did get made were created by covert communists like Chen Liting and Zhang Junxiang (then using the pseudonym Yang Jun).

Several people associated with the pre-war United Photoplay Service (UPS) found their way back to Shanghai in 1946, including its former head Luo Mingyou and his estranged financier Wu Xingcai, and attempts were made to refloat the old company. Luo's own attempt failed, despite being supported by his friends in the KMT, but two others succeeded. The screenwriter Yang Hansheng and directors Cai Chusheng and Shi Dongshan set up a new company, initially under the UPS (Lianhua) banner, soon named The Peak Film Industries Corporation (Kunlun Yingye Gongsi); the studiously apolitical name was taken from the name of one of China's 'sacred' mountains. The new company began its inaugural production in September 1946. This was *Eight Thousand Li under the Cloud and Moon* (*Baqian Li Lu Yun he Yue*, 1947, co-directed by Shi Dongshan and Wang Weiyi), which chronicles the wartime experiences of two students in a touring theatre group putting on anti-Japanese performances and then their post-war experiences as a married couple in Shanghai, brought down by social corruption and their own poverty. The film, which made big stars of its leads Tao Jin and Bai Yang, echoed the best films of the 1930s in setting a Borzage-like romantic tragedy at the heart of a near-documentary exposition.

The Peak's second production was even more ambitious. *Spring River Flows East* (*Yijiang Chunshui Xiang Dong Liu*, 1947) was made and released in two feature-length parts. It, too, starred Tao Jin and Bai Yang and was written and directed by Cai Chusheng and former actor Zheng Junli. (Tao Jin told me in 1979 that Cai had been too scared of the KMT censors to come on set most of the time; he said the film was effectively directed by Zheng … and added that it was only the bribes paid by producer Xia Yunhu to KMT officials which made the film possible at all.) An idealistic young couple in Shanghai are separated by the war in 1937; he goes inland as a volunteer, is imprisoned by the Japanese, escapes to Chongqing – and becomes a dissolute, alcoholic, bigamous wreck. Meanwhile his wife and parents suffer endless tribulations back in Shanghai.

The company went on to make 13 more features, five more before Shanghai was taken by the communist army, two during the transition to communist rule and six in the early years of the PRC. None is without interest, but the two stand-outs have to be *The Winter of Three-Hairs* (*Sanmao Liulang Ji*, 1949, co-directed by Zhao Ming and Yan Gong), a stylised, live-action adaptation of Zhang Leping's celebrated comic-strips about a resourceful urchin, and Zheng Junli's brilliant *Crows and Sparrows* (*Wuya yu Maque*, 1949), in which the downtrodden tenants of a Shanghai boarding house eventually muster the courage to stand up to their KMT landlord and his wife, who are on the verge of absconding to Taiwan. This has the best ensemble acting in any Chinese film, thanks to very clever plotting and very witty dialogue. The company suffered a major setback when Sun Yu's two-part film about a Qing Dynasty philanthropist *The Story of Wu Xun* (*Wu Xun Chuan*, 1950) was attacked for political mistakes in the Party press (it was later revealed that the critic was Mao himself). The company made its last two films in 1953, one directed by Shen Fu, the other by the actor Zhao Dan, and was then absorbed into the state-run Shanghai Film Studio.

The leftist financier Wu Xingcai, who had run UPS's 'second studio' as a pro-communist base in the mid-1930s, went his own way and founded the Wenhua Film Company in 1946. He worked mainly with talents from literature and the theatre. China's foremost modern playwright Cao Yu directed his only film for the company: *Bright Day* (aka *Mr Yin Says No, Yanyang Tian*, 1948), starring Shi Hui as a lawyer who operates as a kind of Robin Hood of the Shanghai slums. Shi, a candidate for any pantheon of great screen actors, appeared in many Wenhua films, often playing characters much older than he was, and turned director too in 1949; the four films he made for the company included the classic *This Whole Life of Mine* (*Wo zhe Yibeizi*, 1950, from a story by Lao She), which charts the successive defeats and disappointments of a policeman in Beijing from the late Qing Dynasty to the eve of the communist victory. The Cambridge-educated theatre director Huang Zuolin (usually credited as 'Zuo Lin') set the pattern for much of Wenhua's output with the first two films he made for the company: *Phoney Phoenixes* (*Jia Feng Xu Huang*, 1947) was a comedy about class snobbery in the vein of Preston Sturges, and *Night Stall* (*Ye Dian*, 1947) transposed Gorky's *Lower Depths* to contemporary Shanghai. His best remembered film is probably *The Watch* (*Biao*, 1949), a leftist fable about an apparently incorrigible delinquent based on a story by Longin Panteleyev which Lu Xun had translated into Chinese.

Like The Peak, Wenhua continued producing films after the communist victory, alongside the state-run Shanghai Film Studio which opened in

1950. And, again like The Peak, it ran into political trouble with some of its films, notably Shi Hui's *Company Commander Guan* (*Guan Lianchang*, 1951). Before it was assimilated by Shanghai Film Studio in 1953 it made a total of 21 features, including such deliciously eccentric oddities as *A Window on America* (*Meiguo zhi Chuang*, 1952, directed by Zuo Lin, Shi Hui and Ye Ming), with class-conflict played out inside an expressionist New York skyscraper, and Chen Xihe's astonishing *Stand Up Sisters* (*Jiejie Meimei Zhanqilai*, 1951), on the state campaign to rehabilitate former prostitutes.

But the film which secures Wenhua's place in world film history was a 'quickie', hastily devised and knocked off to fill a gap in the company's release schedule. Fei Mu's magisterial *Spring in a Small Town* (*Xiao Cheng zhi Chun*, 1948) contains a striking innovation in film grammar – dissolves within scenes – but it's more notable for capturing the mood of post-war anomie better than any other film. A peerless cast – Shi Yu as the impotent husband, newcomer Li Wei as the visitor and especially Wei Wei as the wife torn between them – finds every nuance in writer Li Tianqing's literate dialogue, and Fei Mu crafts an exquisite piece of chamber cinema. Jia Zhangke devotes nearly ten minutes of his essential documentary *I Wish I Knew* (*Hai Shang Chuanqi*, 2010) to *Spring in a Small Town*, including interviews with Wei Wei and Fei Mu's daughter Barbara Fei. The latter speaks for the first time about her father's tribulations with the Communist Party, throwing more light on the 'Second Generation' in a few minutes than I've been able to in this whole essay. ◔

When the People's Republic of China was founded in 1949, the ruling Communist Party, led by Chairman Mao Zedong, set forth on a mission to create a new nation, liberated from Western and Japanese imperialism as well as Chinese feudal tradition. The People's Republic would assert China's independence, not just politically and economically but culturally. The founding of a national cinema, one boldly and uniquely Chinese, was crucial to this mission.

From the beginning, Party leaders understood the power of films to captivate the masses and sway them to adopt their ambitious social programs. The challenge was to devise a cinema that would convey these messages effectively across the nation. By 1949, only a tiny fraction of Chinese had even seen a film, as theatres were mostly in the big cities. Cinema had existed in China since the start of the century, especially in the cosmopolitan city of Shanghai, but the new regime rejected almost all pre-existing films as bourgeois.

A new mandate, conceived in the Communist cultural stronghold of Yan'an, envisioned a revolutionary people's cinema with an infrastructure to match. No longer would films play only in theatres for urban audiences; mobile projection units would bring films to far-flung villages. Films would now be made for everyone, and they had to be simple in concept and straightforward in execution to appeal to as many people as possible. Premier Zhou Enlai stated the terms plainly: "Our films must have a beginning and an ending; plots must be clear; patterns should not be as fast as foreign films. Because we are people from a semi-agricultural society, we can't catch up if it is too fast."

As noted by film scholar Chris Berry, to develop this new medium for the masses, Yan'an's cultural architects looked to one of China's most revered artistic traditions, the opera. Chinese opera, with its clear character types, iconic expressions and overpowering music, provided a blueprint for a people's cinema, one where the camera, like an opera performer, moves through the moment until it freezes in a powerful, monumental gesture. One of the first PRC productions was a dramatic adaptation of a Yan'an opera, *The White-Haired Girl* (*Baimao Nü*, 1950) by Shui Hua and Wang Bin; its strong delineations of heroes, villains and righteous struggle helped establish the new national model for storytelling and character portrayal. Filmmakers also embraced the Soviet model of socialist-realist cinema. These films conveyed positive portrayals of the working masses, promoting collectivism and mass mobilisation, with less emphasis on the individual, the psychological, and the emotional – traits common to Hollywood films that the Party considered decadent.

Wang Bin's *Bridge* (*Qiao*, 1949), the first Communist feature film made in the People's Republic, establishes many of these elements. Nearly 10 minutes pass before a single character is addressed by name – mostly they call each other "comrade". It feels like a bold new vision of collectivist cinema, but eventually it settles into a traditional character-driven narrative about the construction of a strategically vital bridge during the war against the Nationalist army. The film introduces character types that would become mainstays of PRC cinema for years to come. On the one hand, there's the smug, Westernised bourgeois; here he's an engineer who doubts that the bridge can be completed with existing resources. He's matched against a heroic labourer who combines his ground-level expertise and proletarian charisma to rally his comrades to the cause. The ending is a foregone conclusion; the only suspense is in whether the bourgeois engineer joins the struggle. In this case, he is successfully reformed; in subsequent films, his kind usually wasn't so lucky.

舞台姐妹
编剧 谷白林徐
导演 谢进晋谢
摄影 周达明陈祥
主演 谢芳曹银娣
TWO STAGE SISTERS

(Above)
The poster for Wang Bin's 'Bridge' (1949), the first feature film made in the new People's Republic.

(Previous page)
The poster for Xie Jin's epic saga 'Two Stage Sisters' (1965) – perhaps the apotheosis of Chinese Communist cinema.

Bridge is a cornerstone for the filmmaking that prevailed through the 1950s: simple, clear exaltations of workers, peasants, and soldiers. But there was also an undercurrent of films influenced by the May Fourth Movement, a school of leftist critique that predated the Communist revolution. Typically generated by a creative class of Shanghai artists and intellectuals who considered themselves carriers of the May Fourth literary tradition, these films were less propagandistic and more focused on burrowing deeply into the social mechanisms of oppression that plagued China for generations. Many of them were adaptations of May Fourth literature, and yet they featured some of the strongest cinematic work of that time.

These films flourished during brief periods of openness towards cinematic subject matter, only to be rebuked in subsequent periods of backlash. Few films from the 1960s were as initially highly praised and then harshly criticised as Xie Tieli's *Early Spring in February* (*Zao Chun Er Yue*, 1963). This uncommonly nuanced film about an idealistic young teacher who finds himself romantically torn between a headstrong fellow teacher and the young widow of a martyred soldier achieves an emotional delicacy not seen in Chinese films since the pre-Revolutionary masterpiece *Spring in a Small Town* (*Xiao Cheng zhi Chun*, 1948). The film enjoyed initial commercial and critical success, only to be censured during the Cultural Revolution as an exercise in bourgeois sentimentalism.

New Year Sacrifice (*Zhufu*, 1956), directed by Sang Hu, is the story of a widow's exploitation at the hands of a brutal patriarchy, adapted from the work of Lu Xun, a leading light of May Fourth literature. Whereas the source novel uses the nuanced, detached perspective of a bourgeois narrator, the film achieves a direct, first-person portrayal of underclass suffering. This is accomplished largely through a Chinese operatic technique underscoring strength and clarity of image and feeling. The musical soundtrack reinforces the link to Chinese opera, intensifying dramatic and emotional states. Given that the film is about a woman who has no voice in her own fate, the expressiveness of the music, often used in place of dialogue, is especially heartrending. While the widow is given the standard iconic treatment of a suffering peasant, she's ultimately a tragic figure – a dramatic break from the Communist heroes that dominated the screen. The filmmakers added an epilogue to assure audiences that her pre-Revolutionary fate would never happen in the present day.

Such alterations to a film were standard procedure and often reached absurd levels of micromanagement. Scholar Paul Clark relates another instance in the making of *New Year Sacrifice* in which a protracted high-level discussion ensued over the exact manner in which the heroine drops a fish; similar debates occurred over how dogs should behave onscreen or how characters should knock on doors. Everything on screen was susceptible to being interpreted as counter-revolutionary, with films as well as careers on the line.

The most infamous and formative instance of censorship occurred with the release of *The Life of Wu Xun* (*Wu Xun Zhuan*, 1950) by Sun Yu, one of China's most accomplished directors at the time. This historical film of a beggar who gradually saves enough money to open a school for the poor was initially well-received by critics and the public, until an anonymous editorial, published in the *People's Daily* national newspaper in May 1951, accused the film of being insufficiently revolutionary. This unsigned work of film criticism, perhaps the most influential on post-war Chinese cinema, was penned by none other than Chairman Mao, and it triggered a chain of events that changed the industry permanently. An onslaught of similar critiques on *The Life of Wu Xun*

led the film to become the first banned by the People's Republic. The Shanghai studios that produced the film fell into financial ruin, and by 1953 all of the once-powerful, privately operated Shanghai film companies were taken over by the state, answering directly to Beijing.

Given the intense degree of scrutiny levelled at a given film project, an inordinate amount of responsibility fell upon the screenwriter to craft the content in such a way as to appease the censors. Perhaps the most notable of these writers was Xia Yan, a leftist playwright who served as China's vice-minister of culture from 1955 to 1964. Xia, a devotee of the May Fourth writers, sought to popularise their works through film adaptations. In addition to adapting Lu Xun's *New Year Sacrifice*, he also wrote the script for Shui Hua's film of Mao Dun's classic novella *The Lin Family Shop* (*Lin Jia Puzi*, 1959). This adaptation meant to commemorate the May Fourth Movement's 40th anniversary, but was nonetheless risky for featuring shop owner Mr. Lin as a petty capitalist anti-hero. To Mao Dun's story Xia added scenes of Lin's cruelty to poor people to prevent audiences from sympathising with him too much, but these modifications could not protect the film from criticism. Eventually Xia was disgraced and sent to prison for eight years, his 'crime' having known Jiang Qing – later to become Mao's wife – in the 1930s.

While these May Fourth-inspired films tried to espouse the socially progressive sentiments demanded of them by the censors, they often bore a tone of scepticism that rendered them vaguely unsettling, even threatening to the ruling powers. Shi Hui's *This Whole Life of Mine* (*Wo Zhe Yibeizi*, 1950),

adapted from a novel by Lao She, tells the story of an honest, humble Beijing policeman whose unwavering trust in the ruling authorities does nothing to stop the oppression of his family. But a critique of the old regimes could be misconstrued as a critique of the new one. Films like *This Whole Life of Mine* had to find a balance between carrying on the May Fourth critical legacy and functioning as simple, Maoist propaganda. Shi Hui, the director and star of *This Whole Life of Mine*, couldn't manage this balancing act. Just a few years later, he was accused of being a bourgeois sentimentalist who valued artists over the masses. Even when directing himself in a 'safe' role as a patriotic soldier in *Company Commander Guan* (*Guan Lianchang*, 1951), Shi was criticised for giving his character too much individual flavour. Faced with overwhelming criticism throughout the remainder of his career, one of the brightest talents of Chinese cinema drowned himself in 1957.

Given the stifling degree of interference at every level of production, few films reached completion in the first decade of the People's Republic. Rarely would more than a dozen features be produced in a given year, while hundreds of Soviet films were imported to fill the void. Over the course of the 1950s, Chinese audiences grew in size and became more familiar with cinema, and less responsive to the conventions of Maoist propaganda films. Even the hardliners could not ignore the need to keep the masses engaged by bringing variety and freshness to their messages. New genres began to emerge, in some ways corresponding to their Hollywood counterparts.

A breakthrough occurred when the PRC issued its first comedies in 1956, the same year as Mao announced the Hundred Flowers Movement to welcome constructive criticism of the Party. Lü Ban's bold satire *Before the New Director Arrives* (*Xin Juzhang Dao Lai Zhiqian*, 1956) follows a self-serving party official who abuses the bureaucracy to his advantage. But as the Hundred Flowers Movement was followed by the backlash Anti-Rightist Movement, Lü's humorous critique on corruption within the party was spurned as an attack on the party itself, and Lü was eventually exiled from the industry after making two more satires, the last being *An Unfinished Comedy* (*Meiyou Wancheng de Xiju*, 1957). In contrast, Xie Jin's *Big Li, Little Li and Old Li* (*Da Li, Xiao Li he Lao Li*, 1962) uses sly comedy to promote physical fitness initiatives in factories across the country. The film succeeds as both comedy and propaganda because it humorously exploits the inherent awkwardness brought by change, especially among older, more resistant workers. The film's stylistic innovations are fascinating; watching it, you'd think that Xie had been studying his contemporary Frank Tashlin from across the Pacific, even though Hollywood films were still banned in China.

Hollywood film techniques crept into other genres. Military adventure films, mixing action with patriotic ideology, had long followed the Soviet model of square, straightforward filmmaking. But by the 1960s the expressive *noir* light and shadow of Hollywood could be found in films like Shui Hua's *Red Crag: Life in Eternal Flame* (*Liehuo Zhong Yongsheng*, 1965), spotlighting the individual suffering and emotional drama of revolutionary martyrs. There was also a greater sense of exoticism, as many films, such as Lin Nong and Zhu Wenshun's *Mysterious Travelling Companion* (*Shenmi de Lüban*, 1955) and Zhao Shinshui's *Visitors on the Icy Mountains* (*Bingshan Shang de Laike*, 1963) were set along the Chinese border regions, providing geographic escapism for the masses. They also dealt with issues of national identity, examining the relationships between the Han Chinese soldiers guarding the frontier and the ethnic minorities native to these territories, with loyalty and trust on the line. In this sense, they were China's equivalent of Hollywood westerns.

As seen in the example of *The Life of Wu Xun*, historical films were a

dangerous proposition, as they risked indulging in the same dynastic past that Communism had sought to overcome. Still, the impulse to reclaim or rehabilitate certain figures as pre-Revolutionary heroes proved irresistible. Shen Fu's *Li Shizhen* (1956) celebrated a 16th-century pharmacologist's efforts to advance Chinese medicine; Zheng Junli's *Lin Zexu* (1959) and Lin Nong's *Naval Battle of 1894* (*Jiawu Fengyun*, 1962) commemorated Qing dynasty battles against Western opium importers and Japanese invaders, respectively. To avoid having these films perceived as celebrations of feudal-era intellectuals or elites, the scenarios emphasised their protagonists' solidarity with and service to the people. While these films were initially received enthusiastically, their feudal-era subjects eventually drew ire from hardline critics; in their eyes, even the films' endorsement by the masses for their heroes amounted to a contemptuous display of elitism. Ten years after receiving unanimous acclaim for *Lin Zexu*, director Zheng Junli died in prison as a suspected counter-revolutionary.

Animated films rose to prominence with the founding of the Shanghai Animation Film Studio in 1957, which would go on to produce over 100 films in its first decade. A leading talent of the studio was Te Wei, whose 1956 short *The Proud General* (*Jiao'ao de Jiangjun*) draws heavily on Chinese traditional cultural forms such as water ink painting, Beijing opera and folklore, but is also visibly influenced by Disney films in terms of character design, movement and storytelling point of view. The Shanghai animators made their greatest achievement with Wan Laiming and Tang Cheng's *Uproar in Heaven* (*Da Nao Tiangong*, 1964), a feature length adaptation of the classic novel *Journey to the West*. Suppressed during the Cultural Revolution, the film waited 14 years before it first screened internationally at the London Film Festival, where at last it was met with great acclaim.

The first internationally renowned film of the People's Republic was also its first colour production, Sang Hu and Huang Sha's filmed version of the classic opera *Liang Shanbo and Zhu Yingtai* (1954). The film enjoyed rare levels of enthusiasm among the upper ranks (in 1955 a government ministry declared it the best Chinese film made since the founding of the Republic); at a conference in Switzerland Premier Zhou Enlai personally presented it to Charlie Chaplin, who was apparently moved to tears. The film's success belies the difficulties that faced the filming of traditional operas at that time. Operas with fantastical or superstitious elements were deemed antithetical to Communist modernity, while the formal dilemma of how to represent these familiar stage works in cinematic form was highly contested. Nonetheless, the desire to draw from Chinese operatic traditions in forging a distinctly Chinese cinema persisted; when the Cultural Revolution eventually denounced nearly all films as bourgeois indulgences, only films of Maoist 'model' operas were permitted.

Another strain of musical film, the ethnic minority musical, enjoyed great success, providing audiences with a sensory feast of music, dance, and romance. Romantic love was still considered a bourgeois concept, so ethnic Han Chinese were largely forbidden to express it onscreen. But ethnic minorities, with their exotic, non-Han features, were excluded from this restriction. The most successful of these musicals, Su Li's *Third Sister Liu* (*Liu San Jie*, 1960) luxuriates in the breathtaking scenery of the Guangxi karst mountain landscape, where it dramatises an ancient Zhuang minority folktale of a bold young woman who defends her village against greedy landlords. The film's sweeping pictorial and musical qualities turn the particularities of place and ethnic identity into a powerful but generalised parable celebrating the nation's natural beauty and political struggle. In Wang Jiayi's *Five Golden Flowers* (*Wu Duo Jinhua*, 1959), a Bai

minority youth searches for a maiden named Golden Flower whom he had
met but once. In his search, he mistakes four other women, also named
Golden Flower, before he finds the right one. One Golden Flower works
at a foundry, one drives a tractor, another is a stockyard worker, and the
last is "an exemplary manure collector." Far from being merely a comic
farce, this setup enables the government to highlight the active roles
performed by women in work communes during the Great Leap Forward.

The roles of women characters in cinema during this period were
indeed expanding, and yet their emotional life was still restricted. In
contrast to the romantic openness of ethnic minorities, Han Chinese
on the screen often had to sublimate sexual desire for revolutionary
desire. Female characters often showed the most passion. In Lu Ren's
Li Shuangshuang (1962), the title character is a village wife swept up in a
Maoist fervour to have her village meet model standards. She exposes the
lazy, selfish, and reactionary elements among her neighbours, friends and
family, including her own husband. Li Shuangshuang's uncompromising
stance toward her community foretold the kind of behaviour that
would explode full-scale during the sweeping, destructive purification
campaigns of the Cultural Revolution to come just a few years later.

Li Shuangshuang is portrayed by Zhang Ruifang, who prepared
for the role by living in a commune for several weeks. With her aura of
enthusiastic commitment, ideological purity and inner strength, Zhang
was one of the most successful actresses of the Seventeen Years period.
Other performers weren't as fortunate. Zhao Dan, a matinee idol from the
heyday of 1930s Shanghai cinema, was severely criticised for starring in
The Life of Wu Xun; despite starring in subsequent films such as *Li Shizhen*

(*Above*)
*Zhang Ruifang as the village wife
swept up in Maoist fervour in Lu
Ren's 'Li Shuangshuang' (1962).*

(*Opposite, top*)
*Women are central to the
revolutionary struggle in
Xie Jin's 'The Red Detachment
of Women' (1961).*

(*Opposite, middle*)
*The two female opera performers
who follow contrasting ideologies
in Xie Jin's classic melodrama
'Two Stage Sisters' (1965).*

(*Opposite, bottom*)
*The poster for Xie Jin's 'Woman
Basketball Player No. 5' (1957).*

and *Lin Zexu*, his career remained under a cloud of scrutiny. Eventually he was imprisoned and tortured for five years during the Cultural Revolution.

Scholar Julian Ward notes, "unlike their Hollywood counterparts, Chinese film stars were lauded not for their unattainability but for their ability to inspire and be inspired by the masses." Actors were sometimes recruited to star in films based on their actual experiences as workers, farmers or peasants. Li Jun's *Serfs* (*Nongnu*, 1963), a powerful drama about oppressed Tibetans, stars Wangdui, who grew up in such conditions. Huang Baomei, a model worker from a Shanghai cotton mill who was honoured in the presence of Chairman Mao, had her experiences commemorated in a 1958 film titled after her.

The director of that film, Xie Jin, featured outstanding women characters throughout a directing career that was exemplary itself, if tragically interrupted. Xie vigorously explored the revolutionary potential of women, both thematically and cinematically, while moving effortlessly across genres. In *Woman Basketball Player No. 5* (*Nü Lan Wu Hao*, 1957), Xie utilises sport filmmaking to demonstrate an invigorating modern vision of female bodies in motion, displaying more bare flesh than had ever been seen in a Chinese film. In *The Red Detachment of Women* (*Hongse Niangzijun*, 1961), Xie positioned women firmly in violent revolutionary struggle. It was a film so popular that it became adapted into one of the few operas allowed during the Cultural Revolution. In both of these films, Xie's women are vital, dynamic, and expressive. But it was with his next film that he – and the Chinese Communist cinema – achieved an apotheosis.

Two Stage Sisters (*Wutai Jiemei*, 1965) is an epic saga involving two young women opera performers whose evolving relationship parallels the evolution of the Chinese Republic. Like so many films of this era, *Two Stage Sisters* is a national origin story, but more than any of the others, it explicitly puts forward the theme of history as drama. One sister adopts bourgeois capitalism like a stage costume, while the other discovers Marxist humanism through May Fourth art and literature – in one shot, she literally wears it like a mask. One ideology proves to be all style, the other substance.

Two Stage Sisters feels like a culmination of the contradictory forces that shaped Communist Chinese cinema up to that point. It combines May Fourth-style social critique with Maoist optimism. Its narrative chorus pays homage to traditional Chinese folk opera while suggesting the self-reflexive distancing devices of Bertolt Brecht. It infuses Marxist liberation theory into a classic women's melodrama straight out of Hollywood. Above all, *Two Stage Sisters* is a story of how art itself is a means for both societal reconciliation and revolution. One sister is seduced by a conniving businessman, while the other retaliates against the injustices around her. The system eventually stages them against each other in a corrupt, pre-determined court proceeding, but the sisters literally break from the script, causing a revolutionary overthrow of the oppressive order. Accused of promoting "class compromise and bourgeois humanism," *Two Stage Sisters* wasn't released until after the Cultural Revolution. Shangguan Yunzhu, an actress in the film whose character commits suicide, followed her character's fate in the face of persecution.

During this time, Mao Zedong's wife Jiang Qing declared most films to be "poisonous weeds" that threatened to subvert the goals of the Revolution. All but a few movies were banned, and most production halted nationwide. Scores of filmmakers were sent to labour camps. It would be decades before the People's Republic recouped what it had accomplished in developing its own cinema during its first 17 years. In many respects, to this day its legacy remains under-recognised, with many of its lessons yet to be fully learned. ◉

Concerned that the Chinese revolution was backsliding into new class hierarchies and emergent capitalism – and also that he was losing power – Chairman Mao launched the Great Proletarian Cultural Revolution in May 1966. He called for violent armed struggle to root out the new bourgeoisie inside the Party and government. Young people responded by forming Red Guard units and attacking perceived 'capitalist roaders' such as Deng Xiaoping, who did indeed launch the country's market economy and open it up to the outside world 20 years later. Factions and infighting rapidly emerged amongst the Red Guards, and in 1968 the People's Liberation Army had to be mobilised to restore order. At the end of the year, the 'Down to the Countryside' movement was launched. Its official aim was to send city youths to learn from the peasantry, but it also had the benefit of putting the disbanded Red Guards at a safe distance from centres of power. Although the Cultural Revolution waned in the 1970s, its eventual repudiation waited until after Mao's death in 1976. Therefore, the 1966-76 era is often referred to as the Cultural Revolution decade.

What happened to Chinese cinema during the Cultural Revolution? And how has the Cultural Revolution been depicted in cinema since its repudiation? Received wisdom has it that film production came to a halt during the era. The only exceptions, according to this version, were recordings of the eight revolutionary 'model operas' (*yangbanxi*) such as *The East Is Red*, which people were forced to watch repeatedly. After the repudiation of the Cultural Revolution, a cycle of 'scar films' about the traumas of the era was made in the late 1970s. But in 1981, the story goes, the historical account was declared settled, and the topic has been off-limits ever since.

It is true that drastic and fundamental changes happened to Chinese cinema during the Cultural Revolution, and that since 1981 it has become a 'sensitive' topic the authorities prefer filmmakers to avoid. Nonetheless, all of the standard account given above is either exaggerated or wrong. For a start, the film recording of the revolutionary variety show *The East Is Red (Dongfang Hong)* is not a model opera, and it was filmed in 1965, prior to the beginning of the Cultural Revolution. However, it did set the strident but also very popular tone for the model operas that followed soon after.

It is also true that cinema was treated with particular suspicion by the Cultural Revolution hardliners. It was a 'foreign' artform during a time of high xenophobia, and its origins in China were particularly associated with Shanghai. Remembered fondly as the 'Paris of the East' by Westerners, to many Chinese the debauchery and semi-colonial status of pre-revolutionary Shanghai made the city a mark of cultural corruption and shame. Therefore, large numbers of film studio workers were indeed 'struggled' and subjected to other punishments, and production of dramatic features came to a halt for several years.

However, film was far too vital a medium for the regime for all production to cease. Chinese television was in its infancy, and illiteracy was still a problem. Radio and film, both of which could be easily controlled by the authorities, were therefore the primary media of the day. Newsreel and documentary production continued to celebrate not only the Cultural Revolution but also the nation's economic and social progress. Examples included the documentary *The Red Flag Canal (Hong Qi Qu*, 1970), which extols voluntarism in the building of the eponymous irrigation project using huge armies of human labour and few machines, or newsreels on the launch of China's first satellite, also in 1970, and called 'The East Is Red No.1'. Huge numbers of prints were made in all formats from 35 mm down to China's own 8.75 mm, invented in 1966 as part of the era's nationalistic

中國
人民志願軍

emphasis on self-reliance. These were shown all over the country, reaching the furthest villages via bicycle-driven mobile projection teams.

As for entertainment, it is true that the revolutionary operas were the most strongly emphasised form during the Cultural Revolution decade. Developed under guidance from Mao's wife of the time, Jiang Qing, they hybridised traditional Chinese forms with classical Western forms and revolutionary content. For example, the heavy make-up of Chinese opera continues. But where it had been purely conventional and non-realist in pre-modern opera, in the revolutionary model operas, make-up became highly stylised but broadly realist. Characters also wore stylised but realist clothing. Western symphonic instruments were introduced, and the tighter structure of Western drama was also used. A few of these new revolutionary stage productions were not operas at all, but revolutionary ballets. Most of the stories were set during the revolutionary wars before 1949, and class-based struggle was highly emphasised.

Contrary to conventional understanding, the model operas were promoted as ultra-modern and Chinese innovations. Furthermore, many were very popular, especially the more kinetic operas featuring acrobatic fight scenes, such as *Taking Tiger Mountain by Strategy* (*Zhi Qu Weihu Shan*) or those with memorable tunes, such as *Azalea Mountain* (*Dujuan Shan*). The diaphanous red silks worn in the film of the revolutionary ballet version of *The Red Detachment of Women* (*Hongse Nianzijun*, 1970) inspired many young men's sexual awakenings, as testified in various documentaries that have appeared more recently.

The authorities were eager to make films of the revolutionary operas. However, they realised that once released, the film versions would become the authoritative renderings of the operas. Therefore, production was closely monitored and scenes were re-shot until considered perfect. The first films did not appear until 1970. To ensure good aesthetic results in a country short of trained filmmakers, many esteemed directors who had been imprisoned or sent to the countryside at the beginning of the Cultural Revolution were soon called back. For example, the famous veteran Xie Tieli directed the 1970 film version of *Taking Tiger Mountain by Strategy* and also went on to direct *Azalea Mountain* in 1974. The assumption that most filmmakers were imprisoned or working down on the commune throughout the Cultural Revolution decade is wrong.

Furthermore, although it is probably true that many Chinese saw each revolutionary opera film more than once, the saying 'eight films for 800 million people' was never true. In fact, by the end of the Cultural Revolution decade, 18 different revolutionary operas were in circulation, some in both opera and ballet forms.

Two other factors also added to the diversity of film culture during the Cultural Revolution decade. First, production of regular dramatic features started again in the early 1970s, around the same time that the film versions of the revolutionary operas began to appear. The dramatic features were straightforwardly black-and-red presentations of evil landlords and foreign spies versus self-sacrificing PLA soldiers and resolute barefoot doctors. In 1976, the *China Filmography* (*Zhongguo Yishu Yingpian Bianmu*) listed 33 feature-length dramatic films, versus 46 for 1965, indicating that production was returning to pre-Cultural Revolution levels.

Second, foreign films continued to be screened in China throughout the Cultural Revolution decade. In fact, at least half the feature films in circulation were foreign. The general image is of a China hermetically sealed from the outside world. Indeed, regular imports from the United States had stopped after the 1949 Revolution, and

once China decided to stick with Stalinism and therefore cut itself off from Krushchev and the 'revisionists' in Moscow in the late 1950s, imports from the Soviet bloc also came to a stop. But films from North Korea, Albania, Yugoslavia and Romania continued to be available.

This narrow range of imports certainly constituted a restricted cinematic diet. Nevertheless, the films were phenomenally popular. Crowds lined up around the block in the early 1970s for the North Korean 1972 epic, *Flower Girl (Kkot Pa-neun Cheo-nyeo)*, allegedly directed by Kim Jong-il himself. So popular was the film that some cinemas played the film repeatedly in 24-hour screenings. Recently, interviewees in Shanghai told me they loved North Korean films because of their songs and their sad stories – these were films to make you cry. The Yugoslav imports were mostly WWII partisan stories, and were known as the 'fighting films'. In the absence of any access to French cinema, the Albanian capital Tirana became an unlikely fashion capital. I was told that Chinese audiences carefully counted how many changes of costume were performed by Doctor Vera, the protagonist of Albanian director Dhimitër Anagnosti's *Old Wounds (Plagë të Vjetra*, 1968). Finally, and perhaps most intriguingly, I have been told that the Romanian films were known as the 'kissing films'.

From this more complex picture, we can see that a greater number and range of films was made and circulated in China during the Cultural Revolution than is usually thought, and that Chinese filmmakers were active during this period. However, it was also a very unusual period in which a great many people suffered. And so, it is not surprising that the minute a new government was installed in 1976 after Mao's death and the Cultural Revolution itself was repudiated, this was followed by a stream of 'scar films' about suffering during the last decade. Although many foreigners had been taken in by Cultural Revolution propaganda, these mainland 'scar films' had already been preceded by Hong Kong director Cecile Tang Shuen's *China Behind (Zaijian Zhongguo)* in 1974, which painted such a bleak portrait of what was happening over the border that it was banned for several years by the nervous British colonial authorities.

One of China's leading contemporary thinkers, Wang Hui, has stated in his essay 'The 1989 Social Movement and the Historical Roots of China's Neoliberalism' that "… repudiating the Cultural Revolution has become the guardian of the dominant ideology as well as of state policy, and this mode of thinking has flourished ever since: any criticism directed against the present can be cast as regression to the Cultural Revolution, and thus as being wholly irrational."

Wang Hui's insight is crucial to understanding the uneasy tensions around the cinematic representation of the Cultural Revolution ever since it ended. On one hand, if current legitimacy is based on its repudiation, there can be no pretence that the Cultural Revolution did not happen. This makes its status quite different from the Democracy Movement and Tiananmen Square Massacre of 1989, which is totally taboo in films that pass the Beijing censors. On the other hand, although the Cultural Revolution must be acknowledged in order to be repudiated, it is also important to rhetorically place it as an exception and to guard against any spreading of the stain of 'error'.

In terms of numbers, the five years after the end of the Cultural Revolution produced a high tide of films about the decade that has never been matched again. The absolute majority of films produced in this period were about the Cultural Revolution in one way or another. Most were melodramatic, such as Xie Jin's *Legend of Tianyun Mountain* (*Tianyun Shan Chuanqi*, 1979), a story couched in multiple flashbacks

(Above)
The poster for Zhang Nuanxin's 'Sacrificed Youth' (1985), which focuses on a North Chinese city girl 'sent down' to the countryside during the Cultural Revolution.

(Below)
'Fifth Generation' director Chen Kaige's 'King of the Children' (1987) also looked at the 'sent-down' generation.

about the desperate efforts to get an unjust verdict reversed, and the destroyed romantic relationships that resulted from the original injustice. A few were black comedies, like Deng Yimin and Yang Yanjin's absurdist depiction of the life of a journalist in the latter days of the Cultural Revolution, *Troubled Laughter* (*Kunao Ren de Xiao*, 1979). Released from detention, the protagonist finds himself caught between his professional duty and demands from his employers that he lie.

Although these films were highly sentimental, even overwrought, they were also very popular. More worrying for the authorities, not only did some of them depict the most violent fighting among armed Red Guard factions, but also many showed 'errors' that went back well before the Cultural Revolution decade. In *Legend of Tianyun Mountain*, for example, the victim of injustice is first accused of being a Rightist in the late 1950s. Such works challenged the idea that the Cultural Revolution could be seen as an isolated aberration and could be seen as undermining faith in the revolutionary project as a whole. Therefore, it did not come as a surprise when Peng Ning's film *Bitter Love* (*Kulian*, also known as *Unrequited Love* and *The Sun and the Man*, 1981) was banned and a campaign launched around it. Ending with a dying man stamping out a question mark in the snow, it was a particularly pessimistic telling of the Cultural Revolution story. The film's fate signalled that the Cultural Revolution was considered sorted, and no further films on the topic would be needed.

However, in practice, things have been more complicated. Indeed, a number of films made after 1981, including some by members of the so-called 'Fifth Generation', are set in the Cultural Revolution decade. Another such film is by Zhang Nuanxin, whose critical essay, 'Throw Away the Walking Stick of Drama,' co-authored with her husband Li Tuo, inspired the Fifth Generation. Zhang's *Sacrificed Youth* (*Qingchun Ji*, 1985) explores the sometimes frightening and sometimes liberating experiences of a young North Chinese educated city girl sent down to the countryside during the Cultural Revolution. She finds herself in a Dai (Thai) ethnic area of the southwest in Yunnan Province, where not only are the living conditions more basic than she is used to, but the customs and mores are challenging to her. The film's voiceover reflections also made it a primary example of the small contemporary cycle of 'women's cinema' (*nüxing dianying*) that interrogated what it meant to be a woman in post-Mao China.

Chen Kaige is one of the leading lights of the Fifth Generation. His *King of the Children* (*Haizi Wang*, 1987) is also about the sent-down generation, and is also set in Yunnan Province. Based on a novel by Ah Cheng, it focuses on a young man who, despite his lack of qualifications, is prevailed upon to become the village schoolteacher in a poor but spectacular mountain area. Like the girl in *Sacrificed Youth*, he finds his values changing and begins to question his assumptions. He gradually abandons the set textbook and adapts his lessons to the everyday realities of his students.

The movement to send young people 'down to the countryside and up into the mountains' during the Cultural Revolution had a profound impact on a whole generation. They had grown up in the cities being told everything was rosy down on the commune. But once they got there, reality shocked them. For many, the experience was traumatic, and it has inspired numerous novels, films, and memoirs ever since. Although generally seen as a disaster for those involved, both *Sacrificed Youth* and *King of the Children* are more ambivalent, as they show their protagonists unexpectedly adapting to their environment. It could even be said that they really do learn from the peasants, as prescribed by the authorities, albeit perhaps not quite in the way the authorities intended. Furthermore,

(Above)
The denounced performers surrounded by Red Guards in Chen Kaige's 'Farewell My Concubine' (1993).

(Below)
Tian Zhuangzhuang's 'The Blue Kite' (1993) depicts the Cultural Revolution era through the eyes of a young boy.

both films steer clear of the violent clashes and persecution that occurred at the height of the Cultural Revolution in the late 1960s. Perhaps this is why neither of them got into any particular trouble with the censors.

Chen Kaige represented the Cultural Revolution again in *Farewell My Concubine* (*Ba Wang Bie Ji*, 1993), the film that won him the Palme d'Or at Cannes. *Farewell* does represent the persecution and violence directly, in an episode where the adopted son betrays his father to the Red Guards. Chen has said in interviews that this episode in Lilian Lee's novel spoke directly to his guilt about how he had behaved towards his own father, the famous director Chen Huaikai, during the Cultural Revolution. However, most of the film depicts the horrors of pre-revolutionary China, and the current regime is not in any disagreement with the depiction of the Cultural Revolution as it appears in *Farewell My Concubine*, so perhaps this is why this film also avoided serious problems.

The same cannot be said for two other mid-1990s films by Chen's Fifth Generation colleagues, Zhang Yimou and Tian Zhuangzhuang. Zhang's *To Live* (*Huozhe*, 1994) and Tian's *The Blue Kite* (*Lan Fengzheng*, 1993) both fell foul of the authorities and got them into serious difficulty, with Tian prevented from directing films for a number of years. The official reason given in both cases was that the films had been submitted to international film festivals without first receiving permission from the Film Bureau. However, both films also differ from *Farewell* in other ways. Their stories take place almost entirely during the period after the establishment of the People's Republic in 1949, and they show errors and disasters resulting from Communist Party policy not only during the repudiated Cultural Revolution itself, but almost from the new state's very beginnings. *The Blue Kite* tells its quietly devastating story through the eyes of a little boy. He recounts the various men in his mother's life. But she only goes through so many partners because each time she is able to set up a new relationship, a new political movement takes the man in her life away.

Since the Fifth Generation, who are now in their fifties and sixties, new generations of Chinese filmmakers have come to the fore. For them and

for their younger audiences, the Cultural Revolution was not a formative experience. Even if they were alive during it, they were too young to have been sent down to the countryside. In these circumstances, perhaps we should not be surprised to find that it appears far less frequently in their films and with none of the gut-wrenching emotional power it had for earlier filmmakers and older audiences. Perhaps the starkest example of this change is Jiang Wen's *In the Heat of the Sun* (*Yanguang Canlan de Rizi*, 1994). Here, a group of teenagers left alone after their parents have been sent off for punishment go through an almost idyllic coming-of-age process, and the Cultural Revolution is a mere backdrop to their lives.

The most respected of the younger directors for well over a decade now has been Jia Zhangke. Jia's second film *Platform* (*Zhantai*, 2000) follows the fortunes of a cultural troupe that appears at first performing revolutionary songs accompanied by martial poses, but after the end of the Cultural Revolution and the disappearance of state subsidies, gradually transitions towards disco and other market-pleasing entertainments. In *Platform*, the tail end of the Cultural Revolution appears, not as part of a traumatic experience to be relived, but rather as an emblem of the past needed only to define the present of the People's Republic. It even carries a little delicate nostalgia, something surely much more difficult for those with direct memories of participation in the era's politics.

Platform suggests the current transformation in the representation of the Cultural Revolution. The period continues to structure the understanding of history, but with much less of the powerful affective charge it carried through all the final decades of the last century, when both filmmakers and audiences had direct memories of the era. Nevertheless, it remains, as they say in the People's Republic, 'sensitive'. The final years, in small town settings far removed from embarrassing episodes in Chinese Communist Party history like the smashing of the 'Gang of Four', are safe to represent. But even today, no filmmaker will include scenes from the Cultural Revolution era without careful consideration of what is acceptable for the censors and what might be considered as going too far. ◑

A BRIEF HISTORY OF CHINESE ANIMATION

By Li Zhen

The earliest known Chinese animations were made in Shanghai in 1923 by Yang Zuotao (1897-1967). After making at least two films, *Zan Ting* (1923) and *Guo Nian* (1923), Yang went to America in August 1924, where he joined the Walt Disney Company. Yang took an English name, Cyrus S. Young, and participated in the making of at least 18 of Disney's classic features.

Before the establishment of the People's Republic of China in October 1949, there were at least 10 animation teams in China and no fewer than 50 completed animation films that we know of. Alongside Yang Zuotao were such figures as Fu Nandi, who devoted himself to science and education animations; Qian Jiajun (1916-2011), head of the Chongqing Educational Film Animation Studio; as well as some now almost unknown animators such as Huang Wennong, Zhang Huiyuan, Qin Lifan, Li Yunchen, Shen Yanzhe, Mei Xuechou and Dong Xiaoding.

However, the most important early Chinese animation team comprised the four Wan brothers, led by Wan Laiming (1900-97) and Wan Guchan (1900-95). The Wan brothers produced at least 34 animations before 1949. The earliest Wan brothers films held by the China Film Archive are four produced in 1933. Their 1940 film *Princess Iron-Fan* was the first feature-length Chinese animation, and is an acknowledged classic. In their early years, Wan brothers productions deliberately copied the Disney model, but they gradually began incorporating elements of traditional Chinese painting into their work.

The Wan Laiming-directed *Uproar in Heaven* (aka *Havoc in Heaven*, aka *The Monkey King*, 1961-64), an adaptation of the *Journey to the West* story, was a milestone in Chinese animation.

Wan Guchan invented paper-cut animation in 1958 – a breakthrough in animation techniques. His representative works using this technique include *Pigsy Eats Watermelon* (1958), *The Golden Conch* (1963) and *The Ginseng Boy* (1961).

When the PRC was established in 1949, the famous cartoonist Te Wei (1915-2010) accepted the Communist Party's assignment to establish what would become China's biggest and most professional animation institution, the Shanghai Animation Film Studio. Te Wei established two important directions for Chinese animation: first, he encouraged the production of animated films that reflected Chinese artistic styles; second, he promoted the use of comedy – something that was genuinely daring amid the political atmosphere after 1949.

Te Wei encouraged experimentation with materials and techniques, and took part in many such experiments himself. His own films include *The Proud General* (1956) and *Where is Mama?* (aka *Baby Tadpoles Look for Their Mother*, 1960).

The Shanghai Animation Film Studio dominated the production of Chinese animated films up to the mid-1980s. The institution had two branches: one produced normal cartoons, the other produced puppet animations. Jin Xi (1919-97) and Yu Zheguang (1906-91) were two key figures from the puppet animation team. Jin Xi directed *A Young Hero* (1953), China's first colour puppet animation film, as well as *The Magic Paintbrush* (1955), *Who Sings Best* (1958) and *Peacock Princess* (1963). His films call attention to the texture of the materials used in the animation, using their physical characteristics to suggest movement and shape the characters.

'Deer and Bull' (1990)

'Pigsy Eats Watermelon' (1958)

'Uproar in Heaven' (aka *'Havoc in Heaven'*, 1961-64)

Yu Zheguang started out by studying Chinese puppetry. After 1949, using his experience, he directed films like *Mr. Dong Guo* (1955) and *Back to Mother's Home* (1956). He invented origami (paper folding) animation in 1960, and produced five films using this technique: *The Wise Duck* (1960), *Cabbage* (1962), *Entertainment on the Lake* (1964), *Three Wolves* (1980) and *Duckling* (1980).

Another key figure associated with the Shanghai Animation Film Studio after 1949 was the aforementioned Qian Jiajun, considered the founder of animation education in China. Qian was a master of Chinese ink animation. His film *Why the Crow is Black* (1955) was the first animation produced by the PRC to receive an international award, and his *A Chuang Tapestry* (1959) was the PRC's first feature-length animation.

Typically, great importance is placed on the specific materials used in Chinese animation. For instance, Zou Qin's film *Deer and Bull* (1990) uses bamboo as all of its visual elements. Zou was careful to use good quality bamboo from Zhejiang province, making full use of the natural characteristics of each part of the bamboo stalk, such as its skin.

Other talented figures in Chinese animation include A Da (Xu Jingda, 1934-87), who is famous for his bizarre ideas and philosophies. His films include *Three Monks* (1980), *36 Characters* (1983) and *The Super Soap* (1986). Another talent is Hu Jinqing (1936-), who works using paper-cut animation. His films include *The Naughty Golden Monkey* (1982), *Snipe-Clam Grapple* (1983) and *Scarecrow* (1985). His ink paper-cut animation cleverly simulates the effect of traditional Chinese ink painting.

Before 1995, all Chinese animation production was a state-sponsored activity, and many animations made in the 1950s and 1960s were 'collective creations'. Such a division of labour concentrates the wisdom of many people, but the results often have less of a prominent personality.

Some have argued for the existence of a distinctly 'Chinese School' of animation, but though many Chinese animation films have similar characteristics, poetic pursuits and values, that's not entirely accurate. Despite such shared traits, the main creators never sat down together and agreed to follow a single unified theory. ⊙

'Peacock Princess' (1963)

The Rooster Crows at Midnight

You Lei, 1964

Trips to the cinema were the most enjoyable events of my childhood. The film that had the most impact on me was a puppet animation made by You Lei at the Shanghai Animation Film Studio called *The Rooster Crows at Midnight* (*Banye Ji Jiao*, 1964), which I must have seen when I was six years old. It might have been the first film I ever saw.

The film is based on a story about a wicked landlord by Gao Yubao. In those days workers were called to work in the morning by a rooster. In the film, to make them start work earlier, the landlord pretends to be the rooster and crows for day at midnight, not at dawn. Almost all Chinese people of my age must have seen this film in their youth, and still remember it fondly, as I do.

The Cultural Revolution had begun after I got to middle school, and the films we saw came from other socialist countries – from the USSR, from Yugoslavia, from Romania, from Albania. I remember *The Flower Girl* from North Korea, which everybody saw several times. Like *The Rooster Crows at Midnight*, they were all films that taught us about class struggle and rebellion.

5

THE FIFTH GENERATION AND THE NEW CINEMA OF THE 1980s

BY MICHAEL BERRY

第五代导演与
80年代新风格电影

Looking back on People's Republic of China cinema of the 1980s, the shadow of the so-called 'Fifth Generation' looms large – the bold cinematic language, visual gestures, and narrative innovations of filmmakers like Zhang Yimou, Chen Kaige, Tian Zhuangzhuang, Wu Ziniu and Li Shaohong, and the seemingly ubiquitous image of Gong Li, seem to have in many ways dominated this pivotal period of Chinese film history. As the first group of filmmakers to graduate from the Beijing Film Academy after the Cultural Revolution, the Fifth Generation were educated amid the age of openness of the early Reform Era. The combination of their personal experiences growing up during the Cultural Revolution with the diverse Western and classical Chinese influences that poured back into China with the Open Door Policy's liberalisation helped make up the Fifth Generation's unique background, and eventually set them on a path to rewrite the history of Chinese cinema. However beyond the iconoclastic ways in which the Fifth Generation challenged Chinese film history, the 1980s saw many other radical cinematic transformations, from passing fads to more long-term shifts that would also change the face of Chinese film.

Goodbye revolution, goodbye?

Even a cursory examination of Chinese film trends over time will reveal the radical shift away from revolutionary discourse that had so dominated PRC cinema from 1949-76. During this early period, ideologically driven 'Red Classics' focusing upon such topics as the exploitation of peasants under feudalism, the war of 'liberation', the War of Resistance against Japan, the Chinese Civil War and Korean War films were all dominant cinematic forms. From classic titles that enshrined soldier-heroes as revolutionary martyrs like *Dong Cunrui* (1955) and *Lei Feng* (1964) to the model opera films of the Cultural Revolution like *Taking Tiger Mountain by Strategy* (*Zhi Qu Weihu Shan*, 1968) and *The Red Detachment of Women* (*Hongse Niangzijun*, 1970), the cinematic shadow of the soldier loomed large during the socialist era.

With the end of the decade-long Cultural Revolution in 1976, new genres, styles and film forms began to sneak back in. While films from previous decades frequently saw private affections and romantic sentiments repressed in favour of more lofty devotion to the nation, by the late 1970s the power of the collective in cinema seemed to give way and new spaces opened up for audiences to project and imagine their private longings and romantic ideals. Films like *Love on Lushan* (*Lushan Lian*, 1980) depicted romantic love in a way that had not been portrayed on the Chinese screen in decades, but at the same time, the lingering ideological shadow of earlier film models lingered. While state studios' overtly 'revolutionary' fare was on the decline, propaganda films continued to be produced, albeit on a smaller scale, and with waning audience numbers – people were now being seduced by a new crop of Chinese genre films (romances, social problem films, action films, comedies, and critical historical melodramas about the Cultural Revolution) and foreign imports.

But beyond the traditional dichotomy of romance and revolution, which has often been present in the 'Revolution Plus Love' formula, the late 1970s and 1980s also saw a new humanism take form on the Chinese silver screen. Mirroring similar trends that were happening on the literary scene, pioneered by writers like Wang Meng, Dai Houying, Lu Yao, and others, films embracing this new humanism abound. A good representative of this in early reform-era Chinese film can be seen in the work of 'Fourth Generation' director Wu Tianming's *Life* (*Rensheng*, 1984) and *Old Well* (*Lao Jing*, 1986) – films that offered a more complex and introspective reappraisal of recent Chinese history. Both of Wu's films

were adapted from popular works of fiction, *Life* from a novel by Lu Yao and *Old Well* from the fiction of Zheng Yi. *Old Well* was an allegorical film that portrayed the fate of villagers in an impoverished village and their all-consuming quest to dig an active well to solve their water crisis. Earning four major awards at the 1987 Tokyo Film Festival, *Old Well* was a major triumph for Chinese cinema on the international film scene. The film also featured cinematographer/director Zhang Yimou in an award-winning leading role, which further emphasised the collaborative spirit among many filmmakers during this era (Wu had given Zhang the green light to direct his first feature *Red Sorghum* [*Hong Gaoliang*, 1987] the same year).

Like *Old Well*, many films from this period were literary adaptations. In addition to the wave of trauma-laden films reflecting the Cultural Revolution adapted from the literary genre of Scar Fiction, there was also a revival when it came to film adaptations of classic works: *The True Story of Ah Q* (*Ah Q Zhengzhuan*, 1981), *Regret for the Past* (*Shangshi*, 1981), *Rickshaw Boy* (*Luotuo Xiangzi*, 1982) and *My Memories of Old Beijing* (*Chengnan Jiushi*, 1982) were all adapted from May Fourth and other classic modern novels.

The 1980s was also a period in which older generation filmmakers whose creative work had been interrupted, suppressed, or curbed during the era of high socialism now had a revival of creativity. Veteran filmmaker Wu Yonggang, best known for his silent masterpiece *The Goddess* (*Shennü*, 1934) returned in 1980 after a 24-year hiatus from filmmaking to co-direct (with Wu Yigong) *Evening Rain* (*Ba Shan Yeyu*). Fourth Generation filmmakers Xie Fei, Wu Tianming and Huang Shuqin seemed to finally find their voice in the reform era. Huang (the daughter of renowned dramatist Huang Zuolin), offered several breakthrough films like the innovative feminist title *Woman, Demon, Human* (*Ren Gui Qing*, 1987). Other notable feminist works from the era include Zhang Nuanxin's *Sacrificed Youth* (*Qingchun Ji*, 1985), a remarkable film about a young girl's sexual awakening as a 'sent-down youth' in Yunnan during the Cultural Revolution.

One of the most prolific and politically resilient filmmakers
in modern China, Xie Jin returned with a string of humanist
melodramas – *Legend of Tianyun Mountain* (*Tianyun Shan Chuanqi*,
1979), *The Herdsman* (*Muma Ren*, 1982), *Wreaths at the Foot of the
Mountain* (*Gaoshan xia de Huahuan*, 1985), *Hibiscus Town* (*Furong Zhen*,
1986) – that perfected the 'Xie Jin model,' a melodramatic formula
that would have an immense impact on films of the reform era.

Hibiscus Town traced the turmoil and trauma of China's post-1949
political movements, culminating with the Cultural Revolution, as seen
through the eyes of Hu Yuyin (Liu Xiaoqing), a local tofu seller with an
entrepreneurial spirit, and Qin Shutian (Jiang Wen), a rightist relegated
to the role of street sweeper. After Hu loses her shop during a political
campaign, she too is sent to sweep the streets, where she falls in love with
Qin, resulting in further persecution; it is not until the end of the Cultural
Revolution that the couple finally marries and Hu reopens her tofu shop,
but the 'happy ending' does little to curtail Xie Jin's scathing look at the
absurdity of the political movements that had consumed China for decades.

Like many of the aforementioned examples, virtually all of Xie's major
reform-era films were also literary adaptations. It might even be argued
that, in some cases, the political boldness of this older generation's films
went beyond even the radical statement of the Fifth Generation.' The
mad paranoid cries of "another political movement is coming…" and the
silhouette of the evil cadre's government vehicle looming over Jiang Wen's
everyman at the end of *Hibiscus Town* are surely as scathing and direct
an indictment of history as we see even a decade later in the renowned
'banned films' *To Live* (*Huozhe,* 1994) and *Farewell My Concubine* (*Ba Wang
Bie Ji,* 1993) by Fifth Generation masters Zhang Yimou and Chen Kaige.

Yellow Earth and the rise of the Fifth Generation

But looking back at the history of Chinese cinema of the 1980s, the Fifth
Generation continues to dominate. A term generally used to describe
the collective of filmmakers who graduated from the Beijing Film
Academy in 1982, the Fifth Generation is also frequently described as
China's New Wave, and like other cinematic New Waves before it, they
broke conventions, challenged long-standing cinematic moulds, and
offered an innovative new use of cinematic language. They did so not
from the margins, but from within the state-controlled studio system
itself, using smaller provincial film studios like Guangxi Film Studio and
Xi'an Film Studio (and the tutelage of veteran figures like Wu Tianming)
to launch their new cinematic initiative. And while many cite titles like
the collective effort *The Red Elephant* (*Hong Xiang,* 1982), Zhang Junzhao's
The One and the Eight (*Yige he Bage,* 1983) and Wu Ziniu's *Bloody Black
Valley* (*Diexue Heigu,* 1984) as the first works in this new movement,
1984's *Yellow Earth* (*Huang Tudi*) was clearly the game changer.

Yellow Earth borrowed some elements that externally seemed to
be left over from the socialist era – rural setting, a soldier protagonist,
attention to the plight of China's peasants, etc – but director Chen Kaige
reconfigured these standard tropes in a new way that would set Chinese
cinema on an entirely new path. The deceptively simple story, which
depicted a soldier in the Red Army travelling to a backwater in Shaanxi
province to collect rural folk songs, belied the film's more radical content
and form. Part of this new aesthetic vision was the way in which *Yellow
Earth* highlighted the natural environment in a manner that served as a
homage to traditional Chinese landscape painting by presenting diminutive
characters against expansive natural scenes of mountains and valleys.

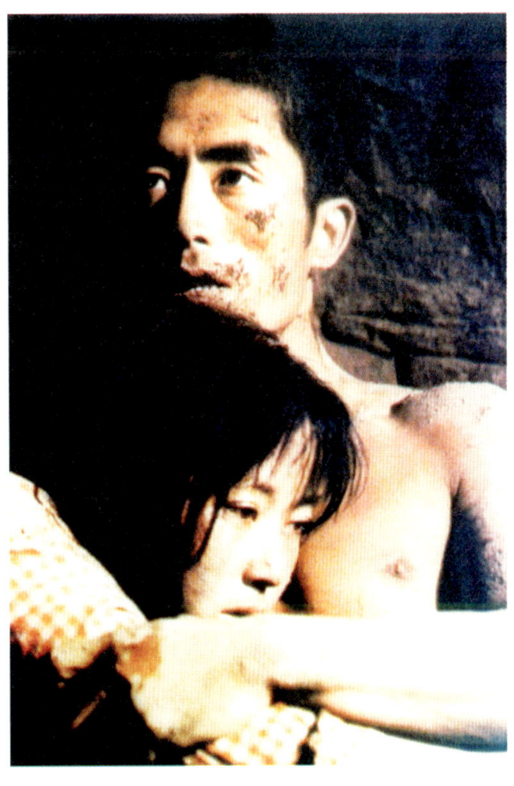

This new cinematic conception of the Chinese landscape – rendered through the very literal domination of the parched yellow earth over the wrinkled dirty peasants – was further augmented by cinematographer Zhang Yimou's bold techniques and unconventional horizon lines.

Yellow Earth also offered renewed attention to folk beliefs and customs, such as traditional arranged marriage ceremonies and the collective prayer to the Dragon God to bring rain to the sun-split land. Such attention to traditional folk beliefs was largely absent in the atheist world of Chinese socialist cinema. And most striking, although the film featured many signifiers left over from socialist cinema, in *Yellow Earth* they have become detached from their original ideological coding. The soldier protagonist is no longer the idealised communist hero from earlier films, just as the happy, healthy, hardworking peasants from countless socialist films are replaced with a new image dominated by impoverishment and silence. Victims of history, tradition and the harsh natural environment, the characters of *Yellow Earth* are not one-dimensional black and white heroes and villains; instead they are imbued with a newfound humanism and a sense of moral ambiguity. Of course, one can also read the film as a larger critique of China's socialist project – the soldier not only collects folk songs, but changes their lyrics into CCP propaganda, at once preserving tradition and destroying it – but more nakedly in the conflict between the CCP's utopian dream to 'liberate China' and the soldier's inability to save even a single poor peasant girl from an arranged marriage and certain fate. All of these qualities, including the collaborative spirit between director Chen Kaige, cinematographer Zhang Yimou, art designer He Qun and composer Zhao Jiping, helped define what would evolve into a major cinematic movement.

Evolution of the Fifth Generation

The critical acclaim and controversy surrounding *Yellow Earth* would help define the early phase of the Fifth Generation.' Many of the movement's early films would also deal with soldier characters – Chen's *The Big Parade* (*Da Yuebing*, 1986) or Zhang Yimou's *Red Sorghum* – but from an angle that consciously distanced them from socialist realist films dealing with similar themes. The Fifth Generation director who went furthest with his explorations of war was undoubtedly Wu Ziniu, whose series of war films *Bloody Black Valley*, *The Dove Tree* (*Gezi Shu*, 1985), *The Evening Bell* (*Wan Zhong*, 1989) and *Nanjing 1937* (1995) each imbued the genre with a reflective pacifist spirit.

Even more prevalent was the experimental avant-garde spirit behind many early Fifth Generation films. For Chen Kaige this experimental vision was best articulated in his films *King of the Children* (*Haizi Wang*, 1987) and *Life on a String* (*Bian Zou Bian Chang*, 1991). Zhang Yimou alternately experimented with documentary-film style aesthetics in *The Story of Qiu Ju* (*Qui Ju Da Guansi*, 1992), and formalistic framing – using an art design heavily indebted to symbolism and colour schemes in the allegorical *Ju Dou* (1990) and *Raise the Red Lantern* (*Da Hong Denglong Gaogao Gua*, 1991).

It was this series of films by Zhang Yimou which, perhaps more than those by any other director, helped put Chinese film on the international map during the 1980s. By the end of the decade, Zhang's films were met with great critical acclaim, received major awards at top festivals, and performed well on the international arthouse circuit. His films from this period, which frequently highlighted the plight of strong female characters struggling against the oppressive patriarchal structure of feudal China, all cast his muse Gong Li in the leading role; over time her image became synonymous with Chinese cinema of this era. Gong Li

(Below, left)
Zhang Yimou used documentary-
like aesthetics in 'The Story of
Qiu Ju' (1992), starring Gong Li.

(Bottom, left)
Gong Li in Zhang Yimou's
international arthouse hit
'Raise the Red Lantern' (1991).

(Below, right)
Zhang Yimou's controversial
'To Live' (1994) once again
starred his muse Gong Li.

(Bottom, right)
Zhang Yimou's sensual 'Ju Dou'
(1990), one of the films that made
Gong Li an international star.

would also go on to star in other major Fifth Generation films, such as Chen Kaige's *Farewell My Concubine* and *Temptress Moon* (*Fengyue*, 1996).

But arguably the most uncompromising voice of the generation was Tian Zhuangzhuang, who famously referred to his early masterpiece *The Horse Thief* (*Dao Mazei*, 1986) as a film made for the 21st century. Shot on location in Tibet using sparse dialogue, *The Horse Thief* depicted the life of Rorbu and his young family as they struggle against illness, poverty and the harsh environment. The film was a sharp turn from earlier portrayals of Tibet in Chinese film, like the 1963 film *Serfs* (*Nongnu*), instead offering much attention to the rites of Tibetan Buddhism, gorgeous cinematography by Hou Yong and Zhao Fei – two of the Fifth Generation's most talented cameramen – and an aesthetic that vacillated between realism and pure visual poetry. Tian's *The Horse Thief*, *On the Hunting Ground* (*Liechang Zhasa*, 1984) and other early films expressed a bold and challenging vision that resonated with the new literary movements of the decade (the search-for-roots movement, misty poetry and new avant-garde literature) and provided the single greatest challenge to prescriptive socialist cinematic moulds. Tian would also later go on to serve as a godfather-type figure to many of the younger 'Sixth Generation' filmmakers a decade later.

The experimental thrust of the Fifth Generation, however, did not last. Gradually most of the major voices of the movement gravitated away from the avant garde and closer to more commercial cinematic models. Cinematographer-turned-director Zhang Yimou always had the strongest commercial instincts among his classmates and seemed to quickly create his own unique filmic model predicated on lavish colours, pre-socialist feudal settings, strong female characters, powerful symbolic elements, and the image of China's first international superstar actress Gong Li. Films like *Red Sorghum*, *Ju Dou*, and *Raise the Red Lantern* became emblematic of the Fifth Generation itself and, in many ways, drove other works of the era that tried to emulate Zhang's formula. At the same time, as the movement developed it became increasingly clear just how tied the group was to the contemporary literary scene, with virtually all of their major works being literary adaptations from novels by leading writers like Mo Yan, Su Tong, Yu Hua and others. The shift from literary adaptation to original stories would eventually become one of the defining traits that would set the Fifth Generation against the independent-minded 'Sixth Generation.'

Although the collective collaborative spirit that dominated early Fifth Generation works like *Red Elephant* and *Yellow Earth* gave way to each of the major directors in the movement asserting their individual spirit, the Fifth Generation continued to follow similar trends. After a series of soldier and war themed films and a flirtation with the avant garde, during the early 1990s the modern historical epic emerged as the Fifth Generation's genre of choice. One by one, the leading representatives – Chen Kaige, Zhang Yimou and Tian Zhuangzhuang – produced *Farewell My Concubine*, *To Live* and *The Blue Kite* (*Lan Fengzheng*, 1993), all modern epics beginning in the pre-liberation era and concluding with the horror of the Cultural Revolution. The films also shared a similar fate as they gained solid reviews and good arthouse performance in Europe, Japan and other international markets while being banned at home.

Farewell My Concubine in particular went on to have a unique status in Chinese cinema – it is the only Chinese-language film to win the Palme d'Or at Cannes and is frequently listed by critics as one of the most influential films in Chinese film history. Adapted from a novel by Hong Kong writer Lilian Lee, produced by former Taiwan martial arts diva Hsu Feng, and featuring a cast that included leading PRC stars Gong Li, Ge You and

(Top)
'The Blue Kite' (1993), by Tian Zhuangzhuang, explored the horrors of the Cultural Revolution.

(Above)
Tian Zhuangzhuang shot his masterful 'The Horse Thief' (1986) on location in Tibet.

Zhang Fengyi with Hong Kong superstar Leslie Cheung, *Farewell* can also be seen as a clear indicator of the Fifth Generation's deeper pan-Chinese cinematic connections during this period. (*To Live* and other films of this period followed a similar production model). The story traced several decades in the lives of two Peking Opera stars, from their childhood during the Republican period and fame during the War of Resistance, ultimately building up to their fate under the red flag in New China. Chen tried to revisit this formula 15 years later with a biopic of opera icon Mei Lanfang in *Forever Enthralled* (*Mei Lanfang,* 2008), with less successful results. The state's ban of *Farewell* would eventually ease up, while *To Live* and *The Blue Kite* remain banned in China today. Collectively these three films stand as an important turning point for the Fifth Generation: moving away from allegory to confront the political horrors of modern Chinese history.

A few years later, members of the Fifth Generation would also dabble in more lighthearted urban-themed films like *Keep Cool* (*You Hua haohao Shuo,* 1997), *Happy Times* (*Xingfu Shiguang,* 2000) and *Together With You* (*He Ni zai Yiqi,* 2002). Eventually they would delve into a series of lavish big-budget films on Qin Shihuang, the First Emperor of China, from Zhou Xiaowen's *The Emperor's Shadow* (*Qinsong,* 1996), to Chen Kaige's *The Emperor and the Assassin* (*Jingke Ci Qinwang,* 1998), and culminating with Zhang Yimou's blockbuster *Hero* (*Yingxiong,* 2002).

In the wake of the unprecedented international box-office success of Ang Lee's *Crouching Tiger, Hidden Dragon* (*Wo Hu Cang Long,* 2000), *Hero* would also set in motion a new trend of big-budget *wuxia* fantasy films with pan-Asian casts and impressive martial-arts choreography augmented by state-of-the-art CGI effects. As Fifth Generation directors and their contemporaries tried to duplicate the *Crouching Tiger* model with varying degrees of success in titles like *House of Flying Daggers* (*Shimian Maifu,* 2004), *Curse of the Golden Flower* (*Man Cheng Jindai Huangjinjia,* 2006), *The Promise* (*Wuji,* 2005) and *The Banquet* (*Ye Yan,* 2006), they again demonstrated a collective will, this time no longer dominated by inspired experiments in cinematic form, but rather in their calculated pursuits of a new global model for Chinese cinema. By the time *Curse of the Golden Flower* and *The Promise* paraded their lavish sets, CGI-laden action sequences, convoluted stories and empty emotional excess across the Chinese silver screen, the original spirit that once produced *Yellow Earth* and *Red Sorghum* seemed like a distant memory.

That is not to say that all members of the group followed the same path. Just as Zhang Yimou and Chen Kaige vied to make more robust martial arts spectacles, Li Shaohong, the most prominent female director of the Fifth Generation, turned to contemporary urban-themed subject matter with excellent films like *Baober in Love* (*Lian'ai zhong de Baobei,* 2004) and *Stolen Life* (*Shengsi Jie,* 2005).

At the same time, long after the original heyday of the Fifth Generation, the collective has been somewhat reinvigorated by 'new old blood'. Some of the most innovative films of the 1990s and 2000s came from actors and technical personnel who cut their teeth on Fifth Generation directors' films before turning to directing much later. Lu Yue and Gu Changwei both made important films like *Mr. Zhao* (*Zhao Xiansheng,* 1998) and *Peacock* (*Kongque,* 2005), respectively, after establishing themselves as two of the representative cinematographers of the Fifth Generation. Even Jiang Wen, director of *In the Heat of the Sun* (*Yangguang Canlan de Rizi,* 1994) and *Let the Bullets Fly* (*Rang Zidan Fei,* 2010), was a figure associated with the movement during the early phase of his career, when he starred in such films as *Red Sorghum* and *Keep Cool.* Therefore, in considering

the long-term impact of this group, it is important not only to consider their own filmographies, but also a more broadly defined group of filmmakers that have been directly fostered by the Fifth Generation.

New commercial forms

During the height of the socialist era, the Chinese film industry was gripped by a set of ideological and generic restrictions. Popular genres that had once thrived in the pre-liberation days now languished, pushed aside to make room for more war films, odes to model heroes, and propagandistic accounts of revolutionary history. With the political thaw and liberalisation of the 1980s came the resurrection of numerous genres. Martial arts films, love stories, satires and comedies, angry youth and coming-of-age films are but a small sample of the new genre forms that greatly expanded the cinescape of China in the 1980s.

The flurry of genre films also led to some of the more idiosyncratic and unexpected films of the 1980s: Tian Zhuangzhuang's teen-angst film about break-dancers and motorcycle rebels, *Rock Kids* (*Yaogun Qingnian*, 1988), or Zhang Yimou's commercial thriller about a highjacked airplane, *Codename Cougar* (*Daihao: Meizhoubao*, 1989). Among this new commercial wave, some of the more innovative and stand-out features include Huang Jianxin's brilliant *Black Cannon Incident* (*Heipao Shijian*, 1985), a breakthrough title whose formal style, black humour and allegorical dimensions left a deep impact on audiences at the time. Huang's film depicts the fate of Zhao Shuxin, whose sending of a simple telegram reading "lost black cannon" leads him into a Kafkaesque labyrinth of bureaucracy and absurdity.

Also of note is the enormous impact of the film adaptations of contemporary writer Wang Shuo. Referred to at the time as a "hooligan writer", Wang captured the dark, whimsical undercurrent of 1980s society through a cast of swindlers, dreamers and outcasts. With four film adaptations released in 1988 – referred to by the Chinese media as Wang Shuo Year – titles like *The Trouble Shooters* (*Wanzhu*, 1988) certainly tapped into the pulse of pre-Tiananmen China. These films also gave rise to a new generation of Chinese comedy stars like Liang Tian and Ge You.

Another major trend in the film industry during the 1980s was the beginning of privatisation and co-productions, and while both trends had a negligible impact in that decade, they planted the seeds for changes that would gradually take root and lead to a monumental overhaul and restructuring of the entire industry in the 1990s and especially the 2000s. The 1980s was the era of *xiahai* (meaning the 'jumping into the sea' of commerce) and saw the privatisation of many industries. Already in the 1980s audiences witnessed the first PRC-Hong Kong co-productions, such as the series of imperial costume dramas helmed by Li Hanxiang, a model that would become increasingly common by the 1997 handover, and eventually completely transform both the PRC and Hong Kong film industries.

By the end of the 1980s, most PRC film productions were still produced by Chinese state-owned film studios, but the writing was already on the wall. Spurred by internal forces of privatisation, external forces of globalisation, as well as ever-increasing ties with pan-Chinese and pan-Asian collaborators, investors, and consumers, the 1980s marked the final years of the 'Chinese National Cinema' as it had existed for the previous four decades. For as China advanced towards the 1990s and 2000s, the industry would be irrevocably transformed by not only privatisation, but by piracy, the rise of independent cinema, the post-1997 integration with the Hong Kong film industry, and by international co-productions, all of which would take the industry into new uncharted waters. ◐

(Top)
'The Trouble Shooters' (1988)
tapped into the pulse of
pre-Tiananmen China.

(Above)
Huang Jianxin's blackly comic
'Black Cannon Incident' (1985).

Eight is a lucky number in Chinese – it's to do with homophones, don't worry about it – so it's a happy accident that 1988 was a watershed year for Chinese cinema. It was the year when the Communist Party, prompted by Deng Xiaoping's strategies for economic reform, announced plans to move the film industry from the state sector into the private sector. It was the year when a 'floating ticket price' was introduced in urban cinemas, producing a 17 per cent increase in box-office revenues despite a sharp decline in film-going in rural areas.

It was also the year that 'Fifth Generation' cinema came to its *de facto* end with the system's effective refusal to distribute Chen Kaige's *King of the Children (Haizi Wang*, 1987) and Hu Mei's *Far from War (Yuanli Zhanzheng de Niandai*, 1987). 'Fifth Generation' stragglers like the films that Zhang Yimou, Tian Zhuangzhuang and Chen Kaige made in the 1990s don't really count in the same way, since they were all foreign-financed and several were at least temporarily banned in China. Not so coincidentally, 1988 was the year when Chen Kaige (the only fluent speaker of English among the 1982 graduates from Beijing Film Academy) moved to New York on a scholarship and began trying to set up an American independent feature. And, most seminally of all, it was the year when the documentary filmmaker Wu Wenguang began filming the lives of independent artists in Beijing.

There are four main reasons why independent filmmaking began in China in the late 1980s, and we'll need to deal with them one by one. Obviously this is a short-hand account; there is much more to say about every reason we identify. The first factor to note is the continuing fall-out from the 'Great Proletarian Cultural Revolution' (1966-76), which had given young people licence to challenge and attack authority figures, including parents and teachers, and had destroyed traditional codes of social courtesy. Even before Mao Zedong's death in 1976, the young people fired up with Maoist fervour had learnt the hard way that Communist Party leaders could themselves be straw idols. Indeed, the Party itself had demonstrated the point by toppling once-favoured sons such as Deng Xiaoping, Liu Shaoqi and Lin Biao. And even before the protest-occupation of Tiananmen Square in the spring of 1989, a new generation of young people, aware of burgeoning changes in the Soviet bloc, felt that it had the right to question authority and distance itself from the established *modus operandi* of communist society. The Cultural Revolution had the side-effect of sparking new attitudes and stances in young people.

The harbingers of this new spirit of independence were the self-styled artists in Beijing's tumbledown alleys and slums who looked for ways to survive outside the system. Wu Wenguang, a refugee from state-controlled television journalism in Kunming, began an informal documentation of the lives of five such artists on 16mm in 1988 without seeking official permission for the project – or having any clear sense of how or when the resulting film would be shown. (Wu was born in 1956, making him much the same age as most of the 'Fifth Generation' directors, but his roots in Yunnan – he had been a primary-school teacher before taking a degree in literature – made him more of an outsider in Beijing than most of the Film Academy crowd.) Wu's two-and-a-half-hour film *The Last Dreamers: Bumming in Beijing (Zuihou de Mengxiangzhe)* was completed in 1990, the first authentically independent film made in China since the communists came to power in 1949. Thanks to help from foreign friends, it was very soon seen in festivals outside China.

The second key factor behind the emergence of independent filmmaking was the reorganisation of the film industry, in direct response to changes in Party policy. In 1988 China had 16 state-run film studios

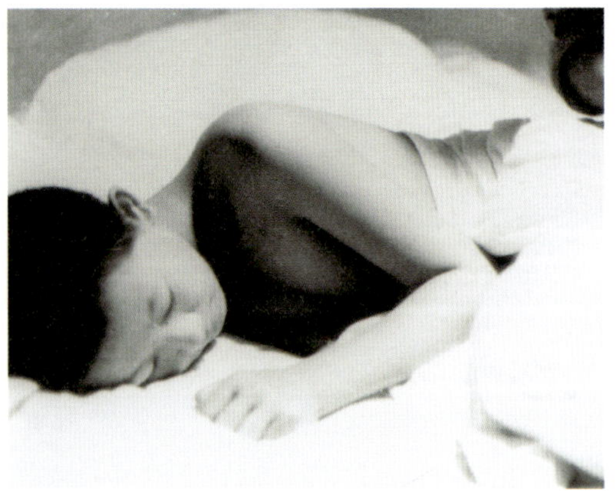

scattered around the country; some of the smaller and more far-flung ones existed mainly to demonstrate the Party's commitment to regionalism and respect for diversity and ethnic minorities. The entire film industry was centrally controlled: the Film Bureau in Beijing set production targets for each studio, rationed out raw film stock and 'advised' on policy and propaganda topics which needed to be covered in the films. Graduates from Beijing Film Academy were routinely assigned to the studios; directors-to-be could generally expect to wait ten years or so to be given a chance to make a feature. Famously, some 'Fifth Generation' directors in the mid-1980s were able to 'jump the queue' because they were assigned to the smaller, less productive studios like the one in Nanning, Guangxi in the deep south-west.

When the authorities announced in 1988 that the film industry would in future have to live on its own profits – and that China Film Corporation, the state-monopoly distributor-cum-sales agent for all Chinese films, would lose its position – most of the studios panicked and all but froze production. Decades of state-commanded filmmaking had not produced personnel with any competence in cost-effective company or production management, much less anyone knowledgeable about distribution or foreign sales, and many of the studios preferred to do nothing rather than risk making unprofitable or potentially disapproved films. Since the larger studios were already massively over-staffed, the new situation led them to refuse to take on new graduates from the Film Academy. The directing-class students who graduated in 1989 found themselves without assigned jobs to go to.

The studios' extreme reluctance to take on new staff was exacerbated by the third factor on our list: the protest-occupation of Tiananmen Square in the spring of 1989, bloodily curtailed on the night of 4 June. All students were regarded with suspicion by the establishment in the aftermath of the massacre, and it was well-known that Film Academy students had been active in the protests, not least for shooting film and video of the demonstration. It must go without saying that the events in Tiananmen Square that spring crystallised the mood of frustration and impatience felt by numerous young people in the years since Mao's death, and that the psychological wounds inflicted by the way the Party ended the protests had lasting effects on the attitudes and behaviour of many. The effect on the independent artists that Wu Wenguang was filming can be seen in the poignantly wordless sequence in *The Last Dreamers* in which they break down in tears.

The fourth factor which gave rise to independent filmmaking was the arrival of China's advertising and pop-music industries. Plenty of Film Academy students – along with under-employed staffers from the TV stations – had been able to earn themselves decent pocket money by working on ads and music videos. This kind of 'casual' work was new in Chinese society, and it bred an openness to the idea of surviving as a freelancer felt by few Chinese since 1949.

The lightweight cameras and recording equipment which made *cinéma vérité* possible had appeared in the US in the 1960s and (thanks to the TV series *The Living Camera*) had transformed the idiom of documentary making virtually overnight. But no such transformation had occurred in China, where the output of the Central Newsreel and Documentary Studio resembled British *Look at Life* programme-fillers with added propaganda. When *The Last Dreamers* first surfaced at 'underground' screenings in 1990, it helped to establish intimate reportage and portrait documentary as viable forms for anyone with access to 16mm or video cameras. Wu Wenguang himself went on to dig up the grass roots of the Cultural Revolution in 1966, in *My Time in the Red Guards* (1992). This provided valuable context and background for the 'Fifth Generation' features of the 1980s; Wu even turned to Tian Zhuangzhuang for some of the testimony. But Wu's initiative with *The Last Dreamers* had already triggered various other reportage documentaries in the independent artist and student milieux. The most notable was *I Have Graduated* (*Wo Biyele*, 1990), which got inside the now heavily guarded campus of Beijing University to ask students how they saw their future after the massacre. The film was signed by 'The Structure, Wave, Youth, Cinema Experimental Group' whose prime mover was Wang Guangli, later to emerge as an interesting independent director under his own name.

The 'First Wave' of Independents

The film that kick-started the first wave of independent fiction filmmaking was *Mama* (1991), a drama in black and white with documentary inserts in colour about a woman's struggle to cope as a single parent with her mentally disabled son. It was directed by Zhang Yuan, recently graduated from the cinematography class at the Film Academy, but the project had been initiated and developed by Wang Xiaoshuai in 1990. Wang (like Chen Kaige earlier, a fluent English speaker), facing unemployment and eager to make a film, saw that UNESCO's upcoming 'Year of the Child' might help him raise private, charitable funds for a child-centred feature. Nobody knows for sure if the Film Bureau got wind of his preparations, but Wang was suddenly and unforeseeably handed instructions to report for duty at Fujian Film Studio in the south. He eventually decided to obey (he worked in Fujian for a year or so as assistant to the 'Fifth Generation' director Wu Ziniu) and handed the *Mama* project on to Zhang Yuan.

Zhang went on to make the film without Film Bureau permission or approval, and then managed to sell the finished film to Xi'an Film Studio, which submitted it to the Film Bureau in the usual way. (Like most studios, Xi'an had produced next to nothing on its own initiative in the depressed climate of 1991.) Before that happened, though, a subtitled print was mysteriously smuggled to Hong Kong and then onward to festivals in Vancouver and elsewhere. It took three years for the Film Bureau to notice what was happening, by which time several more independent features were enjoying international acclaim, but I can report that in 1994 the Film Bureau politely but mistakenly accused me of having smuggled *Mama* into Hong Kong. It was perhaps understandably enraged that an unapproved and uncensored Chinese film had found its way into the international arena. The words 'horse' and 'stable door' come to mind.

Wang Xiaoshuai was motivated by the success of *Mama* outside China to quit his post in Fujian and return to Beijing to make an independent feature of his own. He was also spurred by the fact that the credits of *Mama* made no mention of his preparatory work on the project, a token of ingratitude which sadly turned out to be characteristic of Zhang Yuan. Like Wu Wenguang, Wang had been drawn to Beijing's burgeoning community of independent artists; the painter Liu Xiaodong, soon to be one of China's most celebrated artists, had already acted in Wang's student short *White* (*Bai*, 1987). For his debut feature *The Days* (*Dong-Chun de Rizi*, 1993), Wang chose to focus on the mood of anomie and incipient madness which had taken hold in that community after the massacre. Real-life couple Liu Xiaodong and Yu Hong play painters whose marriage disintegrates when the woman finds a way to emigrate; Wang's classmate Lou Ye appears in a cameo as a student on the run from the authorities after the crackdown in Tiananmen Square. Wang took all these themes further in his second feature *Frozen* (*Jidu Hanleng*, 1995-97,

signed 'Wu Ming' ['Anonymous']), which explores the self-destructive impulses and hypocrisies of Beijing's independent artists across the story of a man who performs a series of ritualised fake suicides.

Motifs of confinement, surveillance and looming mental breakdown dominated other films in the 'first wave' of independent filmmaking. He Jianjun, with a background as a production assistant in the industry rather than a Film Academy training, made *Red Beads* (*Xuan Lian*, 1993), a dark fantasia about a young man imagining that he works as an orderly in a squalid asylum while he waits for his girlfriend in a noisy restaurant, and *Postman* (*Youchai*, 1995), about a young man who reads the mail he delivers and thus accesses the sexual secrets wof the residents on his round. Wu Di, who had photographed part of *The Days* and all of *Postman*, made *Goldfish* (*Huangjin Yu*, 1995), in which a young man planning to emigrate panics at the airport and is reduced to hiding with his fiancée in a farmhouse outside Beijing.

Zhang Yuan meanwhile launched into an association with China's foremost rock star Cui Jian, resulting in four powerful music videos and the feature *Beijing Bastards* (*Beijing Zazhong*, 1993), which chronicles Cui's rehearsals with his band and their struggles to get permission for public performances; it also shows how Cui's music (hugely popular during the Tiananmen Square protests in 1989) provides the soundtrack to the life of a disaffected kid who has got his girlfriend pregnant. It's a safe bet that it was the Cui Jian connection which led the Film Bureau to take action against Zhang Yuan: he was one week into the filming of his third feature, *Chicken Feathers on the Ground* (*Yi Di Jimao*), in December

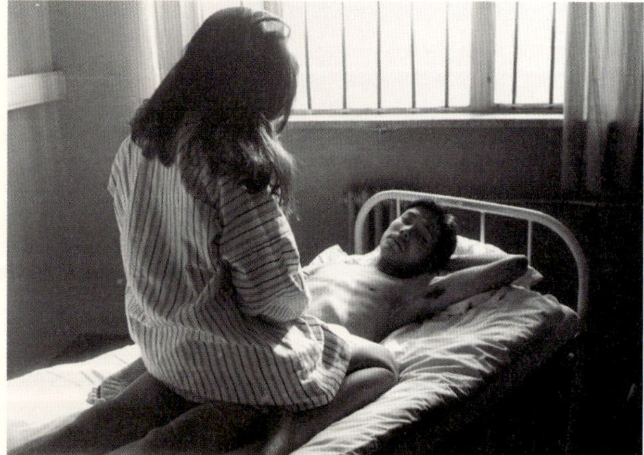

1993 when the authorities brought pressure on his private financier to disinvest – leading to the abandonment of the project. Zhang's then-wife Ning Dai documented both the shoot and its enforced cancellation in her videotape *A Film is Stopped* (*Yibu Yingpian Wei Wancheng Yinqi de Taolun*, 1994). Zhang Yuan and Ning Dai both found their names on a Film Bureau blacklist in the spring of 1994, specifying that no one should rent equipment to them or provide material support for their 'illegal' filmmaking, and that no lab should process their film stock. (Other names on the blacklist included Wang Xiaoshuai – hence the 'anonymity' of *Frozen* – and Tian Zhuangzhuang, named for completing *The Blue Kite* without permission and showing it abroad.) The Film Bureau went on to specifically outlaw independent, unauthorised production from 1 July 1996.

The filmmakers initially responded with defiance. China has many 'back door' ways of getting things done, and no one was deterred by the prohibition on accessing equipment and lab facilities. Zhang Yuan was especially cheeky: immediately after the publication of the blacklist, he teamed up with documentary director Duan Jinchuan to make *The Square* (*Guangchang*, 1994), a 100-minute 'portrait' of Tiananmen Square – the symbolic heart of the communist state – showing how ordinary Chinese use the space and how the authorities police it. He went on to make *Sons* (*Erzi*, 1995), a docudrama about one dysfunctional family which prefigured present-day 'structured reality' shows, and then – prompted by his chance discovery of Beijing's subterranean gay scene – the remarkable *East Palace, West Palace* (*Dong Gong, Xi Gong*, 1996). This multi-layered film started out as a sociological survey of the city's gay subculture – the title invokes the gay-slang names for two public toilets in the Forbidden City, both notorious for cruising – but morphed into a chamber drama about the sado-masochist relationship between a macho cop and an arrested gay man who desires him. It's not hard to see the film as a cipher for Zhang Yuan's own flirtatious (ambivalently submissive and defiant) relationship with state power.

Coupled with the impossibility of getting independent films screened in China's cinemas, the Film Bureau's increasingly agitated suppression of the movement took its toll. By 1997, coincidentally the year that Britain gave up its colonial rule in Hong Kong, all of the main indie directors of the 'first wave' had either stopped making films or were looking for ways to work within the still conspicuously disordered film industry. The heroic exception was Wang Guangli, who used his own advertising film company as a front to make his first fiction feature *Maiden Work* (*Chunü Zuo*) in 1997; the film was almost recklessly indie in spirit, since it picked up Wang Xiaoshuai's focus on independent artists, featured a lesbian affair and had a complicated meta-fictional structure. Tian Zhuangzhuang, always the 'Fifth Generation' director most sympathetic to the younger independents, negotiated an end to his own blacklisting by setting up a quasi-independent production company called Pegase within Beijing Film Studio; its inaugural productions included Wang Xiaoshuai's third feature, his first 'official' film, *So Close to Paradise* (*Biandan • Guniang*, 1998), eventually completed after three years of wrangling with the Film Bureau. After a couple of years of inactivity, Zhang Yuan made his first two 'official' features in 1999. The wave of independent filmmaking seemed to be over.

The 'Second Wave' of Independents

The lull didn't last long. A former art student in Taiyuan and an aspiring novelist, Jia Zhangke had taken a film theory course at Beijing Film Academy in the mid-1990s. While there, in 1995, he founded the 'Youth Experimental Film Group' and made two shorts and the hour-

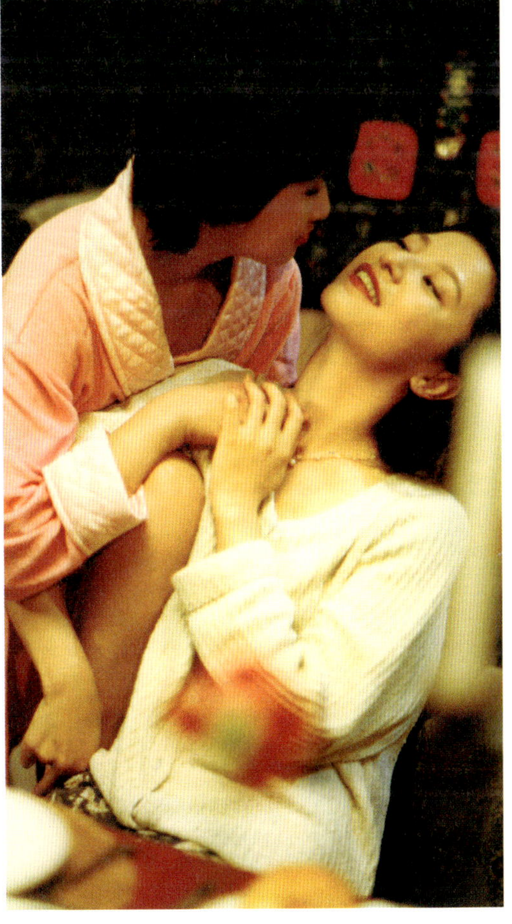

Blind Shaft

Li Yang, 2003

Li Yang's 'underground' film *Blind Shaft* is my favourite Chinese film made since my own career began in the late 1970s. I first saw it on DVD – there was no cinema release at first because of its subject. It gives a very true picture of modern China, exposing the dangers and corruption faced by China's illegal miners.

The opening scene takes us down hundreds of metres into a deep pit. Suddenly, in the middle of a peaceful chat between three miners about their plans for New Year, a brutal murder takes place. The scene is lit only by the torches on the miners' helmets, and the impact is powerful and original.

***Blind Shaft* has courage. It is about more than just expressing a personal filmic style. Its horizons are broader; it scrutinises humanity within a shocking social context. It shows the wicked sides of its characters, but also the potential hope hidden in them. It's a piercing analysis, cutting deeply into our world of hypocrisy and vanity, ideology and propaganda.**

Li Yang lived among the miners for more than a year, getting to know details of their daily lives. He showed tremendous courage to face down the relentless commerciality of the industry and the censorship of the authorities to get the film made, and I salute him for it.

***Blind Shaft* is a record of our times, one that will allow future generations to understand contemporary China better than any 'heroic' or 'beautiful' story will do.**

long film *Xiao Shan Going Home* (*Xiao Shan Hui Jia*, 1995). During a visit to a student film festival in Hong Kong, he met the cinematographer Yu Lik-Wai and producers Li Kit-Ming and Chow Keung; together they hatched the plan for a low-budget independent feature to be shot in Jia's home town Fenyang in Shanxi Province. The result was *Xiao Wu* (aka *Pickpocket*, 1997), which became the foundation-stone for a second wave of independent filmmaking, on a much bigger scale than the first.

Jia's default idiom was realist, but from the start his *mise en scène*, his preference for extended takes and his use of narrative patterning made his work extraordinary. *Xiao Wu* was first screened in the Forum section of the Berlin Film Festival in February 1998 and quickly won so much acclaim that Jia was offered investment for his future projects from Japan and France. He went on to make two more 'illegal' films – *Platform* (*Zhantai*, 2000) and *Unknown Pleasures* (*Ren Xiao Yao*, 2002), both of them also set in Shanxi – before reaching an accommodation with the Film Bureau for his fourth feature *The World* (*Shijie*, 2004). By then Jia's idiom was edging into 'magic realist' territory, with elements of sci-fi and fantasy.

Jia's first three features proved massively influential throughout China; before long there was hardly a city of any size in the country which didn't have at least one independent filmmaker. Why were Jia's films so much more inspirational than the films from the 'first wave' of independents had been in the 1990s? Several reasons. First, people could watch them – thanks to the rapid spread of pirated DVDs. Video piracy began in China's southern provinces, near Hong Kong and Taiwan, and remains based there to this day. The publication and distribution of pirated discs was very open until the authorities cracked down during the run-up to the Beijing Olympics. The high-street shops selling cheap knock-offs of everything from commercial blockbusters to Criterion Collection titles have now gone, but the piracy industry survives underground. Nowadays it takes only a phone call or an SMS text to bring a vendor to your door with cases containing a cross-section of everything cinema has to offer: vintage classics, BBC wildlife documentaries, boxed sets of Godard's near-complete works, Japanese *pink eiga*, you name it. Back in 2004, the owner of a pirate-video store in Beijing told me that he was shifting around 50 copies of *Xiao Wu* every day.

Second, advances in the tech field had brought the means of production into the hands of many more people. Equipped with a camcorder and Edit-pro software, anyone could make a film, and many did. The Film Bureau obligingly turned a blind eye (it decreed that digital films were outside its remit, a position since rethought) and festivals of independent cinema were launched in Beijing, Nanjing, Chongqing and Hangzhou.

Third, and most important of all, on 13 November 1998 Jia Zhangke published his essay 'The Era of Amateur Cinema is Near' in the famously liberal weekly newspaper *Southern Weekend* (*Nanfang Zhoumo*). It's not hard to find this text online, and it's worth seeking it out. It was very widely reprinted after its first appearance, and rapidly became the single most influential essay on filmmaking ever published in China. In it, Jia argues against cinema that panders to critics and credulous audiences and for ethics and truthfulness, no matter how rough-hewn.

The immediate effect of Jia's influence was a small flood of indie movies which looked very much like imitation Jia Zhangke films. The punning term '*jia de Jia Zhangke*' ('fake Jia Zhangke') became current as filmmakers across China picked up on Jia's idiosyncratic style, his use of regional microcosms as ciphers for China's larger social, economic and political changes and his focus on ethical questions. This phase proved to be short-lived, as the better indie directors began to discover their own identities.

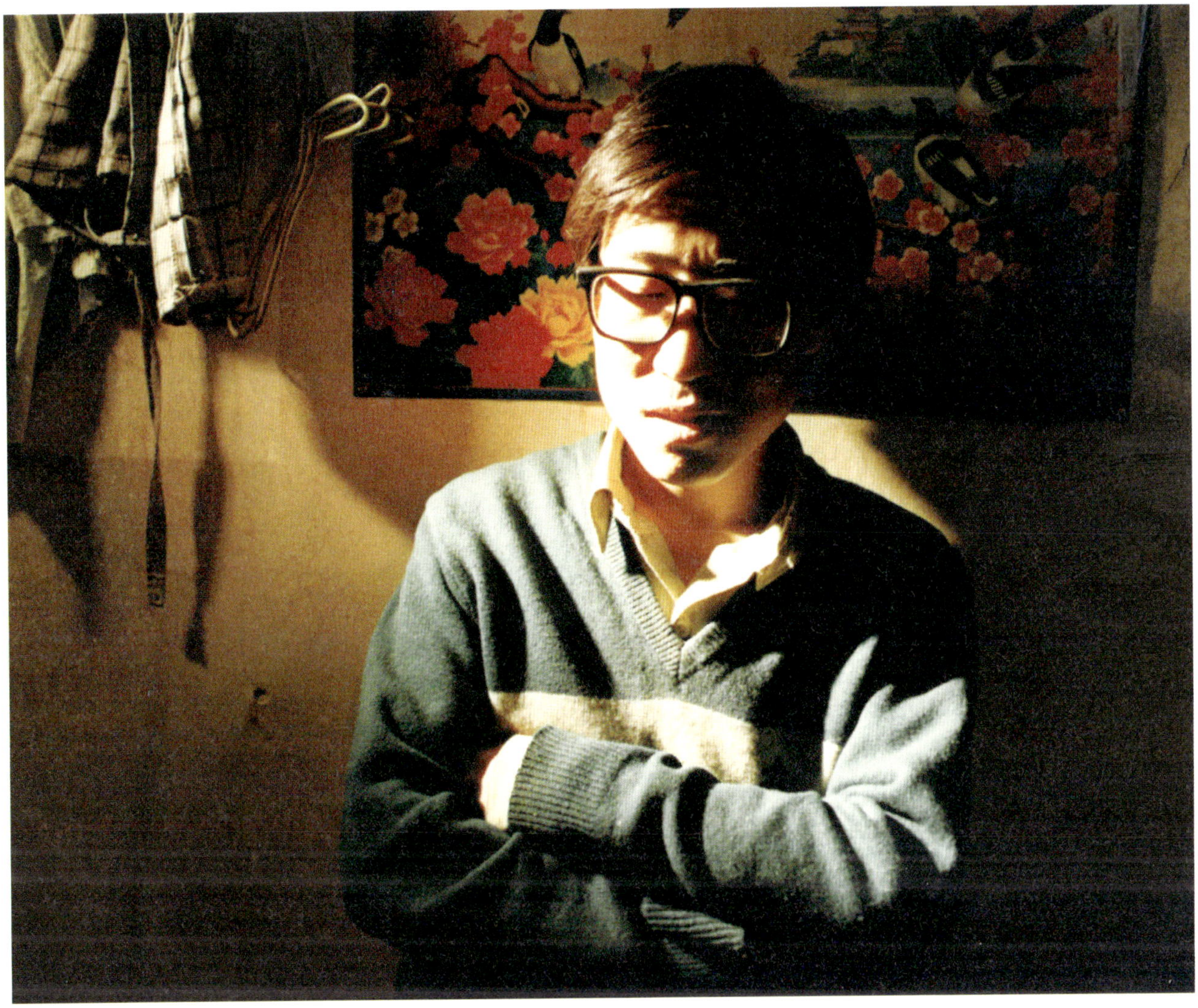

(Above)
Wang Hongwei in Jia Zhangke's 'Xiao Wu' (1997), which launched a second wave of independent filmmaking.

(Below)
Jia Zhangke (centre) during the filming of 'Xiao Wu'.

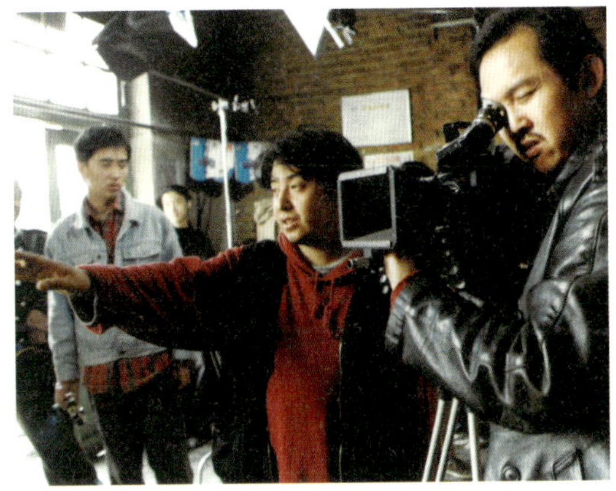

A couple of examples among many. Ning Hao (like Jia, a native of Shanxi), was still a post-graduate student in the Film Academy's cinematography department when he made the Jia-like indie feature *Incense* (*Xianghuo*, 2004), on a Buddhist priest's disastrous attempts to renovate his temple; his subsequent 'legal' black comedies, some of them hugely successful in China, suggest that his real sensibility lies somewhere between Tsui Hark and Sergio Leone. Wang Chao meanwhile stopped working as Chen Kaige's assistant in the industry and went indie to make the Jia-like *The Orphan of Anyang* (*Anyang de Gu'er*, 2001), in which a bicycle repairman and a small-time gangster battle it out over adopting a fatherless infant, and then found backers in France who gave him the freedom to explore his ideas about class conflict in subsequent movies.

Other new filmmakers were less inspired by Jia's films than by his demonstrations that relatively modest indie productions could achieve global distribution and win large audiences. One prime example would be Zhu Wen, born during the Cultural Revolution, who was working in a thermal power plant (he studied electrical engineering) when he began publishing fiction and poetry. In 2001 he enlisted the help of Wu Wenguang and Jia Zhangke's cinematographer Yu Lik-Wai in making his debut feature *Seafood* (*Haixian*), a very sardonic drama of the sex wars featuring a macho cop and a suicidal prostitute, set in the Communist

Party's favourite seaside resort Beidaihe. Zhu went on to make the 'legal' films *South of the Clouds* (*Yun de Nanfang*, 2003) and *Thomas Mao* (*Xiao Dongxi*, 2010), but maintained strong connections with prominent figures in the independent arts scene, such as the 'underground' musician Zuoxiao Zuzhou. Another example would be the Korean-Chinese novelist Zhang Lu (Korean name: Jang Ryeol), who turned filmmaker in 2003 with the droll, minimalist *Tang Poetry* (*Tang Shi*) and deflected the Film Bureau's attentions by identifying it – and his subsequent films – as Korean productions.

Some of the post-Jia surge in independent filmmaking parallels equivalent 'renegade' work in Western countries by giving voice to marginalised groups, such as ethnic and sexual minorities. Cui Zi'en, born in Harbin, was teaching at the Film Academy when he co-scripted the indie feature *Men and Women* (*Nan Nan Nü Nü*, 1999), directed by Liu Bingjian, which splices together an amusing fantasy of gay activism with Chinese characteristics and a realist melodrama about a young man chased by both a woman and her husband. Cui, who also publishes fiction, poetry and criticism, went on to direct a dozen or more indie features himself, exploring gay male desires, problems and fantasies, culminating in the documentary feature *Queer China, 'Comrade' China* (*Zhi Tongzhi*, 2009). Li Yu abandoned her career as a writer-director with CCTV, China's state broadcaster, to make the indie feature *Fish and Elephant* (*Yu he Daxiang*, aka *Jin Nian Xiatian*, 2001), centred on a lesbian relationship which comes under various strains; her later films have been 'legal' but have regularly run into trouble at the Film Bureau.

The foremost ethnic minority independents are the Tibetans: Pema-tseden and his cinematographer Sonthar-gyal have both made remarkably vivid films in their native villages with non-professional actors, grappling with issues of identity, tradition and the generation gap. For obvious reasons, they both avoid direct discussion of China's presence in Tibet and its claim to sovereignty.

There are now so many independent filmmakers in China that any survey of their work risks degenerating into a list of names and dates. It's embarrassing that we have not yet touched on the films of such major figures as Li Hongqi, Zhang Yuedong, Diao Yinan, Liu Fendou, Yang Heng, Ying Liang, Pan Jianlin and Li Luo, not to mention young rebels like Robin Weng and Wu Haohao. We should also have pointed out that women directors remain pretty marginalised, despite the best efforts of Liu Jiayin, Yang Lina, Vivian Qu and a few others, and that independent documentary-making (some of it challengingly investigative) remains important, thanks to Zhao Liang, Wang Bing, Du Haibin and many others. It may be more useful, though, to note two recent developments.

One is that the Chinese film industry has found its feet commercially: new multiplexes are everywhere, audience levels are rivalling those in the US, and investment in film production has never been higher. Many new investors appear every year, most of them industrial entrepreneurs with spare cash, and that has made it easier for such directors as Diao Yinan to make 'legal' films – *Black Coal, Thin Ice* (*Bairi Yanhuo*, 2014), winner of Berlin's Golden Bear – without losing touch with their indie roots. But there is still little or no space in Chinese distribution and exhibition for 'alternative' or 'arthouse' titles, and it's safe to assume that streaming sites and the purveyors of pirated DVDs will go on meeting the needs and tastes of the niche audiences who want to see something more than mainstream entertainment. The current economic and cultural climate has closed off many possibilities for indie and ex-indie directors, The shining exception is Jia Zhangke, now with many uncompromised features to his credit,

but his latest film *A Touch of Sin* (*Tian Zhuding*, 2013) has hit a roadblock. Although initially passed by the Film Bureau, its release in China has been indefinitely postponed – and the pirates have moved in to make it available through 'underground' channels, robbing Jia of his paying audience.

The other significant development in the last two years is that the Film Bureau has renewed its attack on the independent fringe, the indie filmmakers who never aspired to commercial distribution either at home or abroad. In 2012-13, all of China's festivals for this kind of cinema were forced to close or suspend their activities. Li Xianting's Film Fund, the major institution supporting grass-roots independents, has been prevented from holding its annual festival and its other programmes of teaching and publishing have been curtailed. There is no new motivation for these attacks: they spring from the Party's fear of dissidence and its horror of what it calls 'chaos' or 'instability'. Independent filmmakers are not the only victims of these attacks: the independent artist community was forced out of three 'artist districts' in East Beijing, as documented in Zheng Kuo's tape *The Cold Winter* (*Ai Dong*, 2012)… which was produced by Li Xianting's Fim Fund. Anyone who follows China's politics knows that tolerance and suppression run in cycles; it would be melodramatic to suggest that the authorities are succeeding in their clamp-down. The situation is currently grim for the independents, but it's inconceivable that they'll be silenced. ☉

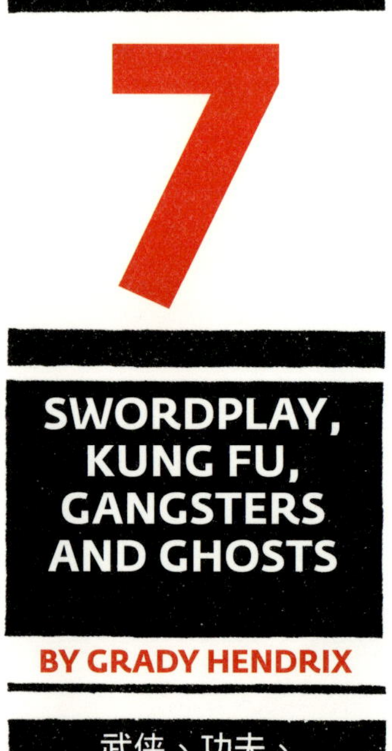

A Chinese genre whose roots go back over 2000 years, *wuxia* (which translates very roughly as 'martial hero') relates the feats of wandering swordsman whose martial arts are so highly developed that they can internalise their *qi* (life force) to fly, shoot swords, and even blast adversaries with 'palm power,' emitting bolts of force from their hands.

Wuxia stories typically take place in the *jiang hu* (literally 'rivers and lakes') – a mythic underworld in which swordsmen, jugglers, pimps, kidnappers, bandits, wandering monks, bodyguards and burglars cross paths. Those in the *jiang hu* are governed by a strict code of honour and obligation, resulting in the proverb: "In the *jiang hu*, a man cannot decide for himself."

The modern *wuxia* genre arose during the Tang Dynasty and experienced a surge in popularity after the May Fourth movement of 1919. It took a while for *wuxia* to make it on to film, but in 1928 *Burning of the Red Lotus Temple* (*Huoshao Honglian Si*) opened the gates. An epic adaptation of the popular 100-chapter story *Legend of the Strange Hero*, the film was, for its time, a special-effects extravaganza. The story concerns a property conflict between two villages, but it was really just an excuse for duelling martial artists to unleash their 'Thunder Palms', 'Shout Weapons' and 'Weightless Leaps.' *Red Lotus* spawned 17 more instalments, all filled with booby-trapped labyrinths, underground fortresses, and special effects painted directly on to the film.

Between 1928 and 1930, *wuxia* made up more than half of all Chinese films. Believing that these pictures encouraged rebellion, China's Nationalist government banned *wuxia* films outright in 1931. As Japan tightened its grip on China, filmmakers fled Shanghai for Hong Kong and in 1938 the first Hong Kong *wuxia*, *The Adorned Pavilion,* was produced. Screens in the British colony were soon playing films like *The Strange Hero Yi Zhimei* (*Guai Xia Yizhimei*, 1940) based on *The Mark of Zorro*, and remakes of 1920s Shanghai *wuxia*, such as *Female Security Escort* (*Nü Biao Shi*, 1941).

Sword-slinging heroines

In the mid-1950s a new school of *wuxia* novel began to appear in Taiwan and Hong Kong. Penned by writers such as Jin Yong, and later Gu Long, their plots shifted from warring schools and sects to lone swordsmen making their way in the *jiang hu*. Gu Long's novels, such as *Sentimental Swordsman, Ruthless Sword* (*Duoqing Jianke Wuqing Jian*), focused on disillusioned, isolated heroes who sought nothing more than to leave the world of the *jiang hu* behind. Hong Kong's *wuxia* trend was reignited in 1961, when the three-film series *The Secret Book* reawakened audience appetites.

The new *wuxia* were more visually elegant than viscerally exciting, and mostly populated by female knights. Chinese cinema's biggest stars had always been women, a tradition dating back at least to 1925 when Chin Tsi-ang, a 16-year-old martial artist, shot to fame as a sword-slinging heroine in dozens of Shanghainese *wuxia*. In 1960s Hong Kong cinema, actors Connie Chan (often cross-dressing as the male hero) and Josephine Siao (often playing the heroine) co-starred in numerous *wuxia* while fans of the two teenage heroines rumbled in the streets over whose idol was the better actress.

In 1957, Run Run Shaw had been summoned from Shaw Brothers' Singapore studios to Hong Kong to do battle with the family's major Hong Kong rivals, MP&GI. His biggest weapon in this cinematic cold war was Movietown, a vast studio in Clearwater Bay that took five years to

build. When it was completed, Run Run Shaw controlled everything, from production to film distribution to running fan clubs for his stars. Twelve soundstages shot day and night, filming scripts from Shaw's 15 full-time writers. Movietown's processing labs allowed them to develop eight hours of film every day, and they never stopped running.

By the mid-1960s, half of Hong Kong's population was under 25, and the biggest local box-office hits were the James Bond films, Sergio Leone's spaghetti westerns and Japanese samurai films; but Shaw was mostly turning out elegant historical dramas, musicals and romances. Such films felt increasingly out of step with the times: in 1966, the Cultural Revolution engulfed Mainland China; the following year, in May 1967, Hong Kong police used excessive force to break up a strike, kicking off a year of riots, bombings and bloodshed between leftists and the colonial police.

That same year, Shaw Brothers released *The One-Armed Swordsman* (*Dubi Dao*, 1967), and it helped spawn modern Hong Kong *wuxia* cinema.

Young men dressed in blood

In 1965, Shaw's film magazine, *Southern Screen*, ran an article bragging that the studio was to launch a "colour *wuxia* offensive." "Shaws will break with tradition," it crowed. "Creating a new vista for martial arts films. The fake, fantastical, and theatrical fighting and the so-called special effects of the past will be replaced by realistic action and fighting that immediately decides life or death."

It had mostly been a failure. The first three films flopped, production on the fourth was delayed, the fifth was completed but shelved, and only King Hu's *Come Drink with Me* (*Da Zui Xia*, 1966) was a hit. But the seventh was *The One-Armed Swordsman*. Raymond Chow, then head of production at Shaw, had lobbied Run Run Shaw to give a directing job to his latest discovery, Chang Cheh (Zhang Che). Born in Mainland China in 1923 to a warlord father, Chang had fled to Taiwan with the Nationalists, become embroiled in political intrigue, and wound up writing scripts in Hong Kong. Desperate to direct action films, Chang believed that, in the words of one collaborator, "when a sword goes in, blood comes out." He thought audiences – particularly women – were tired of seeing female heroes onscreen. An admirer of James Dean and Marlon Brando, Chang wanted to work with unknown actors who were difficult to manage and didn't have pretty-boy looks. He found one in Jimmy Wang Yu, a charismatic Taiwanese contract actor at Shaw.

In an interview about his career, Chang Cheh said, "The whole world is immersed in violence. How can the cinema avoid it?" *The One-Armed Swordsman* revelled in it. Jimmy Wang Yu plays the son of a servant of the Golden Blade sect, who is bullied by the sect's wealthier students. After the master's spoiled teenage daughter hacks off his arm, Wang Yu's character goes into exile and teaches himself a one-armed fighting style, returning just in time to save the Golden Blade sect from destruction. The film ends with him dying heroically in a courtyard paved with fresh bodies. It became a massive hit, and even though it wasn't technically the first Hong Kong film to break the million-dollar mark at the box office, Shaw hyped it as such.

Where previously *wuxia* had been about sophisticated swordsmen and women dressed in silk, wielding mystical weapons, Chang Cheh gave audiences young, male, working class heroes, stripped to the waist and smeared with blood, dying with an axe in their guts. Utilising a stylistic arsenal of slow motion, sudden zooms, handheld cameras and blood squibs, Chang Cheh, Jimmy Wang Yu, and action choreographers Lau Kar-leung and Tong Kai went on to make nine more

films together, in varying combinations, before 1970. By the time they were finished, Hong Kong cinema belonged to the angry young men.

Following a dispute, Raymond Chow left Shaw in 1970 and with Leonard Ho, founded the Golden Harvest studio. Suddenly, Shaw had a rival and when Bruce Lee came back to Hong Kong in 1971 he signed with Golden Harvest. His four films launched a wave that replaced the *wuxia* sword with the kung fu fist.

Yet Chang Cheh held on, directing almost 75 more films for Shaw, sometimes *wuxia*, sometimes kung fu, but always about *xiongdi*. A Chinese term meaning 'brother', *xiongdi* was a blood bond with another man that was stronger than family, marriage, patriotism, even death. Chang turned actors David Chiang and Ti Lung into stars with *xiongdi* films such as *Vengeance* (*Baochu*, 1970) and *The New One-Armed Swordsman* (*Xin Dubi Dao*, 1971), in which the two men often start as rivals, but finally come to recognise their unique bond.

In Taiwan, King Hu had parlayed his success with *Come Drink with Me* into another hit, *Dragon Gate Inn* (*Longmen Kezhan*, 1966). He then called in all his markers to make the spectacular, three-hour *A Touch of Zen* (*Xia Nü*, 1969). A throwback to the pre-1967 school of *wuxia*, *Zen* is told through the eyes of a meek male scholar, and features a ferocious female swordswoman, but it's also a film about a very 1960s idea of consciousness. From the small moment when the scholar devises a clever trap, laughing at its effectiveness, before the laughter dies in his throat as he witnesses the carnage it has wrought, to the finale when the characters must transcend the conflict-filled world of the *jiang hu* to embrace a Buddhist idea of peace and harmony, it's a film about growth. The first Chinese film to win a prize at the Cannes Film Festival, *A Touch of Zen* was nonetheless a box-office flop that heralded the beginning of the end of Hu's commercial fortunes. His film may have been about growth and change, but his audience was already changing.

The 'New Wave' comes ashore

By the early 1980s, audiences were growing tired of Chang's angry young men. Hong Kong's increasingly sophisticated audiences wanted to watch contemporary action flicks and kung fu comedies. *Wuxia* was passé. Shaw Brothers was too controlling to attract top talent and too old-fashioned to attract audiences. Run Run Shaw threw production into overdrive, trying every genre he could imagine, but it was too late. The 'New Wave' was about to wash him away.

The name coined for a generation of Chinese directors who were mostly educated overseas, the 'New Wave' owed a great debt to Selina Chow (now a prominent Hong Kong politician), the head of television programming at the TVB (Television Broadcasts Limited) commercial channel in the late 1970s. Chow hired a number of aspiring Chinese filmmakers who had studied at overseas film schools and gave them their first directing jobs.

Tsui Hark was one such filmmaker who got his break in TV, but over at the CTV channel, where his 1978 series *Gold Dagger Romance* (based on a Gu Long novel) had been such a success that when he got a chance to shoot his first film he opted for another *wuxia*. *The Butterfly Murders* (*Die Bian*, 1979) was a Gothic whirlwind of warring martial arts sects, killer butterflies, secret tunnels and armoured steampunk warriors who rely on grappling hooks and gunpowder, not internalised *qi*, to fly.

The film flopped, but Tsui returned to the genre in 1983 when he made *Zu: Warriors from the Magic Mountain* (*Xin Shu Shan Jianxia*). Determined to give Chinese films production values that could compete

King Hu

with Hollywood, Tsui brought in Hollywood effects technicians to update *wuxia*, advancing the use of wirework to portray gravity-defying swordsmen, and using blue screens, stop-motion animation and optical printing to reimagine genre chestnuts like Sky Mirrors and palm power.

Seven years later Tsui Hark turned again to *wuxia*, as producer of *Swordsman* (*Xiao'ao Jianghu*, 1990), an adaptation of a Jin Yong novel. Released in the wake of 1989's Tiananmen Square incident, which traumatised a Hong Kong populace who were starting to look ahead to the 1997 handover from the British to the Chinese, its breakneck story of evil eunuchs from the imperial court trying to crush a free-spirited wandering swordsman, played by Canto-pop star Sam Hui, captured the mood of the times.

The sequel, *Swordsman II* (*Xiao'ao Jianghu: Dongfang Bu Bai*, 1992), was a surreal phantasmagoria that replaced Hui with the then much cheaper Jet Li, and set him against Asia the Invincible, a swordsman who castrated himself to attain supremacy in the *jiang hu*. Slowly turning into a woman, Asia was played by Taiwanese actress, Brigitte Lin.

In the aftermath of Tsui Hark

Swordsman launched a wave of 1990s *wuxia* that featured a phantasmagoria of grotesque imagery: human beings fired like arrows from giant bows, superpowered warriors tearing off opponent's faces, swordsmen with pet killer whales named Sea Wayne... Turning out close to 300 films per year in the mid-1990s, Hong Kong was caught in an over-production bubble, propped up by pre-sales to foreign territories. When foreign markets stopped buying and the Asian economic crisis hit, the industry imploded. By 1998 production had dropped to 85 films.

But the 1990s also gave us three of Hong Kong's best *wuxia*. The first was Wong Kar Wai's adaptation of the Jin Yong novel, *The Eagle Shooting Heroes* (*She Diao Yingxiong Chuan*), starring seven of Hong Kong's most bankable stars. It was supposed to be a Chinese New Year's film, the prime slot for big releases, but after spending two years shooting hundreds of thousands of feet of film, Wong turned in *Ashes of Time* (*Dong Xie Xi Du*, 1994) a moody, oblique meditation on memory, loss and masochism with action filmed as expressionistic blurs.

To keep Wong from being sued by their investors, his business partner Jeff Lau quickly shot another film with the same cast, only as a comedy called *The Eagle Shooting Heroes* (*She Diao Yingxiongzhi Dong Cheng Xi Jiu*, 1993) that was a throwback to the campy *wuxia* of pre-*The One Armed Swordsman* Chinese cinema. Two years later, Lau made an even more direct response to Wong's *Ashes of Time* with his two-part Stephen Chow adaptation of the Buddhist classic *Journey*

(Above)
Maggie Cheung (left) and Zhang Ziyi in Zhang Yimou's 'Hero' (2002).

(Below)
Ang Lee's 'Crouching Tiger, Hidden Dragon' (2000) sparked a wave of lavishly produced wuxia films.

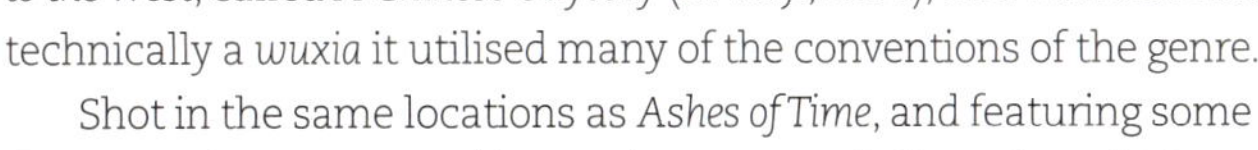

to the West, called *A Chinese Odyssey* (*Xi Youji*, 1995), and while it's not technically a *wuxia* it utilised many of the conventions of the genre.

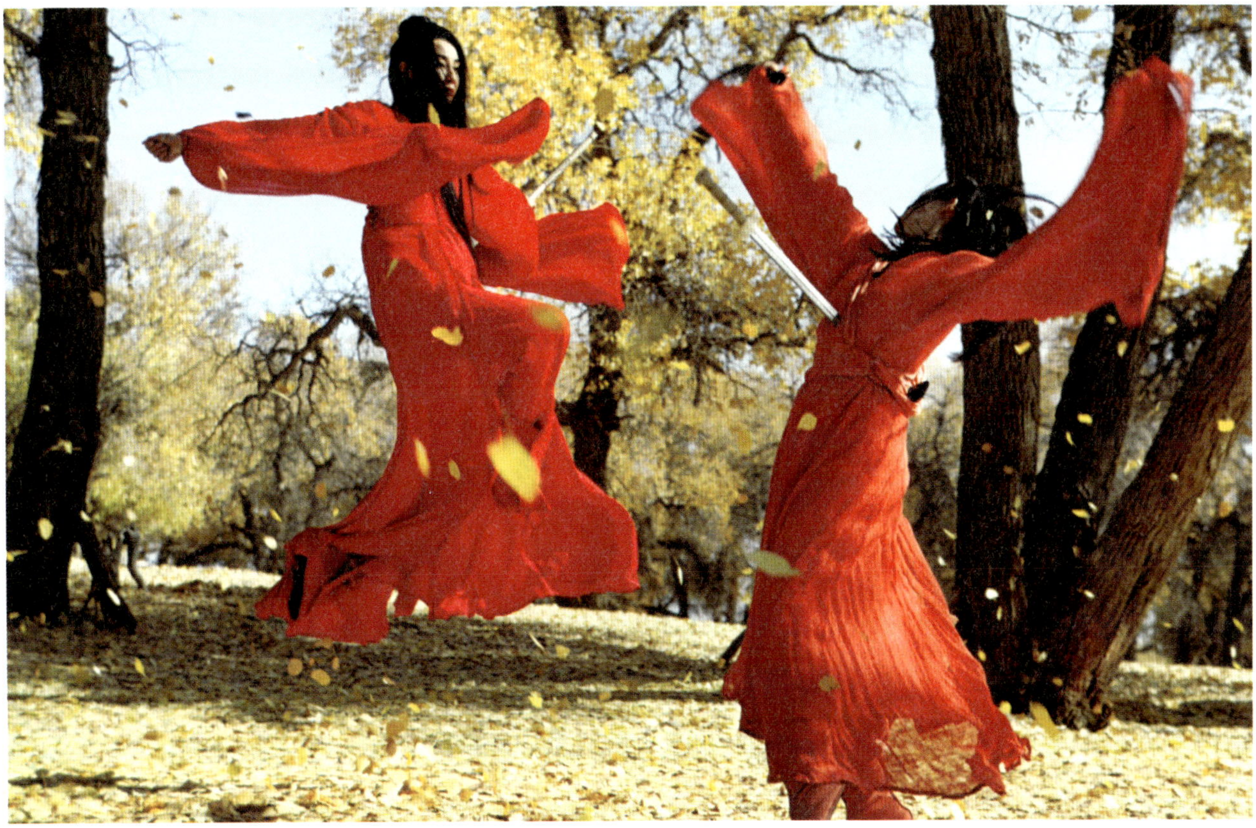

Shot in the same locations as *Ashes of Time*, and featuring some of the same characters, *A Chinese Odyssey* starred Chow, then the hottest comedian in Hong Kong, as the reincarnation of the legendary Monkey King who travels through time to save the life of his lover. *A Chinese Odyssey* is a rare combination of surreal slapstick and genuine pathos.

Another late creative success was *The Blade* (*Dao*, 1996), Tsui Hark's deconstruction of Chang Cheh's *The One-Armed Swordsman*. Tsui's vision of the *jiang hu* was a world in which the strong take and the weak die. If *Ashes of Time* was an elegant exploration of the intellectual side of *wuxia*, Tsui's film was a muscular examination of its addiction to violence.

Wuxia in the new millennium

Ang Lee's *Crouching Tiger, Hidden Dragon* (*Wo Hu Cang Long*, 2000) helped kick off an early 2000s revival of *wuxia*, delivering high production values and nuanced performances to a genre then in decline, and going on to make a fortune at the international box office. Its success sparked a wave of lavishly produced *wuxia*, mostly shot in Mainland China, and usually featuring multi-national casts. The most satisfying of these was Zhang Yimou's *Hero* (*Yingxiong*, 2002), a film that can be simultaneously read as an endorsement of a unified China (including Taiwan and Tibet) or as a subtle critique of same. The rest of these films, from Zhang Yimou's *House of Flying Daggers* (*Shimian Maifu*, 2004), to Chen Kaige's *The Promise* (*Wuji*, 2005) and beyond, were so worried about running foul of censorship that their stories typically played it numbingly safe. The result was a series of visually extravagant films that clipped the wings of a genre whose multi-gendered, rabble-rousing heroes are more used to soaring through the sky.

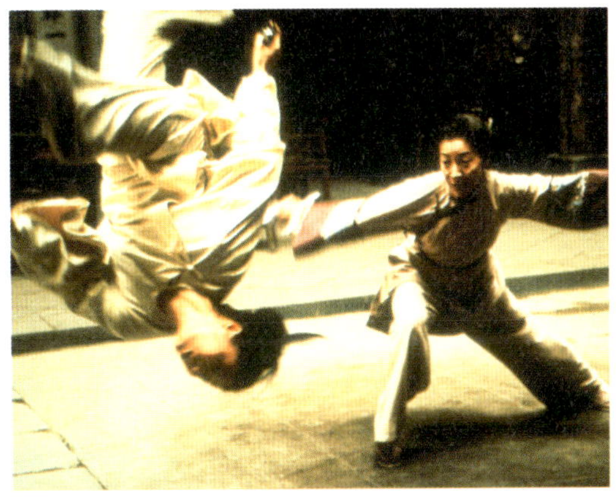

The kung fu film has been arguably Chinese cinema's most popular export, and at its heart is the figure of Wong Fei-hung. A real-life martial arts master who died aged 76 in 1924, Wong was a Chinese folk hero, a symbol of tradition and Confucian values. His life inspired a hugely popular Hong Kong Cantonese film series that started with *Wong Fei-hung: The Whip that Smacks the Candle* (*Huang Feihong Zhuan: Bianfeng Mie Zhu*, 1949), and concluded in 1970 with *Wong Fei-hung: Bravely Crushing the Fire Formation* (*Huang Feihong Yongpo Liehuo Zhen*). For 77 of these films Wong was played, or rather embodied, by the Cantonese Opera star Kwan Tak-hing, an actor who became so identified with the character that he refused to ask for a raise because it would be immodest. In 1970, Kwan was apparently still making what he made in 1949: $520 per film.

With an emphasis on actual martial arts instead of the flying swordsmen and palm power of *wuxia* films, the Wong Fei-hung films launched a generation of kung fu film talents, including Simon Yuen, whose five sons would each become major action filmmakers, most notably Yuen Woo-ping, who would later choreograph *The Matrix* (1999) and *Kill Bill: Vol 1* (2003). The most important of the Wong Fei-hung alumni was Lau Kar-Leung, who worked on the films thanks to his father, an action choreographer, and a third-generation disciple of Wong Fei-hung himself.

The job of action choreographer didn't officially exist until 1961, but even before then Lau and his partner, Tong Kai – who also worked on the Wong Fei-hung series – were two of the first and best. Lau and Tong were hired by Shaw Brothers to work with director Chang Cheh on numerous *wuxia* films, including *The One-Armed Swordsman*, but they found their skills especially in demand after Run Run Shaw, worried that the *wuxia* boom was about to burst, put Jimmy Wang Yu to work as director and star – with Tong Kai as action choreographer – on *The Chinese Boxer* (*Longhu Dou*, 1970). *The Chinese Boxer* is one of the first modern kung fu films, with a bare-bones revenge plot that involves evil Japanese killing Wang Yu's teacher, and Wang Yu slaughtering them in return. Its success helped launch a wave of kung fu movies in the 1970s.

Quickly realising that he was the box-office draw, not Shaw Brothers, Jimmy Wang Yu broke his contract and moved over to Golden Harvest. Shaw sued, and the case was only settled when Wang Yu agreed not to make films in Hong Kong for three years, decamping to Taiwan where he went on to shoot almost 50 films including *One-Armed Boxer vs. Zatoichi* (*Dubi Dao Dazhan Mang Xia*, 1971) and *Beach of the War Gods* (*Zhanshen Tan*, 1973).

The return of the dragon

The kung fu craze really went into overdrive in 1971 when former child star Bruce Lee returned to Hong Kong from America and signed a deal with Golden Harvest. Lee had a magnetic, rebellious charisma, and an appeal that transcended national and language barriers. He was typically cast as a valiant upholder of justice: in his first kung fu film, *The Big Boss* (*Tangshan Da Xiong*, 1971), which shattered box-office records, he plays an oppressed Chinese worker in Thailand who fights back against his Thai oppressors; in *Fist of Fury* (*Jingwu Men*, 1972) he plays an oppressed Chinese kung fu student in occupied China who fights back against his Japanese oppressors; and in *Way of the Dragon* (*Meng Long Guo Jiang*, 1972) he plays an oppressed Chinese waiter in Italy who fights back against Chuck Norris. In his final completed film, *Enter the Dragon* (1973) Lee isn't oppressed by anyone, but is instead closer to a James Bond-type figure.

Lee's early death in 1973 didn't slow down the craze he had sparked. Instead, it launched the Bruceploitation industry, as Bruces Li, Le, and Leung starred in low-budget films like *The Clones of Bruce Lee* (*Shenwei San Meng Long*, 1981) and *Bruce Lee Fights Back from the Grave* (1976).

In 1975, Shaw Brothers offered their ace action choreographer Lau Kar-leung a chance to direct *The Spiritual Boxer* (*Shen Da*), which quickly became a hit. His next film was *Challenge of the Masters* (*Liu Acai yu Huang Feihong*, 1976), a Wong Fei-hung film. Determined to depict kung fu with authenticity and respect, it kicked off a string of films directed by Lau that redefined the soul of the kung fu film. Putting the emphasis on the master-student relationship, Lau's Shaw Brothers films are thoughtful, classy – yet still ass-kicking – epics. *The 36th Chamber of Shaolin* (*Shaolin Sanshiliu Fang*, 1978) sees a brash young man seek sanctuary inside the Shaolin monastery. The centrepiece of the film is a series of training sequences that are an hour-long cinematic tone poem about discipline, focus and commitment. Lau's films eschewed revenge for respect – as in *Heroes of the East* (*Zhonghua Zhangfu*, 1978), in which a Chinese husband and Japanese wife gleefully destroy their new home as each tries to prove the superiority of their homeland's martial arts, offering a rebuttal to the anti-Japanese xenophobia of *The Chinese Boxer* and *Fist of Fury*. Their duels end not with bloody mayhem, but with mutual respect. Lau was making his best films as Shaw Brothers entered its most difficult period, turning out classic titles like *Dirty Ho* (*Lan Tou He*, 1976), *The Lady is the Boss* (*Zhang Men Ren*, 1983) and *Eight Diagram Pole Fighter* (*Wang Lang Ba Gua Gun*, 1984). But after Run Run Shaw shut down his film arm in 1986 and devoted all his resources to television, Lau was a man without a studio. His final six films were mere shadows of the stunning work he did while sheltered at Shaw.

Jackie Chan and the Golden Harvest years

Meanwhile, noting the success of Lau's *The Spiritual Boxer*, Yuen Woo-ping decided to direct a kung fu comedy featuring an actor with a string of low-budget flops behind him, Jackie Chan. The film was *Snake in the Eagle's Shadow* (*She Xing Diao Shou*, 1978), in which Chan's loser servant is taught the Snake Fist style by a drunk old beggar (played by the director's father, Simon Yuen). It was so successful that director Yuen, his father and Jackie teamed up again for *Drunken Master* (*Zui Quan*, 1978), with Jackie playing a young, dumb Wong Fei-hung. The film was an even bigger success, and Golden Harvest came calling, signing Chan up as its next big star.

Golden Harvest may have footed the bill and distributed the pictures, but it was Sammo Hung who really created Jackie Chan. Grandson of *wuxia* star Chin Tsi-ang, Hung had attended the China Drama Academy, a tough

Chinese opera school run by the demanding Master Yu Jim Yuen, where he was 'elder brother' to Chan and another actor named Yuen Biao. The three grew up together, but it was Hung who first found fame as a stuntman and action choreographer. With Chan and Yuen on board to provide the action, Sammo Hung launched his Lucky Stars series with *Winners & Sinners* (*Qi Mou Miao Ji: Wu Fuxing*, 1983). These globetrotting, cosmopolitan comedy kung fu flicks, choreographed and produced by Hung, captured the "What, me worry?" mood of Asia's booming, urban middle class, and became hits.

Hung, Chan and Yuen Biao became known as the 'Three Dragons' of kung fu comedy, but Chan's fame rapidly outstripped that of his 'brothers', and when he directed and starred in big-budget blockbusters such as *Police Story* (*Jingcha Gushi*, 1985) and *Project A Part II* (*'A' Jihua Xuji 2*, 1987) he didn't invite them along for the ride. After one final film together, *Dragons Forever* (*Fei Long Meng Jiang*, 1988), the three went their separate ways. Chan eventually made his way to Hollywood. Yuen found himself in increasingly cheap films, while Hung called in all his favours to direct and star in three spectacular action classics, *Millionaires Express* (*Fugui Lieche*, 1986), *Eastern Condors* (*Dongfang Tuying*, 1987) and *Pedicab Driver* (*Qun Long Xi Feng*, 1989).

Meanwhile, Yuen Woo-ping tried to make lightning strike twice, recruiting Donnie Yen, a young kid from Boston, to star in *Drunken Tai Chi* (*Xiao Taiji*, 1984) and then a breakdancing comedy called

Mismatched Couples (*Qingfeng de Sao*, 1985), but both films flopped.

By the end of the 1980s, the kung fu genre looked to be dead when Tsui Hark launched his big-budget Wong Fei-hung film, *Once Upon a Time in China* (*Huang Feihong*, 1991), starring Mainland martial artist Jet Li, then a relative unknown. Li portrayed Wong as a Chinese everyman trying to do the right thing in a country torn between Western encroachment and Chinese corruption. To everyone's surprise, the spectacular *Once Upon a Time in China* revived the genre, spawned five sequels, and made Jet Li one of Asia's biggest stars.

Goodbye, Wong Fei-hung. Hello, Ip Man

As Jackie Chan and Jet Li left behind period films for contemporary action pictures in the 1990s, the kung fu film went into decline again. When the Hong Kong film production bubble burst in the mid-1990s, Sammo Hung, Jackie Chan and Jet Li all left for Hollywood, and the cry went out: who would replace the kung fu stars of yesteryear? The answer turned out to be Donnie Yen. After a career spent playing good guys in small films and bad guys in big films, Yen was almost 42 years old when he made *Kill Zone: S.P.L.* (*Sha Po Lang*, 2005) with director Wilson Yip. A modern day crime film, it featured kinetic hand-to-hand action with a focus on Yen's eye-catching fighting style that mixed kung fu, judo, mixed martial arts and boxing. It led to a series of award-winning collaborations between Yen and Yip, climaxing with their Hong Kong-Mainland co-production, *Ip Man* (*Ye Wen*, 2008).

Desperate to save its failing film industry, in 2003 Hong Kong signed the Closer Economic Partnership Agreement with China. CEPA allowed Hong Kong filmmakers to co-produce and distribute films on the Mainland as long as they followed Mainland censorship rules. Hong Kong filmmakers now had access to an audience of more than one billion, as long as they avoided making anything that might be considered controversial. *Wuxia*, set in the distant past and portraying righteous heroes, found new life as the safest co-production genre.

The Mainland market was soon over-saturated with period *wuxia* epics, so Yip and Yen's *Ip Man* landed like a hurricane. The holy grail of Hong Kong kung fu films has long been a Bruce Lee biopic, but tight control of Lee's image has thus far rendered that dream impossible. Instead, filmmakers have turned their attention to the story of his teacher, *wing chun* master Ip Man. With action choreography by Sammo Hung, Donnie Yen played Ip Man as a picture of tolerance and Lau Kar-leung-esque virtue, teaching his disciples the philosophical value of martial arts, and slaughtering dozens of Japanese soldiers in the process.

Ip Man spawned the successful sequel *Ip Man 2* (*Ye Wen 2*, 2010), set in Hong Kong, that traded evil Japanese for evil colonial British, and it turned Donnie Yen into an international action icon. There have been numerous Ip Man spin-offs, sequels, TV series and remakes. Even Wong Kar Wai has made an Ip Man film, winning several Chinese film awards with *The Grandmaster* (*Yidai Zongshi*, 2013), his typically elliptical take on the Ip Man legend. However, the most distinctive version has been Hong Kong filmmaker Herman Yau's *Ip Man: The Final Fight* (*Ye Wen – Zhongji Yi Zhan*, 2013), which portrays Ip as a humble man caught up in the turmoil of Hong Kong's political and social unrest of the 1960s. When one of Ip Man's friends, recently emigrated from China, begins to sob that he had to sell one of his children to buy food, Ip Man's response is to sit impotently, then pour him another drink. It's a moment that undermines the old heart of the kung fu film, suggesting that mastery of the martial arts is in the end useless when it comes to dealing with real life. ◓

Shanghai in 1921 was awash in pulp fiction and detective magazines, so when the time came to make the first feature film in the city the topic was obvious. The previous summer, the city had been rocked by the murder of a well-known prostitute at the hands of one of her flashy young clients, Yan Ruisheng. Casting a friend of the killer in the title role, Ren Pengnian's true-crime film *Yan Ruisheng* (1921) was an immediate hit.

However it was after *wuxia* films were banned by the Chinese government in 1931 that the detective film became a sought-after replacement. The husband-and-wife team of Zhang Huimin and Wu Suxin were popular as a Shanghainese Nick and Nora Charles, and the period also saw the production of titles such as Li Pingqian's *The Casebook of Sherlock Holmes* (*Fuermosi Zhentan An*, 1931) and locked room mysteries such as *Shadow on the Window* (*Chuangshang Renying*, 1931).

Hong Kong melodramas of the 1950s featured the occasional murder, but Taiwanese and Hong Kong authorities had made it clear that disrespectful portrayals of police officers (even the wearing of an untidy uniform by a character) could get a film pulled from screens. Hong Kong's answer was to focus on plainclothes detectives, the most famous of whom was middle-aged actor Walter Tso Tat-Wah. Following the success of *Dr. No* (1962), Tso was given a James Bond makeover in films like *The Spy* (*Tian Zi Jiandie Wang*, 1963) and *Secret Codes* (*Mima Jiandie Zhan*, 1964). But there was little spark with audiences, so director Chor Yuen (Chu Yuan) decided to take a cue from gaudy contemporary European titles like *Modesty Blaise* (1966) and made *The Black Rose* (*Hei Meigui*, 1966).

The Black Rose kicked off what came to be known as the 'Jane Bond' films. The heroines of these movies were good girls by day, but when darkness fell they put on their all-black 'night-walking suits' to steal from the rich and give to the poor, sneak down secret passages, fire lipstick guns, wear ultra-violet sunglasses and scale high-rise buildings. Their adventures felt irrelevant after the 1967 riots, however, and Lung Kong better captured the mood of the times with *The Story of a Discharged Prisoner* (*Yingxiong Bense*, 1967), a tough and influential film about an ex-con trying to go straight while tormented by bullying cops and dangerous criminals.

All-shocking! All-daring! All-true!

In the 1970s, Shaw Brothers turned to the true-crime film with *Kidnap* (*Tian Wang*, 1974). Shot on location in Hong Kong, and oozing authenticity, the film was based on an actual recent kidnapping case. Sweaty and desperate, it spawned a rash of true-crime films that served as showcases for some of Shaw's most inventive directors. The outstanding five-part true-crime anthology series *The Criminals* (1976 - 77) saw Mou Tun-fei and Kuei Chih-hung turn in sleazy, savage shorts in which serial rapists stalk crumbling apartment complexes and teenagers go on kill-crazy crime sprees.

Shaw's crime films tried to lure audiences away from their televisions by offering generous helpings of lurid violence and nudity. Director Sun Chung mixed guns, girls and bare breasts in *The Sexy Killer* (*Du Hou Mi Shi*, 1976), a knock-off of the Pam Grier vehicle *Coffy* (1973), followed by more of the same in *Big Bad Sis* (*Sa Dan Ying*, 1976).

Then there was shockmeister Kuei Chih-hung, director of *The Delinquent* (*Fennu Qingnian*, 1972). Co-directed with Chang Cheh (who really only lent his name to reassure Shaw), it opens with young star Wang Chung screaming as he smashes through giant photos of Hong Kong and ends with a POV shot from his dying eyes after he's jumped out of a 20th-floor

(Above)
Kuei Chih-hung's films, such as 'Big Brother Cheng' (1975), set the template for future triad dramas.

(Below)
Johnny Mak's brutal 'Long Arm of the Law' (1984).

window. Kuei was then tasked with making *Bamboo House of Dolls* (*Nü Jizhongying*, 1973), a depraved, big-budget picture about a Japanese prison camp for women that was exactly as sleazy as it sounds. Kuei turned out hit after hit for Shaw, with pictures including *The Teahouse* (*Chengji Chalou*, 1974) and *Big Brother Cheng* (*Da Ge Cheng*, 1975) – contemporary crime films that set the template for future triad dramas. After directing close to 40 films for Shaw, Kuei tried to direct an independent production, which earned him a letter from Run Run Shaw's lawyers. Bitter over his treatment, Kuei retired to California and opened a pizza parlor.

The long arm of the handover

In 1979, Britain and China began talking about the future of Hong Kong, resulting in the Joint Declaration of 1984, which promised to return Hong Kong to Chinese rule in 1997. It was an anxious time, with Deng Xiaopeng threatening to invade Hong Kong if Britain didn't agree to key concessions. Kung fu comedies helped Hong Kongers embrace blissful denial, but nihilistic crime films were where their anxieties were manifest. Terry Tong's *Coolie Killer* (*Sha Chu Xiying Pan*, 1982), about a blank-faced assassin, was a poke in the eye to notions of manly heroism. After a young girl nurses our hero back to health, he repays the debt by shooting her in the head. Alex Cheung's *Cops and Robbers* (*Dian zhi Bing Bing*, 1979) features a cop even more violent than the criminals he hunts, and his *Man on the Brink* (*Bian Yuen Ren*, 1981) focuses on an undercover officer who almost cracks up when his superiors force him to infiltrate a triad gang.

One of the era's most critically acclaimed and influential thrillers was *Long Arm of the Law* (*Sheng Gang Qibing*, 1984), an intense and brutal film that follows a gang of Mainland criminals who hit Hong Kong for 48 hours of smash-and-grab armed robbery. Director Johnny Mak makes sure our loyalties stay with the ruthless gang even as other criminals betray them. The film's only bright spot is the gang's brotherly bond, or *xiongdi*.

In a world where Hong Kongers felt controlled by events, rather than in control of them, the idea of the mythical *jiang hu* underworld was ripe for reinvention, and it came a few years later when John Woo and Ringo Lam released two very different crime films back to back, defining what became known as the 'heroic bloodshed' genre, and cementing the image of two of Hong Kong's most recognisable cinematic characters: the desperate undercover cop and the cool triad gangster. At the time, John Woo was a washed-up comedy director, but he had talked with Tsui Hark about their shared admiration for Lung Kong's *The Story of a Discharged Prisoner*. Sensing an opportunity, Tsui funded Woo to direct a loose remake of Lung's film entitled *A Better Tomorrow* (*Yingxiong Bensè*, 1986). Shaw Brothers veteran Ti Lung was cast as an honorable gangster, Leslie Cheung as his younger brother, and Chow Yun-Fat played their mutual best friend, a flashy triad gangster who wore sunglasses, a black trenchcoat, lit his cigarettes with $100 bills, and wielded a .45 in each hand. The result was a massive hit that came to define Chow Yun-Fat's image.

A Better Tomorrow was a return to Chang Cheh's macho *wuxia*, centered on the bonds of *xiongdi* and set in an updated version of the *jiang hu* in which triad gangs stand in for martial arts clans and guns for swords. Woo would go on to make a sequel, fall out with Tsui Hark over *The Killer* (*Diexue Shuang Xiong*, 1989) and ultimately go his own way. Woo's searing *Bullet in the Head* (*Diexue Jietou*, 1990), about three Hong Kong men trapped in Vietnam during the war, featured scenes from the 1967 riots, and he followed it with *Once a Thief* (*Zongheng Sihai*, 1991) and *Hard Boiled* (*Lashou Shentan*, 1992), both again starring Chow Yun-Fat. By this time

Woo's films had become so huge that he was lured away to Hollywood.

Ringo Lam's *City on Fire* (*Lunghu Fengyun*, 1987), released soon after *A Better Tomorrow*, paired Chow Yun-Fat with a former Shaw Brothers actor, Danny Lee. Chow plays an undercover cop unwillingly assigned to infiltrate a gang led by Lee, and the film is grim and fatalistic where *A Better Tomorrow* is triumphant and heroic. Lam then found huge box office success with *Prison on Fire* (*Jianyu Fengyun*, 1988), also starring Chow, about a prison torn between warring triads and sadistic guards, but lost his box-office clout with *School on Fire* (*Huexuiao Fengyun*, 1988), a controversial film that depicted high schools as little more than training grounds for future triad members, junkies and prostitutes.

Triads and big timers

Triad members had long viewed themselves as modern-day equivalents of the kung fu icon Wong Fei-hung, supporting virtue and standing for tradition, and *A Better Tomorrow* launched a wave of films – among them *Flaming Brothers* (*Jiang Hu Long Hu Men*, 1987), *Rich and Famous* (*Jiang Hu Qing*, 1987) and *Tragic Hero* (*Yingxiong Hao Han*, 1987) – that starred Chow Yun-Fat as a righteous triad who teams up with his blood brothers to fight unscrupulous, drug-dealing triad bosses.

As the heroic bloodshed trend peaked, the so-called 'Big Timer' films appeared to take their place. Set in the 1920s and 1930s, these films, such as *To Be Number One* (*Bo Hao*, 1991) and *Lord of the East China Sea* (*Shanghai Huangdi zhi Suiyue Fengyun*, 1993), were

MANNESMANN

historical epics that mythologised the lives of real triad bosses.

With film production booming, the boundaries between crime on screen and on the streets blurred, and triads began to see filmmaking as a way to launder money. In 1990, actress Carina Lau was abducted for refusing to appear in a triad-funded film, Jet Li's manager, a man with rumoured triad connections, was murdered for reportedly refusing to lend Li to a triad-produced film, and triads conducted armed raids on film processing labs to steal the negatives of their rivals' films. Finally, in 1992, hundreds of Hong Kong stars and film industry workers marched to demand protection from the police and get the triads out of the film business.

Even after the Hong Kong film bubble burst, triad films hung on, as unkillable as a cockroach. In 1996 producer Wong Jing hired noted cinematographer Andrew Lau to direct a film about righteous young triad boys in leather pants and flowing locks. Shot on the fly, *Young and Dangerous* (*Gu Huozi: Ren zai Jiang Hu*, 1996) went on to spawn numerous sequels, prequels, spin-offs, two all-female versions, a parody film and a reboot. Surprisingly, the series got better with each instalment, ripening into a layered, complex saga.

Across the Milkyway

As the handover approached, and with the market for Hong Kong films at rock bottom, director Johnnie To and a TVB scriptwriter named Wai Ka-fai formed Milkyway Image, vowing to make dark, complicated, formally daring films. Between 1996 and 1999 they turned out ten nihilistic, elegantly crafted crime films, among them *The Longest Nite* (*An Hua*, 1998), a jet black *noir* about a corrupt cop, and *A Hero Never Dies* (*Zhenxin Yingxiong*, 1998), a tongue-in-cheek rebuttal to the John Woo heroic bloodshed films.

However it wasn't until *Running Out of Time* (*An Zhan*, 1999), a caper flick examining the bond of *xiongdi* between a cop and a criminal, that Milkyway found success at the box office. The company's crime film output peaked with Johnnie To's masterpieces, *Election* (*Heishehui*, 2005) and its sequel *Election 2* (*Heishehui Yi He Wei Gui*, 2006). A sober look at the secret history of Hong Kong as told through the triads, the two films stripped away decades of mythmaking to expose the triads as little more than criminal murder mills. Big hits in Hong Kong, neither film has ever been released in Mainland China, as *Election 2* in particular pulls no punches in depicting links between Mainland politicians and overseas triads.

Milkyway productions have alternated between New Year's comedies, populist romances, and black-as-coal crime films, but their holy grail has long been to break into the Mainland Chinese market. They finally found success with *Drug War* (*Du Zhan*, 2013), one of the first Mainland Chinese-Hong Kong co-productions to deal with contemporary crime.

The Hong Kong crime film's two iconic characters – the slick triad in his impeccable suit, and the harried undercover cop trying to keep it together – came face to face in Andrew Lau and Alan Mak's's trilogy *Infernal Affairs* (*Wujian Dao*, 2002-03). Canto-pop star Andy Lau plays an undercover triad mole who has infiltrated the police force to try to root out an undercover cop (Tony Leung Chiu-wai), who has in turn infiltrated the triads. At a time when many Hong Kong films looked cheap and soulless, *Infernal Affairs* was a polished, sophisticated epic. The trilogy became an international hit, inspiring an English-language remake in Martin Scorsese's *The Departed* (2006). Few people noticed, however, that the films marked a shifting of sympathies – that it was Leung's blue-collar cop who was cast as the victim, whereas Lau's sleek, sophisticated triad was a soulless hustler taking the slow bus to Hell. ↻

Any discussion of Chinese horror films or fiction must begin with Pu Songling's classic collection of nearly 500 supernatural stories, *Strange Tales from a Chinese Studio (Liao Zhai Zhi Yi)*. In 1679, then a struggling tutor, Pu Songling began circulating his manuscript containing tales of Taoist priests, fox spirits, dwarves, cannibals, sea monsters, ghostly beauties romancing scholars and vengeance from beyond the grave that he had collected over the years. Pu continued to update the collection for the rest of his life, and over the centuries since, *Strange Tales* has become the ur-text for Chinese horror – a cultural touchstone that is Edgar Allan Poe, *Tales of 1001 Nights* and Aesop's fables rolled into one.

All of which means that it's perhaps a surprise that China's first horror film was instead inspired by a European classic. The very first sound adaptation of Gaston Leroux's *The Phantom of the Opera* was *Song at Midnight (Yeban Gesheng*, 1937), a sophisticated Gothic that owed a lot to the shadowy romance of James Whale's Universal horrors. It became a big hit, prompting its director Ma-Xu Weibang to turn out further horror productions like *Walking Corpse in an Old House (Guwu Xingshi Ji*, 1938) and *The Leper Girl (Ma Feng Nü*, 1939). Ma-Xu turned to Mary Shelley's *Frankenstein* and H.G. Wells's *The Island of Doctor Moreau* for inspiration for a 1941 sequel to *Song at Midnight* – which some rate as superior even to the original film. Ma-Xu wound up making films such as *The Opium War* for the occupying Japanese army, which got him labelled as a collaborator. He fled to Hong Kong after the war where he continued to make films – including a number of horror titles – until he was run over by a tram in 1961.

After 1949, the new PRC government took a dim view of the supernatural, but by the 1950s stories from Pu Songling's collection had begun to reach the screen via Hong Kong-made films like Doe Ching's *Beyond the Grave (Ren Gui Lian*, 1954), based on the ghost story 'Lian Suo', in which a young man is sent to his deserted ancestral house where he meets and falls in love with the beautiful Lian Suo, only to find out that she is, in fact, a ghost. The film's stylish art direction by Chan Ki-yui showed the influence of German expressionism in its bold shadows.

The most famous adaptation of a Pu Songling story in Hong Kong cinema of this period was 1960's *The Enchanting Shadow (Qiannü Youhun)*, filmed in lush colour by Shaw's premiere director of elegant historical films, Li Hanxiang. The story of a young scholar who spends the night in a haunted temple where he falls in love with a ghost, it fit perfectly with Shaw's then-popular brand of restrained historical productions and set a pattern for adaptations of Pu's stories throughout the 1960s.

That refined, elegant approach began to change in 1974, when Shaw teamed up with Britain's Hammer Films to make *Legend of the Seven Golden Vampires*, a kung fu Dracula movie co-directed by the UK's Roy Ward Baker and Chang Cheh, with Peter Cushing coming to China to hunt Dracula.

Released the same year was Golden Harvest's anthology film *Blood Reincarnation (Yin Yang Jie*, 1974), by director Ting Shan-hsi (Ding Shanxi). Largely abandoning ethereal romance in favour of jump scares and onscreen gore, this three-parter used the techniques of Western horror films to present Chinese ghosts. Its three stories range from the viscerally gory 'The Treasure', in which a couple murder an elderly lady and attempt to steal her fortune, through to the blackly comic 'The Wanton', in which the dead body of an adulterous woman's husband refuses to be disposed of, and finally to the mournful title story, in which a wrongly executed doctor uses a 'blood reincarnation'

spell to return as a ghost to right the injustice he has suffered. *Blood Reincarnation* wasn't a huge hit, but it paved the way for what came next.

In 1975, Shaw director Ho Meng-hua went even further with his hit *Black Magic* (*Jiangtou*, 1975), which brought a new gore and grotesquerie to Hong Kong horror cinema. Stirring together folk magic, true-crime stories and a dose of xenophobia, *Black Magic* tells of a Chinese woman living in Malaysia who hires a local wizard to brew up a love potion – whose ingredients unfortunately require tongue removal and human bodies boiled down for oil. But that was just a warm-up for *Black Magic 2* (*Jiangtou 2*, 1976), which featured immortality serums made from breast milk and pubic hair, and worms wriggling out of open sores.

For most of the next decade, Shaw churned out numerous films about 'civilised' Hong Kongers travelling to 'primitive' foreign countries where all manner of unspeakable things happen, namely filthy local wizards doling out blood curses on unsuspecting Hong Kongers. Kuei Chih-hung took Ho Meng-hua's brand of horror and made a series of films – *Hex* (*Xie*, 1980), *Hex versus Witchcraft* (*Xie Dou Xie*, 1980), *Hex After Hex* (*Xie Wan Zai Xie*, 1982) and *The Boxer's Omen* (*Mo*, 1983) – that upped the gross-out, exploitation ante. Things came to a truly traumatic end with Yeung Kuen's outrageous, gore-filled *Seeding of a Ghost* (*Zhong Kui*, 1983), in which a taxi driver turns to a sorcerer to enact supernatural vengeance after his wife is raped and murdered.

Kung fu gets spooked

While Shaw was making gross-out horror films and Lau Kar-leung films, Sammo Hung was looking to spice up his action movies, and the result was *Encounter of the Spooky Kind* (*Gui Da Gui*, 1980), a period kung fu comedy about a philanderer who hires a magician to knock off the idiot husband of his lover. The film made much of the 'hopping vampires' first seen in Lau Kar-leung's Shaw Brothers production *Spiritual Boxer II* (*Maoshan Jiangshi Quan*, 1979). Vampires in Chinese cinema are not commanding 'Princes of Darkness' looking for blood, but are instead rotting corpses, so stiff with rigor mortis that they can't bend their knees or elbows and have to hop after their prey, arms extended, until someone punches them back into their grave.

The hopping vampire formula was perfected with *Mr. Vampire* (*Jiangshi Xiansheng*, 1985), directed by Ricky Lau and co-produced by Sammo Hung, which added stunt man Lam Ching-ying as a stern Taoist priest who does battle with the hopping horrors, using everything from kung fu to his cherrywood sword. Hong Kong cinema soon went hopping vampire mad, and the eight years between 1986-94 saw dozens of *Mr. Vampire* knock-offs, all of them low budget but the best of them exhibiting a kind of deranged inventiveness – such as the Africa-set *Crazy Safari* (*Feizhou Heshang*, 1991), by director Billy Chen.

It wasn't all hopping vampires though. In 1987 Tsui Hark produced a remake of *The Enchanting Shadow* directed by Tony Ching (Ching Siu-Tung) called *A Chinese Ghost Story* (*Qiannü Youhun*), whose mixture of special effects-driven scares and swoonsome romance spawned countless imitators. In Ching's updating of Pu Songling's story, which made full use of special effects by Tsui's in-house workshop, Cinefex, the love-sick scholar was played by Leslie Cheung, and the ghost who fluttered through the blue-lit forest – trailing miles of billowing silk – was played by Joey Wong. Another huge hit for Tsui, it led to two sequels which boasted ever more elaborate effects that stretched Cinefex to its limit, as they conjured up mile-long centipedes and giant drooling monsters.

The dawn of Category III

Hopping vampires and graceful ghosts gave way to chopped-up corpses in 1988 when Hong Kong's film classification system was established. With it came a new rating: Category III, the equivalent of the X or NC-17 certificates in the UK and USA. Permitted to depict nudity and gore more graphically than ever before, producers smelled money. The first Category III film was *Sentenced to Hang* (*San Lang Qi'an*, 1989), a bloodier remake of Shaw Brothers's first true-crime movie *Kidnap* (*Tian Wang*, 1974).

Danny Lee and Billy Tang's *Dr. Lamb* (*Gaoyang Yisheng*, 1992) took true-crime further still. Based on the real-life serial killer Lam Go-wan, it focuses on a no-holds-barred performance from Simon Yam as a taxi driver who butchered four women in the tiny apartment he shared with his extended family – who all claimed they never had a clue about his crimes.

Serial-killer films were the latest trend. *The Untold Story* (*Baxian Fandian zhi Renrou Chashaobao*, 1993), from director Herman Yau, saw star Anthony Wong play a killer who grinds his victims into mincemeat for the 'roast pork' buns he then serves to cops. Successive films attempted to outdo the last in terms of sadistic horror – Billy Tang's *Red to Kill* (*Ruo Sha*, 1994), about a necrophiliac serial rapist running a school for mentally disabled adults, plumbed new depths of human depravity.

The next horror boom was sparked by Japanese director Nakata Hideo's 'J-Horror' hit *The Ring* (*Ringu*, 1998). Hong Kong producers were inspired to unleash a flood of low-budget horror flicks – a few of which were actually good. Wilson Yip's *Bio-Zombie* (*Shenghua Shoushi*, 1998) was a stoner take on George Romero's *Dawn of the Dead*, and Bob Cheng (aka Soi Cheang) turned in a string of claustrophobic gems like *Horror Hotline…Big Head Monster* (*Kongbu Rexian zhi Datou Guai Ying*, 2001).

Hong Kong horror hasn't been hot in years, but director Juno Mak updated the hopping vampire with *Rigor Mortis* (*Jiangshi*, 2013), which might yet herald the revival of the genre, back from its shallow cinematic grave.

In Mainland China, government regulations banning "content about murder, violence, terror, ghosts and the supernatural…" limits the production of horror films. Nonetheless, since the 1980s some very low-budget movies have included horror elements, but any hint of the supernatural had to be given a plausible real-world explanation. It wasn't until *Painted Skin* (*Huapi*, 2008), a big-budget fantasy starring Donnie Yen, that a film focused on the supernatural was allowed a wide release. Its success generated a sequel and paved the way for more supernatural content, such as a Mainland remake of *A Chinese Ghost Story* (2011). The argument that allowed *Painted Skin* to slip by the censors? It was presented as a showcase for traditional culture, based on a national literary treasure, Pu Songling's *Strange Tales from a Chinese Studio*. ☯

CHINESE DOCUMENTARY FILMMAKING

BY KEVIN B. LEE AND YUQIAN YAN

中国记录片制作

The first film made in China by Chinese filmmakers, 1905's *The Battle of Dingjunshan*, records a performance of the titular Beijing opera, which depicts a battle steeped in ancient Chinese historical legend. While the film no longer physically exists, its historical precedent poses a question: does the recording of a performance count as documentary reality or filmed fiction? This longstanding yet oft-ignored conundrum informs films of all origins, but the history of Chinese documentary dramatises a singular tension borne by China's perilous journey through the 20th century into the present. From the very first instance, Chinese documentary exemplifies China's striving for modernity through the advanced technology of the cinema, while also seeking to preserve the country's cultural essence. The waves of social and political upheaval that have rippled throughout China in the modern era can be viewed as successive attempts to redefine its relationship to past legacies, present challenges, and to reality itself. Throughout this saga, Chinese documentaries reveal as much about these evolving tensions as they do about their nominal subjects.

As described in the seminal research of scholars Fang Fang and Yingchi Chu, early non-fiction filmmakers pursued a broad range of subjects: from the lives of political and cultural leaders to the lifestyles of ethnic minorities; from natural landscapes to urban social activities. Such a diverse spectrum of topics suggests a collective captivation with cinema's power to portray the splendours of a land newly freed from dynastic rule and seeking to build a new society. This cinematic national pride was prolifically represented in the films of educational publisher Commercial Press, which made films on such progressive topics as destroying opium supplies and teaching proper hygiene. Lai Man-Wai (Li Minwei), who would go on to pioneer the Hong Kong film industry, made several hagiographic portraits of Nationalist leader Sun Yat-sen in an effort to rally people behind the nascent Republic.

The power of documentary was such that it could lend its aura of authenticity to fiction films. Cheng Bugao's *Wild Torrent* (*Kuang Liu*, 1933), considered the first leftist Chinese film, builds its story of social awakening around documentary footage of a flood. The soccer-themed love story *Kicking Out* (*Yi Jiao Ti Chuqu*, 1927) incorporated footage of actual football matches. Sport was a prominent documentary subject, emphasising strong, athletic bodies that could project the strength of a nation. The modernism of cinema could also preserve the enchantments of traditional culture in filmed performances of Chinese operas.

One of the major figures to advance the practice at this critical period was Sun Mingjing, who has drawn comparison to British documentary pioneer John Grierson for their efforts to institutionalise documentary making in their respective nations. Working for the Council for Film Education at Jinling University, the first film department in a Chinese school, Sun focused on cinema's educational impact and technological advancement, helping to produce the first Chinese colour film, *Solar Eclipse* (*Rishi*, 1936), and the first film to use both sound and colour, *The Frontline of Democracy* (*Minzhu Qianfeng*, 1947). Sun's wife and colleague Lü Jin'ai was a pioneer in her own right, having created the first film stock made in China.

As a technology hailing from the West, cinema in China inevitably drew the participation of foreign filmmakers in a variety of non-fiction capacities, from tobacco company-produced actualities on Chinese social life (featuring cigarette-holding socialites) to Joseph F. Rock's pioneering ethnographic studies of Chinese minorities. With the Japanese invasion of China, sympathetic Westerners such as Edgar Snow, Harry Dunham, Joris Ivens and Roman Karmen made newsreel-type reports of the

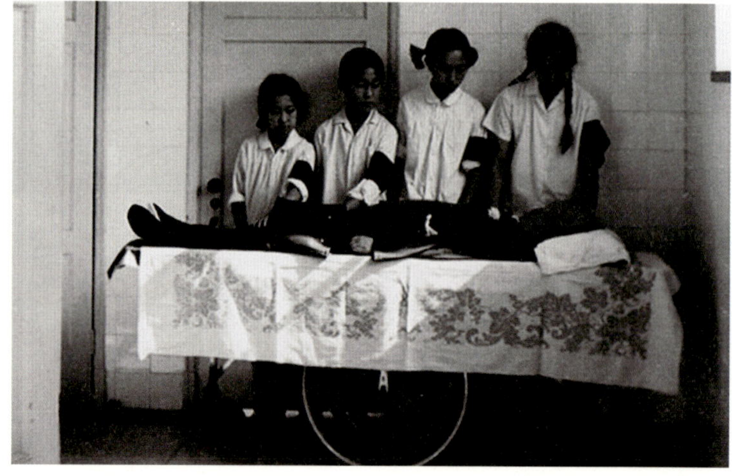

Chinese resistance. Both the Nationalist and Communist factions of the anti-Japanese war effort utilised documentary as a mobilising force. In making the first Communist Chinese documentary, *Yan'an and the Eighth Route Army* (*Yan'an Yu Balu Jun*, 1940), director Yuan Muzhi travelled to the Soviet Union to complete post-production, only to lose much of the footage amidst the tumult of the German invasion. Nonetheless, the shooting methods adopted by the production, using staged events rather than observational filming, provided an influential model of non-fiction filmmaking in China for years to come. This pre-planned approach afforded an economic remedy to the relative lack of film stock in the post-war years.

In one exceptionally extravagant instance, the Sino-Soviet collaboration *Victory of the Chinese People* (*Zhongguo Renmin de Shengli*, 1950) spent eight months restaging a historic battle in the war against the Nationalists. As noted by scholar Ying Qian, this restaged 'documentary' is in fact also a remaking of *Million Heroes Crossing the Yangtze* (*Baiwan Xiongshi Xia Jiangnan*, 1949), a documentary with actual footage of the battle filmed solely by Chinese filmmakers, but deemed insufficiently dramatic for commemorating such a historically significant event. This docu-dramatic impulse paved the way for an aesthetic of 'revolutionary romanticism' (*Geming Langman Zhuyi*) to prevail in Maoist documentary films.

The aesthetic struggle over documentaries came to a head with the Great Leap Forward of 1958, an ill-conceived mass-industrialisation campaign that urged every corner of society to produce its way into modernisation. Some 352 documentaries were made in 1958, more than the total of the previous ten years combined, celebrating military, social, political and economic achievements. Proletarian romanticism prevailed in these films, while other aesthetic modes suffered; the very notion of 'art' was targeted as bourgeois decadence. In *Yangtze River Bridge* (*Wuhan Changjiang Daqiao*, 1957), a single line of voiceover that compares the bridge to "a handsome art work" was harshly criticised. *Jiangnan in Spring* (*Xinghua Chunyu Jiangnan*, 1956), a rare instance of a lyrical Maoist documentary, drew ire for excessively emphasising the idyllic countryside scenery while neglecting the toil of farm labourers.

Communist writer He Jingzhi found fault in other films: "Witnessing the touching scenes of people's hard work… I felt very unsatisfied with just seeing a few small trees and a small patch of irrigated rice field at the end of the film." Realistic depictions were deemed insufficient in portraying a Communist vision of reality; He wondered, "Why can't documentaries document tomorrow?" Accordingly, any hint of the disastrous effects wrought by Mao's campaigns (famines that killed tens of millions during the Great Leap Forward, and millions more persecuted during the Cultural Revolution) were never shown. It would take another 50 years before the historical exposés *In Search of Lin Zhao's Soul* (*Xun Zhao Lin Zhao De Ling Hun*, 2004) and *Though I Am Gone* (*Wo Sui Si Qu*, 2007) by Hu Jie uncovered the horrifying realities hidden from these utopian images.

Revolutionary romanticism would find its ultimate object of disgust through a foreign lens, just as Mao was warming up to the West. Michelangelo Antonioni's *Chung Kuo – China* (1972), the product of a diplomatic détente between China and Italy, was an unprecedented glimpse of the Cultural Revolution from a Western eye. Antonioni's film, with its long takes patiently trained on the unvarnished, grey-hued beauty of mundane life, scandalised its commissioners, who found it visually ugly and deeply offensive as a representation of the nation. Thus *Chung Kuo – China* sparked the largest denunciation campaign ever directed against a documentary, with an 18-page Party pamphlet mobilising people across China to write critical essays against a film they weren't even allowed to see. By Antonioni's own admission, *Chung Kuo – China* is a work whose gaze scratches the surface of Chinese society, made over a three-week visit. Joris Ivens and Marceline Loridan started filming their China documentary the same year as Antonioni but finished three years later; their result, *How Yukong Moved the Mountains*, is a far more immersive work, nearing 13 hours. In contrast to Antonioni's lengthy silent gazes at Chinese people, Ivens and Loridan engage their subjects, soliciting them to express their views and emotions. Despite this more empathetic method, the film still elicited a 61-point critical memo from Mao's wife Jiang Qing.

Mao's passing opened the way for his successor Deng Xiaoping to implement social reforms that sparked the beginning of China's economic ascendance in the 1980s. Gains in personal incomes led to an increase of televisions in private households, and China Central Television (CCTV) became the country's most powerful broadcaster and producer of documentary programming. New technocratic visions of prosperity through scientific and economic advancement pervaded these programmes, guided by Deng's slogan 'we must seek truth from facts' in place of Mao's dogma 'facts serve politics'. The pursuit of advanced production quality in documentary film yielded international co-productions like *The Silk Road* (1980) and *The Yangtze River* (1982), serving foreign interest in China's exotic appeal while portraying the nation with an unprecedented commercial lavishness.

The heated Chinese reform efforts of the 1980s reached boiling point at the end of the decade, with a TV documentary playing a pivotal role. *River Elegy* (*He Shang*, 1988), a six-hour series, inspired fierce public debate, and criticised traditional Chinese culture as an obstacle to social progress with an outspokenness unseen before or since in a nationally televised programme. The show had a galvanising effect on the student-led democracy movement of 1989, culminating in the June 4 Tiananmen Square Incident. Following that tragedy, the documentary was censored and a number of its creators either fled China or were arrested.

In the wake of Tiananmen and *River Elegy*, CCTV tightly regulated its content to avoid political controversy while also consolidating its position as the nation's most powerful non-fiction programmer; in 1993 it officially absorbed the state Central Newsreel and Documentary Film Studio. At the same time, a new generation of documentary filmmakers sought to work outside the strictures of the system. Around the time of Tiananmen, CCTV filmmaker Wu Wenguang borrowed equipment to interview artist friends

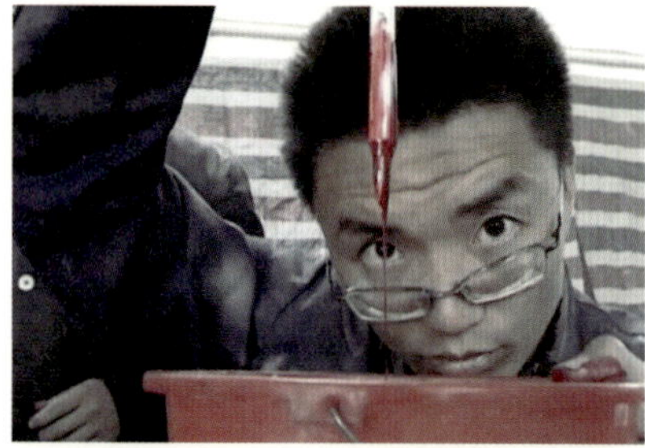

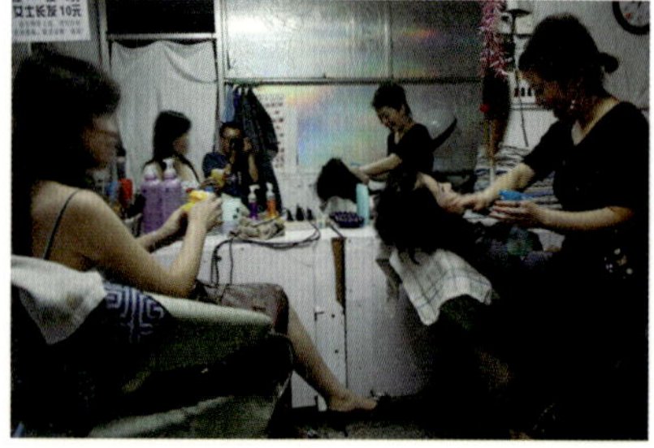

struggling to make a living. The resulting film, *The Last Dreamers: Bumming in Beijing* (*Zuihou de Mengxiangzhe*, 1990), laid the blueprint for a new independent aesthetic that contrasted sharply with the scripted realities of the studio. With its famous scene of a woman experiencing a nervous breakdown on camera, Wu's film embraced an aesthetic of immediacy (*xianchang*) whose spontaneity and indeterminacy expressed both the disillusionment and the search for freedom within post-Tiananmen China.

The Last Dreamers: Bumming in Beijing heralded a change not only in documentary but also in Chinese independent films, as the upstart 'Sixth Generation' filmmakers sought a street-level aesthetic and a realistic engagement with everyday subject matter. While often characterised as narrative directors, they squarely belong within the documentary practices of the time. Zhang Yuan's *Mama* (1991), cited as the first Chinese independent narrative film made after the Communist Revolution, features documentary interviews of women with mentally disabled children; *The Square* (*Guangchang*, 1994), co-directed by Zhang and Duan Jinchuan, is a documentary of Tiananmen Square that reveals its fictional nature: how the site's monumental presentation celebrates China's national glory while erasing its recent traumas.

Perhaps no filmmaker has explored the interplay of reality and fiction in contemporary China more thoroughly than Jia Zhangke. Many of his films, such as *Xiao Wu* (1997), 24 City (*Ershisi Cheng Ji*, 2008) and *I Wish I Knew* (*Hai Shang Chuanqi*, 2010) count as docu-fiction hybrids by virtue of their extraordinary sensitivity to the fictional, constructed nature of China's history and social landscape over recent generations of cultural upheaval. In his documentary *Dong* (2006), Jia filmed painter Liu Xiaodong's interactions with labourers on the Three Gorges Dam; this work led to a second feature, *Still Life* (*Sanxia Haoren,* 2006), which transforms footage from the documentary into the foundations for poetic fiction.

Although the majority of these films could not pass censorship, other films made within the system employed ethnographic realism, such as *The Story of Qiu Ju* (*Qiu Ju Da Guansi*, 1992) and *Ermo* (1994). Chinese documentary scholar Lü Xinyu points out that this *xianchang* aesthetic appears in CCTV productions like *Odyssey of the Great Wall* (*Wang Changcheng,* 1991), which features unscripted interviews that were a novelty to mainstream programming. As a 'reality' aesthetic and concern for ordinary lives pervaded mainstream Chinese film and media, independent documentaries largely languished in the margins, confined to overseas festivals or private salon screenings.

But with the new century, their production would prosper exponentially with the advent of digital technology. Portable DV cameras and cheap videotape enabled filmmakers to achieve new levels of intimacy and immersion with their subjects. These qualities are exemplified in two epic achievements of Chinese independent documentary, Wang Bing's nine-hour *West of the Tracks* (*Tiexi Qu*, 2003), which winds its way through the desolation of post-industrial northern China; and *Petition* (*Shangfang*, 2009), in which filmmaker Zhao Liang spends 12 years chronicling the ordeals of destitute Chinese seeking justice in Beijing. The availability of recordable DVDs enabled filmmakers to cheaply distribute their own works, while the internet allowed them to educate themselves on films and connect with others around the country.

By the early 2000s, a loose network of underground film festivals emerged with hubs in Yunnan, Beijing and Nanjing, enabling filmmakers to intensify their interactions and principles. New controversies emerged regarding the ethical responsibilities of the filmmaker: Xu Tong's *Wheat*

Harvest (*Mai Shou*, 2009), a portrait of sex workers, received severe scrutiny when one subject complained that her privacy had been compromised by the film's public release, to which she had not consented. This is but one of numerous instances where the filming of socially marginalised people raises questions about the motivations of the filmmakers; in Fan Lixin's *Last Train Home* (*Gui Tu Lie Che*, 2009), one of the most internationally acclaimed and commercially successful Chinese social documentaries, the subject, caught in the middle of a family argument, turns to the camera and cries, "Isn't this what you want?" It's a stunning moment that breaks the film's veneer of objective observational reality, casting scrutiny upon the subjective interests of those behind the camera.

A more recent crop of directors have addressed the dilemma of documentary ethics by exploring their own subjectivity. In *Tape* (*Jiao Dai*, 2010), performance artist Li Ning records five years of his own life, an obsessive project that pushes the boundary between public and private to disturbing extremes. Other films, such as the collective city symphony project *San Yuan Li* (2005), adopt experimental approaches to challenge the direct cinema reality aesthetic that has dominated the field. Huang Weikai's found footage remix *Disorder* (*Xianshi Shi Guoqu de Weilai*, 2009) was compiled from over 1,000 hours of underground videotapes of strange occurrences in China's streets, incidents that would never be reported on television, though today they might be viral videos on the internet. As exemplified by Cao Fei's virtual documentary *i.Mirror by China Tracy* (2007), recorded entirely within the online social platform Second Life, the web represents a bold new frontier for documentary practices to define China's reality once again, just as it has from the beginning. ◑

Since the making of the first Chinese fiction films – shortly after the Republic was founded – cinema became a stage on to which questions pertaining to the role of women in the new society could be 'performed'. In 1913, Lai Man-Wai (Li Minwei, 1893-1953) produced and co-directed a two-reeler, *Zhuangzi Tests His Wife* (*Zhuangzi Shi Qi*, 1913). Following a 1772 edict prohibiting men and women from appearing on stage and performing together, Lai played both the role of Zhangzi and, in full costume and make-up, that of his wife. In a bold move, however, Lai entrusted the small part of a maid to his wife, Yan Shanshan (1896-1952), who thus became the first actress in Chinese cinema. The same year, another young man named Zhang Shichuan (1889-1953) co-directed a four-reeler, *The Difficult Couple* (*Nan Fu Nan Qi*). The film was a critique of the practice of arranged marriage, but the cast was entirely male. Yet the trail opened by Lai would soon prove to be beneficial to Zhang, as the codes of realism enacted in the new film industry required the bodies of 'real women' to perform female roles.

In 1922 Zhang Shichuan founded his own production company, Mingxing (Star), and set out to recruit the most beautiful women in Shanghai. For his first feature-length film, *Orphan Rescues Grandfather* (*Gu'er Jiu Zu Ji*, 1923), Zhang cast the part of a model wife, mother and daughter-in-law against type by entrusting it to Wang Hanlun, a 'modern girl' who spoke English perfectly and was working as a typist in a tobacco company. The film was a spectacular success and soon many more 'glamour girls' were 'discovered'. Among the new actresses in his roster, Zhang was particularly proud of having 'stolen' Hu Die (aka Butterfly Wu, 1907-89) from a rival production company, Tianyi (Unique). Hu would become Zhang's biggest star and the highest-paid actress at the time.

Hu was cast in Zhang's film *Burning of the Red Lotus Temple* (*Huoshao Honglian Si*, 1928-31), an epic spread over 18 episodes that triggered the martial-arts movie (*wuxia pian*) craze. A number of these *wuxia pian* revolved around the presence of a *xia nü* (woman warrior): actresses were recruited not only for their beauty and their acting skills, but also for their ability to enact or suggest martial arts feats with the help of still-rudimentary special effects.

One of Zhang's discoveries was Xuan Jinglin, whom he had rescued from a low-class brothel to turn into one of the first martial-arts heroines in *The Nameless Hero* (*Wuming Yingxiong*, 1926), as well as cashing in on her real-life story in *An Amorous Story of the Silver Screen* (*Yinmu Yanshi*, 1931). Of the early films celebrating the fighting powers of the *xia nü* two are still extant: Wen Yimin's *Red Heroine* (*Hong Xia*, 1929) and Chen Kengran et al's *Swordswoman of Huangjiang* (*Huangjiang Nüxia*, 1930).

The 1930s: the 'golden age' of the female star system

The 'Golden Age' of filmmaking in Shanghai in the 1930s was also the golden age of the female star system. The urban environment of Shanghai provided countless employment opportunities for women – from bilingual secretaries to dance-hall hostesses to movie stars – but the connection between city life and moral turpitude was still prevalent, and movie stars, while worshipped, were subjected to acute scrutiny and criticism. The nascent film industry was ambivalent in its treatment of women. The female star system, while giving independence and autonomy to actresses, also turned them into commodities – their images were sold in fan magazines and used in advertisements.

The melodramatic plots in which these women were cast played a double function. For some, such as Zhang Sichuan, they were simply ploys to attract the female audience: women – at least urban women – were

given agency as buyers of tickets, the same way publicity campaigns using the images of famous actresses gave them agency as consumers. On the other hand, for left-wing writers and directors melodrama was a way to attract the public's attention to the socio-political problems that plagued the country. As the situation worsened throughout the 1930s with civil war, unemployment and the Japanese invasion, the figure of the 'suffering woman' became a metaphor for the suffering of China, her prostitution and powerlessness signifying China's fate at the hands of imperialist powers.

In 1930, in collaboration with the exhibitor/distributor Luo Mingyou (1900-67), Lai Minwei founded Lianhua (United Photoplay Service), which became one of the most influential production companies in Shanghai. Shortly afterwards, Hu Die's rival at the box office, the legendary Ruan Lingyu (1910-35), joined Lianhua, where she collaborated with the best filmmakers of the era: Bu Wancang (1903-74), Fei Mu (1906-51) and Sun Yu (1900-90).

The Goddess (*Shennü*, 1934) by Wu Yonggang (1907-83), in which she plays a prostitute who raises her son alone and eventually kills her pimp, has remained Ruan's most famous performance. In her penultimate film, *New Women* (*Xin Nüxing*, 1934), Cai Chusheng (1906-68) cast her as a modern young woman, a music teacher, a writer and a mother, who commits suicide after being subjected to malicious gossip. The film was loosely inspired by the suicide of the actress Ai Xia (1912-34) – who was incidentally the second female filmmaker in China after the actress Xie Caizhen, who had directed *An Orphan's Cry* (*Guchu Beisheng*) in 1925, having scripted, directed and starred in *A Modern Woman* (*Xiandai yi Nüxing*, 1933). The release of Cai's *New Women* was overshadowed by Ruan's own suicide, after she had been attacked by the yellow press for her private life.

Along with another Ruan vehicle, Bu Wancang's *Three Modern Women* (*San'ge Modeng Nüxing*, 1933), these films articulated a debate that fascinated all levels of society in the Republican era: what should the 'New Woman' (*xin nüxing*) be? Many thought that the future of China depended on the evolution of the condition of women. Yet it was hard to break the Confucian mould of the 'three obediences' (to one's father, husband and son), and also, while intellectual/political trends such as the May Fourth Movement (that had started as a May 4 1919 protest of students, artists and intellectuals against the conditions imposed upon China by the Versailles Treaty) wanted to initiate a social and cultural renaissance in China, they deliberately promoted a form of modernity that they felt would not turn the country into a cultural colony of the West, and the *xin nüxing* into a copy-cat of the flapper.

Of the actresses that adorned the marquees of Shanghai theatres during the Republican era, many, such as Hu Die, Wei Wei, Li Lihua and Zhou Xuan, fled to Hong Kong after 1949. Many more stayed – the lovely Chen Bo'er even became culture minister before her untimely death in 1951. Others, alas, were persecuted during the Cultural Revolution, as was the case with Bai Yang and Shangguan Yunzhu.

The 'new woman' in the New China

After 1949, the question of the *xin nüxing* was displaced and reformulated: women's social and sexual exploitation was caused by feudalism and imperialism; socialism would give women professional equality, and the 'new woman' would be working to implement revolutionary goals.

However, issues of 'women's rights' and the 'women's movement' were not articulated through grass-roots mobilisation, but unfolded under the centrally supervised aegis of the Women's Federation: 'women's

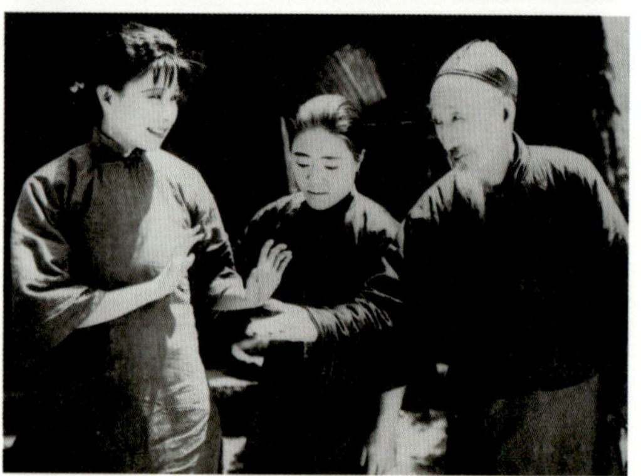

rights' were often not clearly distinguished from a barely feminised version of the rights of the proletariat, as defined by the Party.

In the film industry, the transition was slow at first, and the first female directors to work in the new China had no formal training. Wang Ping (1916-90) had started her career as an actress in leftist films and stage productions in the Republican era and was fired from the school where she was teaching for having played Nora in a production of Ibsen's *The Doll's House*. An active member of the Communist Party during the war with Japan, she was subsequently invited to make an instructional film for the army in 1952, then became the first woman to direct a feature in Communist China with *Breaking Through the Darkness Before Dawn* (*Chongpo Liming Qian De Heian*, 1956). Wang worked on a number of films celebrating the revolution, such as the drama *Story of Liubao Village* (*Liubao de Gushi*, 1957) and the pageant of revolutionary songs *The East is Red* (*Dongfang Hong*, 1965). Other women directors in the 'Seventeen Years' period include Wang Shaoyan (1924-), who made one of the most famous revolutionary opera films, *Red Coral* (*Hong Shanhu* 1961); Dong Kena (1930-), whose *Grass Grows on the Kunlun Mountain* (*Kunlun Shan Shang Yike Cao*, 1962) has remained a classic, and Yan Bili, famous for the children's film *Little Football Players* (*Xiao Zuqui Duiyuan*, 1965).

As the Shanghai Animation Film studio was experiencing a golden age in the 1950s and 60s, a young woman trained as a painter, Tang Cheng (1919-86) joined the company. She was modest, often in poor health, and the 'co-directing' credits scattered about her illustrious career may have been the result of her aversion to the spotlight. She is mostly known for having crafted, in collaboration with Te Wei, *Where is Mama?* (aka *Baby Tadpoles Look for Their Mother*, *Xiao Kedou Zhao Mama*, 1961), China's first animated ink-and-wash film, and for having co-directed the second part of *Uproar in Heaven* (*Da Nao Tian Gong*, 1961-64) with Wang Laiming.

After 1949, actresses were paid a proletarian salary and cast as 'cultural workers' involved in the task of turning cinema into a popular art. The glamorous lifestyles of the 1930s may have been no more, but some still attained stardom, such as Tian Hua (1928-), the unforgettable star of *The White-Haired Girl* (*Baimao Nü*, 1950, Wang Bin and Shui Hua) – another film which equated female suffering with the dismal fate of the people under feudalism, and attracted audiences of more than 150 million.

The 'new woman' after the Cultural Revolution

The Cultural Revolution halted the careers of many filmmakers of both genders, but Wang Ping and Dong Kena eventually bounced back. They were joined by women who had graduated from film schools in the mid-1960s, but had to wait until the end of the 1970s to start directing, such as Zhang Nuanxin (1940-95), whose 1985 feature, *Sacrificed Youth* (*Qingchun Ji*) sensitively renders the emotional dilemma of a young woman 'sent down' to a minority rural area for re-education during the Cultural Revolution.

Another landmark in positioning issues of female identity within a socialist society was *Woman, Demon, Human* (*Ren Gui Qing*, 1987) by Huang Shuqin (1940-). The film follows the travails of a young actress/singer (inspired by the life story of a famous opera actress, Pei Yanling) who dreams of playing, in full 'painted face' make-up, the part of a benevolent male ghost on a Beijing Opera stage.

Huang Shuqin continued to make films till 2002, including *The Soul of the Painter* (*Hua Hun*, 1994), starring Gong Li and fictionalising the life of a prostitute-turned-painter who lived in Paris. Zhang Nuanxin directed *Good Morning Beijing* (*Beijing Nizao*, 1990), the first film to tackle the new youth urban culture, before dying of cancer.

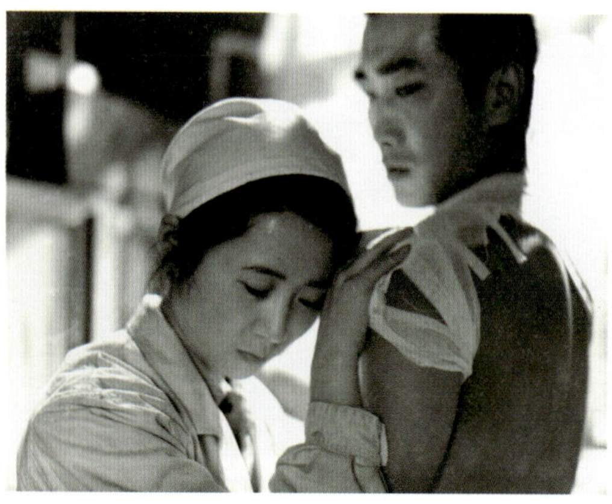

In the 1980s, as 'Fifth Generation' female directors arrived on the scene – having attended the Beijing Film Academy after it reopened its doors in 1978 – China boasted a higher proportion of female directors than any other country. Among them was Hu Mei (1956-), who reached notoriety with her first feature, *Army Nurse* (*Nüer Lou*, 1985), a film that explores the contradiction between the heroine's professional duty and her romantic attraction for a patient.

Another key Fifth Generation member, Peng Xiaolian (1953-), became famous with her second film, *Women's Story* (*Nüren de Gushi*, 1987), which details the resistance of three peasant women to the fate decided for them (including one case of forced marriage). However, a Western newspaper described the film as having criticised China's one-child policy, and in the spring of 1989 Peng left the country for New York on a scholarship. She was eventually able to return to her home city of Shanghai, and has continued to make films describing the female condition, such as *Shanghai Women* (*Jiazhuang Mei Ganjue*, 2002).

Li Shaohong (1955-) completed the controversial *Bloody Morning* (*Xuese Qingcheng*) in 1990, at a time when her adaptation of Gabriel Garcia Marquez's *Chronicle of a Death Foretold* was interpreted as an allusion to the bloody incidents of June 1989 – and was banned for a couple of years. Her fourth feature, the visually sumptuous *Blush* (*Hong Fen*, 1995), recounts post-communist history from the point of view of two prostitutes who were 'liberated' against their wishes in 1949.

The youngest member of the Fifth Generation was also a woman, Li Miaomiao, from the Hui Muslim minority, who had entered the Beijing Film Academy at 16, and directed her first feature, *Stories of the Voyage* (*Yuangyang Yishi*, 1985), when she was 23. She is mostly known for *Women on the Long March* (*Mati Shengcui*, 1987), about eight female fighters in the Red Army, and *Chatterbox* (*Zazuizi*, 1993), a film she directed for the Children's Film Studio and took to the Venice Film Festival where it won an award. Like Hu Mei and Li Shaohong, Li Miaomiao is currently active in television.

In the years following the Cultural Revolution, Liu Xiaoqing (1951-), mostly famous for her performance in Xie Jin's *Hibiscus Town* (*Furong Zhen*, 1986), was long considered the best actress in China, closely followed by Siqin Gaowa (1950-), who has acted equally in Mainland and Hong Kong productions. Yet it was the positive reception received abroad by the first films of the Fifth Generation that turned Gong Li (1966-) into the first Chinese actress to be known by international audiences, for her roles in such Zhang Yimou films as *Red Sorghum* (*Hong Gaoliang*, 1987), *Ju Dou* (1989) and *The Story of Qiu Jiu* (*Qiu Jiu Da Guansi*, 1992), due to the publicity campaigns launched by their Western distributors. She became an icon of a certain kind of Chinese woman, playing – some contend – into Orientalist fantasies, combining suffering, glamour and rebellion.

Post 1989 renaissance

The year 1989 marked a historical break, a pause and a springboard. The repression was followed by an intense period of artistic and intellectual activity, during which the New Documentary Movement emerged. Li Hong's epoch-making *Out of Phoenixbridge* (*Hui Dao Fenghuang Qiao*, 1997) was the first, and for a while the only, 'new documentary' made by a woman. As digital cameras and home computer editing systems spread in the 1990s, making documentaries became easier and more women got involved, such as Yang Lina (a former actress in the Red Army troupe), director of *Old Men* (*Lao Tou*, 1999), *Home Video* (2001) and *The Love of Mr. An*, (*Lao An*, 2008); Ma Li, director of *Born in Beijing* (*Jing Sheng*, 2012); Ji Dan, director of *Spiral Staircase* of Harbin (*Haerbin Xuan Zhuan Lou Ti*, 2008) and *When the Bough Breaks* (*Wei Chao*, 2011); the environmentalist/activist Shi Lihong, director of *Voice of the Angry River*, 2004); Yang Rui, creator of original hybrids of anthropological documentary and fiction *The Bimo Records* (*Bimoji*, 2006) and *Crossing the Mountains* (*Fanshan*, 2009); and the feminist academic/activist Ai Xiaoming, who received the Prix Simone de Beauvoir in 2010, and whose films include *White Ribbon* (*Bai Sidai*, 2004), and *Our Children* (*Women de Wawa*, 2009).

Digital, light modes of recording have also given a mode of visual expression to China's generally invisible and/or repressed queer community. Female directors active in the field include Ying Weiwei aka Echo Y. Windy, director of *The Box* (*Hezi*, 2001); Shi Tou, director of *Dyke March* (*Nütongzhi Youxingri*, 2004) and *We Want to Get Married* (2007); and Yang Yang, director of *Our Story – 10-Year 'Guerrilla Warfare' of Beijing Queer Film Festival* (*Women de Gushi*, 2012).

The 'digital revolution' also prompted an intermingling of artforms and unorthodox collaborations, some with hybrid modes of financing (sometimes benefiting from Western art-world commissions), and in which women have played a role. Collectives such as U-theque in Guangzhou produced groundbreaking experimental documentaries about the displacement of urban populations, among them *San Yuan Li* (2003) and *Meishi Street* (*Mei Shijie*, 2006), in which installation artist Cao Fei and experimental filmmaker Tan Tantan participated.

In Sichuan, Peng Shan produced and scripted her partner (now husband) Ying Liang's films, including the multiple-award winning *The Other Half* (*Ling Yiban*, 2006). In 2008 Beijing critic/curator Zhang Yaxuan co-directed *A Disappearance Foretold* (*Qianmen Qian*) with her husband, Belgian documentarist Olivier Meys. Dancer/choreographer Wen Hui directed *Listening to Third Grandmother's Stories* (*Ting San Nainai Jiang Guoqu de Shiqing*, 2011), part of the 'Folk Memory Project' she initiated with veteran documentary filmmaker Wu Wenguang, and though which a number of young people, including such women as Zou Xueping, Zhang Mengqi, Li Xinmin and Guo Rui, have made films about the history of their villages or families – in particular recording an oral account of the great famine of 1959-61.

The spring 1989 movement was complex, contradictory and multi-layered, as the claims for 'democracy' didn't mean the same thing for all participants. Some argued for an opening to a more fluid market economy, and they eventually got what they wanted. State-owned studios gradually lost their monopoly, and independent production companies appeared. In the early 1990s independent productions were still illegal, but businessmen started investing, albeit modestly, with unexpected results in terms of gender: the equal opportunity system advocated by the studios was no longer relevant, and investors shied away from female filmmakers. Until the early 2000s, aside from the New Documentary Movement and artists' films and videos, the post-1989 'Sixth Generation' was mostly a men's club.

Ning Ying (1959-) is a transitional figure: having graduated from the BFA in 1982, she is a member of the Fifth Generation, but her younger age and urban sensibility made her closer to the work of the 'Sixth Generation.' She also studied cinema in Rome, worked as an assistant to Bernardo Bertolucci on *The Last Emperor* (1987) and founded her own Italo-Chinese independent production company. Ning directed the critically hailed *Beijing Trilogy: For Fun* (*Zhao Le*, 1992); *On The Beat* (*Minjing Gushi*, 1995); and *I Love Beijing* (*Xiari Nuanyangyang*, 2000) about the fate of men (retired opera lovers, cops, taxi drivers) in a rapidly changing urban environment, before drawing an insightful portrait of four women for her first digital feature, *Perpetual Motion*

(Below)
Gong Li in her debut role in Zhang Yimou's 'Red Sorghum' (1987).

(Bottom)
Films like Zhang Yimou's 'Raise the Red Lantern' (1991) made Gong Li the most internationally known Chinese actress of the 1990s.

(*Wu Qiong Dong*, 2005). Still fascinated by masculinity, she recently shot another cop story in Inner Mongolia, *To Live and Die in Ordos* (*Jincha Riji*, 2014).

The new millennium saw the arrival of two female talents from the 'Sixth Generation.' Directed in 16mm by a former TV anchor turned journalist turned television documentary maker, Li Yu (1973-), *Fish and Elephant* (*Jinnian Xiatian*, 2001) was the first Chinese lesbian underground feature. Starring Shi Tou as a market vendor who leaves her boyfriend for a female zookeeper, it was banned in China, but shown at 70 international film festivals. It launched Li Yu's career; her subsequent works (in particular *Lost in Beijing* (*Ping Guo*, 2007) have continued to explore the female condition. Her 2010 feature, *Buddha Mountain* (*Guanyin Shan*), starring two major actresses, Sylvia Chang from Taiwan and Fan Bingbing from China, was the first independent art film to reap commercial success in the PRC.

Produced by a small Hong Kong company in order to bypass censorship, *Conjugation* (*Dongci Bianwei*, 2001) by Tang Xiaobai (aka Emily Tang) was the first film shot (underground) in China about the aftermath of Tiananmen Square. In her following two films, *Perfect Life* (*Wan Mei Shenghuo*, 2008) and *All Apologies* (*Ai de Tishen*, 2012), Tang has developed and expanded her mixture of documentary and fiction, acutely reproducing small changes in the texture of Chinese society as they affect the female migrant population, or the discrepancy between rich and poor.

In the early 2000s, the female producer Lola launched the 'Yunnan Project', comprising ten films by ten female directors. The first two productions, Wang Fen's *The Case* (*Xiang Zi*, 2007) and Yin Lichuan's *The Park* (*Gongyuan*, 2007), were critical successes, but the project was eventually abandoned. Another female producer, Vivian Qu, turned to directing with the neo-*noir Trap Street* (*Shuiyin Jie*, 2013), which uses a doomed love story to allude to the 'black jails' where Chinese citizens can disappear after their arrest.

Around 2005, Jia Zhangke started producing the work of young filmmakers, a number of them women. Song Fang's *Memories Look at Me* (*Ji Yi Wang Zhe Wo*, 2012), an elegant autobiographical mix of fiction and documentary, won an award in Locarno, and Quan Ling's *Forgetting to Know You* (*Mo Sheng*, 2013), which finely depicts a crumbling working-class marriage in the Chongqing area, was shown in Berlin.

The most original female directorial voice of the new millennium is that of Liu Jiayin, who deconstructs the 'intimate family drama' in a robust and exhilarating manner. At 23, while a BFA student, she won the FIPRESCI Award in Berlin for *Oxhide* (*Niupi*, 2004), shot with a small DV camera but in a widescreen ratio, in her parents' small apartment. *Oxhide II* (*Niupi Er*, 2009) pushes the formal radicalism one step further: it breaks down a smaller domestic space into nine shots of uneven lengths and varied angles that go around a workshop/dinner table in 45 per cent increments, reorganising the balance of power between the three protagonists (Mum, Dad and the filmmaker-daughter) as they make and eat dumplings in real time.

The post-2000 revival of the star system

With the reintroduction of the market economy a solid star system was rekindled in China, which became fully established by the late 1990s; fashion models and would-be starlets were soon competing for roles with actresses with serious training.

The four *dan* actresses (*dan* denoting a female role in opera) noted by the Chinese press are Zhou Xun, who had a double role in Lou Ye's *Suzhou River* (*Suzhou He*, 2000); Zhang Ziyi, discovered by Zhang Yimou for his *The Road Home* (*Wo de Fuqin Muqin*, 1999); Xu Jinglei (a role model

(Below)
Ning Ying's insightful portrait of four women, 'Perpetual Motion' (2005).

(Bottom)
Liu Jiayin's exhilaratingly original 'Oxhide' (2004).

(Opposite)
The four 'dan' actresses of post-2000 Chinese cinema: (clockwise from top left) Zhang Ziyi in 'Crouching Tiger, Hidden Dragon' (2000); Xu Jinglei in 'Letter from an Unknown Woman' (2004); Zhou Xun in 'Suzhou River' (2000); Zhao Wei in 'Red Cliff' (2008).

for the new urban youth); and Zhao Wei, who has worked equally well
with filmmakers from the Mainland as those from Hong Kong. Zhang
Ziyi is the one who has succeeded in crossing over to international
audiences, having appeared in such transnational productions as Ang
Lee's *Crouching Tiger, Hidden Dragon* (*Wo Hu Cang Long*, 2000), Zhang
Yimou's *Hero* (*Yingxiong*, 2002) and Wong Kar Wai's *The Grandmaster* (*Yidai
Zongshi*, 2013), as well as Hollywood films like *Memoirs of a Geisha* (2005).

The most significant presence for Chinese audiences is that of Xu
Jinglei, who truly embodies what a *xin nüxing* could or should be in
contemporary society. Xu started her career as a teenager with a small
part in Zhang Yuan's *Beijing Bastards* (*Beijing Zazhong*, 1993). She became
known on television, and later cashed in on her success in cutting-edge
urban films directed by Zhang Yang, Zhang Yibai and Zhang Yuan to write,
direct and produce her own vehicles, starting with the intimate drama
My Father and I (*Wo he Baba*) in 2003. In *Letter from an Unknown Woman* (*Yige
Mosheng Nüren de Laixin*, 2004) she transposed Stefan Zweig's original
novella to Republican China. Where Max Ophüls's 1948 Hollywood version
constructed a female victim, Xu's heroine suffers but bites; she never
becomes a respectable housewife, but is instead a witty courtesan.

With *Go Lala Go!* (*Du Lala Shengzhi Ji*, 2010) Xu adapted an internet
novel about an ambitious young woman's survival strategies and
setbacks in the corporate world (including but not limited to sex with
her boss), and became the first Chinese female director to hit the
million mark at the box-office. Xu publishes one of the most visited
blogs on earth, has edited a magazine, and is contemplating producing
the work of young directors. Other actresses are following suit: in
2013 Zhao Wei directed the romantic melodrama *So Young* (*Zhi Women
Zhong Jiang Shiqu de Qingchun*), which became a huge box-office hit.

The 'new woman' controversy is not closed, as the film industry
is booming in China, it is now clearly marked by the double question
of who controls women's bodies and who controls their images.
But it is now the women themselves, instead of Party leaders,
philosophers or social reformers, who are providing the answers.

THE EVOLUTION OF CHINESE QUEER CINEMA

By Cui Zi'en with Michael Berry

Cui Zi'en is associate professor at the Beijing Film Academy and a leading activist in the Chinese queer rights movement. He is co-founder of the Beijing Queer Film Festival, and the author of numerous books. He is also an actor, a prolific screenwriter and the writer/director of several dozen independent films including *The Old Testament* (*Jiuyue, 2002*), *Withered in a Blooming Season* (*Shaonian Huacao Huang*, 2005), *Refrain* (*Fuge*, 2006) and the documentaries *Queer China, 'Comrade' China* (*Zhi Tongzhi*, 2009) and *We Are the... of Communism* (*Women shi Gongchanzhuyi Shengluehao*, 2007). The following comments are drawn from an interview between Michael Berry and Cui Zi'en on 30 April 2014 at the University of California, Santa Barbara, where Berry asked Cui to describe the development and evolution of Chinese queer cinema from his unique perspective as a filmmaker, scholar and festival programmer.

Usually when we think about the history of gay film in China we begin with Zhang Yuan's *East Palace, West Palace* (*Dong Gong Xi Gong*, 1995), which is generally considered the first Chinese queer film. Before that there had been other films with queer themes, or which depicted same-sex relations, like *Farewell My Concubine* (*Ba Wang Bie Ji*, 1993), which used Chinese opera and the theatre world to imply a certain type of male-male relations, but films like this were more about homosocial relations, and not necessarily homosexual relationships, and therefore should be looked at differently.

East Palace, West Palace is also directly linked to China's first sociological study of gay culture in China, Wang Xiaobo and Li Yinhe's *Their World* (*Tamen De Shijie*, 1992). After collaborating on that book, Wang Xiaobo worked with Zhang Yuan on the screenplay for *East Palace, West Palace*. *Farewell My Concubine*, on the other hand, was adapted from a popular bestselling novel by Lilian Lee, so the film was the product of a marriage between film and literature, whereas *East Palace, West Palace* was the product of the union between sociology, literature and cinema.

In the ensuing years, other important gay-themed films in China were made, including Liu Bingjian's *Men and Women* (*Nannan Nünü*, 1999), on which I collaborated, and Li Yu's *Fish and Elephant* (*Jinnian Xiatian*, 2001), one of the first Chinese lesbian films. From there, I directed *The Old Testament* (*Jiuyue*, 2001) and Stanley Kwan directed *Lan Yu* (2001), which was shot on location in China. These films, along with *East Palace, West Palace*, were the five titles screened in 2001 at the first Gay and Lesbian Film Festival in Beijing.

By the time we put on the second Gay and Lesbian Film Festival in 2005 (which had by then been renamed the Beijing Queer Film Festival), we screened more than 30 titles. Included were two films by the Shanghai-based director Anthony Chen (Chen Yusu): *Shanghai Panic* (*Women dou Haipa*, 2002) and *Destination Shanghai* (*Mudidi Shanghai*, 2003). Comparing the first two festivals, one clear shift was that many of the directors featured in the 2005 festival may have been portraying queer themes in their films, but they themselves were not gay. Because they were approaching queer themes from a non-queer perspective, one can see two traps that many of their films fell into. One set of films tended to praise everything queer, presenting an overly positive spin on all gay characters and their relationships – similar to the phenomena of 'queer fandom.' The other set offered a fantastical, embellished and imaginary vision of what a queer lifestyle is like – one quite distant from reality and not terribly deep or insightful.

In 2008, when we put together the third Queer Film Festival, we started to see a much greater diversity in terms of styles and genres. Many more individuals who self-identify as gay or lesbian

'Queer China, 'Comrade' China' (2009)

were picking up cameras to make films themselves. Naturally, many of these new works may not have reached the same artistic standards that we might expect from more seasoned filmmakers, but their work began to take us inside a more authentic vision of queer life in China, in all its layers and complexities.

There is a Shanghai director named Han Chen, born in 1986, who began making films while a student at Tongji University. He is quite prolific and usually shoots between two to three films a year. Many of his films take the form of American-inspired genre films – something the Chinese LGBT film community hadn't really seen before.

Another shift in Chinese queer cinema has been the complex relationship between documentary and narrative film. More and more queer-themed films are blurring the lines between documentary and narrative, non-fiction and fiction, fact and fantasy. Zhang Hanzi is one director who has taken this to a brilliant new level in queer film. Lesbian-themed films and films by lesbian filmmakers on the other hand are still quite few. One of the more interesting Chinese lesbian filmmakers goes simply by the name Julia (Zhuliya), but she only made two or three films before disappearing off the scene.

This year [2014] we are beginning the selection process for another festival and some new trends are already apparent, such as the rise of *wei dianying* or 'micro-films' – educational films sponsored by various NGOs, many of which are narrative shorts. It is also apparent that fewer filmmakers are making feature-length queer films and that the short film is beginning to dominate.

I have mostly excluded my own films from this narrative. That would be an entirely separate history of queer cinema! I also refrain from screening my work at our festivals, which have only limited screening slots; I don't want my own films to get in the way of the younger filmmakers whose work we are trying to highlight. ◐

In 2013, the Motion Picture Association of America (MPAA) released statistics that served to confirm what many industry observers had predicted for some time: China had surpassed Japan to become the world's second-largest film market with a cinema audience worth $2.7 billion per year. This is still some way off that of the US, with its current audience value of $10.8 billion, but nonetheless shows that China's theatrical exhibition sector is growing at an unprecedented rate.

Much of the media coverage of China's rapidly expanding multiplex market – which in 2013 reportedly saw 10 cinema screens being built every day – has focused on the eager consumption of 3D-equipped Hollywood blockbusters, some of which achieve box-office grosses in China that exceed their domestic revenues due to a constant demand for effects-heavy spectacles from Chinese audiences.

However, the Chinese market is more multi-faceted, not only with regards to its relationship with the major Hollywood studios, but in terms of national output. The years since the millennium have seen a run of crowd-pleasing, Chinese-made films that have responded to the ever-shifting taste of local audiences in ways that American producers with dreams of controlling this lucrative market can only dream of emulating.

The long march to prosperity

The thriving film industry that exists in China today is the result of three decades of initiatives that have been intertwined with gradual ideological shifts. In the years that followed the end of the Cultural Revolution, the industry was slow to rebuild. Production of escapist cinema was initially encouraged, with the animation *Nezha Conquers the Dragon King* (*Nezha Nao Hai*, 1979), love story *Romance on Lushan Mountain* (*Lu Shan Lian*, 1980) and sci-fi adventure *Death Ray on Coral Island* (*Shanhu Dao Shang de Siguang*, 1980) among early forays into popular narrative; but such entertainments were soon deemed unacceptable by the authorities. Instead, the directors of the 'Fourth Generation' turned out 'Scar Dramas' that reflected the sustained trauma that was being experienced by much of the population, and 'Fifth Generation' directors such as Chen Kaige and Zhang Yimou forged a new path through phantasmagoric landscapes and a focus on the struggle of the individual.

Sustainable models for commercially viable cinema started to fall into place in the late-1990s, with the widespread popularity of low-cost comedies by directors Zhang Yang and Feng Xiaogang. Zhang's early outings *Spicy Love Soup* (*Aiqing Mala Tang*, 1997) and *Shower* (*Xizao*, 1999) have a mellow sense of humour which stems from observation of daily minutiae: *Spicy Love Soup* is a multi-character piece about life in modern Beijing, while *Shower* focuses on a bathhouse based in an area of the capital that was scheduled for redevelopment.

Feng Xiaogang became a household name by delivering a run of popular and fitfully amusing satires, such as *The Dream Factory* (*Jiafang Yifang*, 1997), *Be There or Be Square* (*Bu Jian Bu San*, 1998), *Sorry Baby* (*Meiwan Meiliao*, 1999) and *Big Shot's Funeral* (*Da Wan*, 2001). Each poked fun at China's rapidly changing value system in the era of economic acceleration, with quick-witted dialogue that played on the official language. Feng would later try his hand at action with *A World Without Thieves* (*Tianxia Wu Zei*, 2004), Civil War recreation with *Assembly* (*Jijie Hao*, 2007), romance with his pair of *If You Are the One* dramas (*Feicheng Wurao*, 2008/*Feicheng Wurao 2*, 2010) and tragedy with the earthquake survival saga *Aftershock* (*Tangshan Da Dizhen*, 2010). Some of these films were allocated huge budgets due to Feng's unrivalled box-office track record,

although disappointing returns for his famine epic *Back to 1942* (*Yi Jiu Si Er*, 2012) prompted him to return to comedy with *Personal Tailor* (*Shiren Ding Zhi*, 2013), which takes jabs at corrupt officials, the value of art in a commercial society and the objectionable behavior of the *nouveau riche*.

Feng's journey from creator of small-scale entertainments to grand spectacle and back again is emblematic of China's film industry over the past decade. Much of the 2000s found local studios being swept up by global ambition as producers sought to emulate the success of Ang Lee's *wuxia* epic *Crouching Tiger, Hidden Dragon* (*Wo Hu Cang Long*, 2000), which grossed $213 million worldwide. Large sums were spent on a succession of martial-arts adventures that required revenue from international sales to show profit. Better examples of this trend, such as Zhang Yimou's *Hero* (*Yingxiong*, 2002) and *House of Flying Daggers* (*Shimian Maifu*, 2004), suggested that the *wuxia* revival could be more than just a production cycle, but interest in the genre was soon flagging due to sub-par efforts like Chen Kaige's lavish *The Promise* (*Wuji*, 2005), which was ridiculed for its poor special effects.

Nonetheless, adventures set in ancient times are still produced. The likes of *Painted Skin* (*Huapi*, 2008), *The Sword Identity* (*Wo Kou De Zong Ji*, 2011), *Painted Skin: The Resurrection* (*Huapi 2*, 2012), *Tai Chi 0* (2012), *The Four* (*Si Da Mingbu*, 2012) and *The Four 2* (*Si Da Mingbu 2*, 2013) provide a spectacle that stands apart from Hollywood due to its roots in history or folklore, even if liberties are frequently taken with regards to period accuracy.

However, the late-2000s onwards has seen the Chinese film industry become ever more diverse, producing films in a range of genres, at more manageable budget levels. Mainland multiplexes are currently filled with comedies and dramas, while thrillers and horror films are creeping in as mainstream directors attempt to work within – or around – censorship restrictions regarding sex, violence or the supernatural.

Attempts are also made to safeguard the domestic industry by limiting the share taken by foreign titles – regular 'blackouts' have been conducted, during which Hollywood releases are barred from the marketplace and a strict quota on releases of foreign films each year is maintained. That quota increased to 34 in 2012, and as a result 'blackouts' have become

less common, although individual Hollywood titles have still fallen victim to such politics: *Avatar* (2009) was pulled from non-3D cinemas in order to make way for the biopic *Confucius* (*Kongfuzi*, 2010); the release of *Transformers: Dark of the Moon* (2011) was held back until the propaganda epic *The Beginning of the Great Revival* (*Jiandang Weiye*, 2011) had reached its box-office target; comic-book blockbusters *The Amazing Spider-Man* (2012) and *The Dark Knight Rises* (2012) were allocated the same release date in what seemed to be an attempt to sabotage these franchises by forcing fans to chose between two superheroes on opening weekend; and actress Zhao Wei made a successful appeal to the film bureau to have the release of *Iron Man 3* (2013) postponed so that her directorial debut *So Young* (*Zhi Women Zhong Jiang Shiqu de Qingchun*, 2013) would have the market to itself.

Occasional unfair advantages aside, China's film industry has realised that the best way to compete with Hollywood is to not do so directly: the mainstream audience will always be tempted to binge on the global popcorn of *Mission: Impossible – Ghost Protocol* (2011) or *Pacific Rim* (2013), but Chinese offerings can comfortably co-exist if their content caters more to popular local taste.

The legend of *Crazy Stone*

The vitality of commercial production in the 2000s would receive a much-needed boost from the work of new directors, the most successful of whom – and the heir to Feng as his generation's foremost popular satirist – is Ning Hao. Ning's rambunctious comedy *Crazy Stone* (*Fengkuang de Shitou*, 2006) parlayed a shaggy dog story about multiple parties trying to gain possession of a piece of priceless jade into a surprise box-office sensation. In contrast to the slickness of most studio features, the low-budget *Crazy Stone* used crude digital photography and made no effort to disguise its debt to the British crime caper *Lock, Stock and Two Smoking Barrels* (1997). This vulgar but undeniably amusing collage led to such imitators as *One Night in Supermarket* (*Ye Dian*, 2009) and *Welcome to Sha-ma Town* (*Juezhan Shama Zhen*, 2010), both of which turned a swift profit, although audiences were more receptive to Ning's sports comedy *Crazy Racer* (*Fengkuang de Saiche*, 2009).

The success of his comedies enabled Ning to shoot *No Man's Land* (*Wu Ren Qu*, 2013), a vicious neo-western in which a city lawyer (Xu Zheng) finds his life under threat when travelling through a desolate region. Although completed in 2010, the film would not be released for a further three years due to the censors objecting to the supposedly depraved nature of its social representation. Ning would return to comedy with *Guns and Roses* (*Huangjin Da Jiean*, 2012), a chaotic heist movie set in Japanese-occupied 1930s Manchuria, before reshooting scenes for a revised version of *No Man's Land*, which was approved for belated release. Despite its troubled journey to the screen, *No Man's Land* shows that Ning is capable of delivering a provocative vision in propulsive fashion, even if he cribs flourishes from Sergio Leone and Quentin Tarantino to facilitate a frenzied vision of moral decay.

But what I really want to do is direct

Some of the biggest hits in recent years been directed by actors. Jiang Wen, who came to prominence as a performer in the 1980s, achieved early success behind the camera with *In the Heat of the Sun* (*Yangguang Canlan de Rizi*, 1994), an adaptation of Wang Shou's coming-of-age novel set in Beijing during the Cultural Revolution. Jiang's subsequent *Devils on the Doorstep* (*Guizi Lai Le*, 2000) and *The Sun Also Rises* (*Taiyang Zhaochang Sheng-qi*, 2007) were aimed at international arthouses, but he returned to commercial prominence in China with *Let the Bullets Fly* (*Rang Zidan Fei*, 2010), a riotous

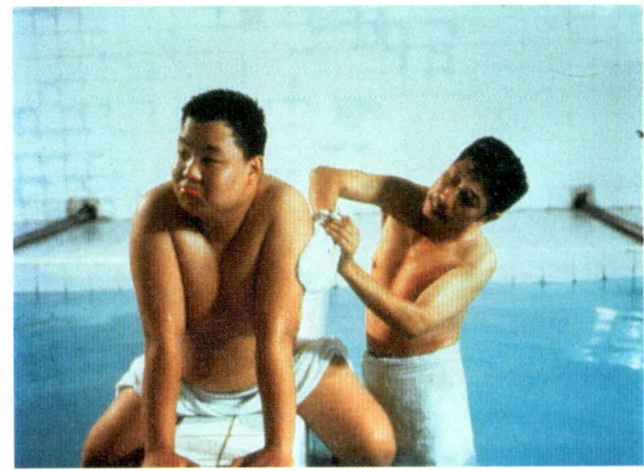

(Top)
'Shower' (1999), by Zhang Yang, is set in a bathhouse in a Beijing area scheduled for demolition.

(Above)
Zhang Yang's multi-character piece 'Spicy Love Soup' (1997) looks at life in modern Beijing.

(Below)
Ning Hao's low-budget comic caper 'Crazy Stone' (2006) became a surprise box-office sensation.

action-comedy set during the 1920s, which pits a bandit (Jiang) against a corrupt public official (Chow Yun-Fat) in a gleefully violent battle of wits. While aimed firmly at the domestic market, *Let the Bullets Fly* was still peppered with satirical humour and shot with panache. It shattered box-office records at the time of release, enabling the local industry to start its campaign to wrestle dominance back from Hollywood by blending the pyrotechnics of imported blockbusters with subject matter, landscapes and archetypes that have more resonance with Chinese cinemagoers.

Xu Jinglei, who rose to stardom alongside Zhao Wei and Zhou Xun, was one of the first performers of her generation to make the career shift. As with Jiang, she initially courted festival acclaim with her dramas *My Father and I* (*Wo he Baba*, 2003) and *Letter from an Unknown Woman* (*Yige Mosheng Nüren de Laixin*, 2004), before crafting an unabashed star vehicle in the form of *Go Lala Go!* (*Du Lala Shengzhi Ji*, 2010). This cheerful comedy set the tone for the lifestyle fantasies that are now a multiplex fixture by adapting Li Ke's novel *Du Lala's Promotion*, widely seen as the unofficial handbook for Chinese women seeking success in the corporate world. *Go Lala Go!* focuses on the titular young professional (Xu) and her efforts to get ahead in an international company despite the inevitable office rivalries. As with most lifestyle fantasies, it is packed with product placement, although Xu is smart enough to play with the obligatory presence of luxury brands as a means of noting how Lala's bubbly personality gradually deflates with the accumulation of status symbols, notably her purchase of a car. The director-star's subsequent feature *Dear Enemy* (*Qin Midiren*, 2012) found her continuing in this vein, reuniting her with *Go Lala Go!* co-star and off-screen partner Stanley Huang for a battle-of-the-sexes comedy set in the international banking sector.

Zhao Wei would follow in Xu's footsteps with *So Young*, a sentimental nostalgia piece adapted from the bestselling novel by Xin Yiwu that concerns the university experiences of a group of friends, and the life obstacles that they encounter in the years that follow graduation. After coming to fame in the television series *Princess Pearl* (*Huanzhu Gege*, 1997), Zhao alternated between the small screen and features while also releasing a number of pop albums. The wildly successful *So Young* marked her directorial debut, developed from her graduation project after a much-publicised period of study at the Beijing Film Academy.

An increasing number of actor-director talents have crossed over to film from television. Among them is Chen Sicheng, whose series *Beijing*

Love Story (*Beijing Aiqing Gushi*, 2014) was spun off into a feature, keeping the title and some of the key performers from the small-screen version, but jettisoning the original storylines in favour of new scenarios.

However, it was another actor-turned-director, Xu Zheng, who would be responsible for China's biggest comedy to date, the culture-clash farce *Lost in Thailand* (*Ren Zai Jiongtu zhi Taijiong*, 2012), in which two businessmen suffer through a series of mishaps while searching for a company shareholder.

There may not have been many overseas buyers for *So Young*, *Beijing Love Story* or *Lost in Thailand*, but with their respective domestic box-office grosses of $116 million, $62 million and $208 million, not to mention low production outlays, these are not films that need to travel in order to recoup.

Chinese dreams in China

The appeal of many recent releases has been their cultivation of China's self-image at a time when the economically thriving nation no longer uses the US as a barometer for success. *American Dreams in China* (*Zhongguo Hehuoren*, 2013), by the Hong Kong filmmaker Peter Chan, tells the true story of Beijing New Oriental School, a language-learning empire that was founded by three friends after their hopes of overseas study were dashed. Chan takes David Fincher's *The Social Network* (2010) as a structural model, with a framing device focusing on a lawsuit levelled against the school's founders by US education authorities for helping Chinese students cheat on entry exams. The economic reforms of the 1980s are seen as a force of liberation while the founders' eventual triumph over the American plaintiffs plays like a jingoistic endorsement of questionable Chinese tactics in a global market. Despite his prestige status, Chan did not have final cut and was forced to keep a scene that

he did not believe in – one of the founders throwing a pile of money
in the air when realising that he had become wealthy – while the film
was subject to a number of Hollywood-style test screenings in order
to ensure that it was hitting the right notes with its target audience.

While this rags-to-riches saga was warmly received, the youth
market pandering of *Tiny Times 1.0* (*Xiao Shidai*, 2013) was more divisive.
Adapted by first-time director Guo Jingming from his series of novels
about young women pursuing high-flying careers in Shanghai, it was
heavily criticised for promoting materialism through the rampant
consumerism of protagonists for whom matching Valentino bags are
a symbol of friendship. Still, *Tiny Times 1.0* was hugely popular with a
young audience that idolises Guo due to the media notoriety that he had
already achieved from his fiction and furthered through his use of social
media, while *Tiny Times 2.0* (*Xiao Shidai 2*, 2013) was in cinemas just two
months later. Further upbeat dramas that celebrate China's meteoric rise
and revel in the trappings of its consumer culture should be expected.

Love is in the air

Yet the genre that just keeps giving is the romantic comedy, with audiences
flocking to 'date movies' that bend the conventions of their Hollywood
models to fit more specifically Chinese notions of love or maintenance
of social status. The genre romance really took flight with the surprise
success of *Love is not Blind* (*Shi Lian 33 Tian*, 2011), a sentimental tale of a
wedding planner (Bai Baihe) who plunges into depression after breaking
up with her long-term boyfriend, only to find unexpected support from
a co-worker (Wen Zhang). Bai has since become synonymous with
romcoms, taking the lead in such largely interchangeable films as *A
Wedding Invitation* (*Fenshou Heyue*, 2013) and *The Stolen Years* (*Beitou Zou de
Na Wu Nian*, 2013), which have established her as a consistent box-office
draw within a relatively low-cost niche, making her a valuable commodity
when other actresses are busy developing their own directing vehicles.
Bai's recurrent character is that of a hopeless romantic with a distinct
lack of material impulses, although the scenes around her are filled with
designer brands and fabulous decor. This illustrates the dual nature of
China's romantic comedies, in that the genre at once revolves around
traditional values yet permits the audience to revel in luxurious fantasy.

Some romantic comedies tweak Hollywood models to make them
more relatable to the local audience. *One Night Surprise* (*Yiye Jingxi*, 2013)
takes the premise of Judd Apatow's *Knocked Up* (2007) and reconfigures it
to provide a topical comedy on the subject of the 'leftover woman'. Fan
Bingbing is a single thirtysomething advertising executive who discovers
she is pregnant after an alcohol-fuelled birthday party and must figure
out who the father is from three suspects. The film takes place in a glossily
globalised world where everyone is impeccably styled, while the protagonist
is both a career-minded professional and dutiful expectant mother who
suffers various embarrassments to establish the father's identity.

Finding Mr. Right (*Beijing Yushang Xiyatu*, 2013) sends a barrage of mixed
messages through a simple romantic conceit: a materialistic mistress
(Tang Wei) falls pregnant and is sent by her wealthy lover from Beijing
to Seattle, where she is to give birth in an illegal maternity centre, only
to become involved with a former doctor (Wu Xiubo) who now helps at
the clinic. The main location of the film pays tribute to *Sleepless in Seattle*
(1993) and a number of narrative contrivances are taken directly from
Hollywood romances, but *Finding Mr. Right* is very much a product of
China in that its leading character's desire to possess nice things is seen

as a common aspect of modern life, with personal development coming from accepting that she should pay for such items herself. If the romantic comedy has been used to launch new stars such as Bai, it is here used to 'rehabilitate' the versatile Tang. The actress is rather wasted in the role of a shrill trophy girlfriend, but needed to reestablish herself following time in industry exile due to her sexually explicit breakthrough role in Ang Lee's period thriller *Lust, Caution* (*Se, Jie*, 2007). Tang then appeared in such Hong Kong productions as *Crossing Hennessy* (*Yueman Xuannishi*, 2010) and *Dragon* (*Wuxia*, 2011), with *Finding Mr. Right* proving to be a safe choice as a mainland comeback vehicle due to the innocuous nature of its genre.

China does not have a crime problem… or ghosts

Censorship continues to shackle commercial filmmakers who wish to work in genres such as thriller or horror. Johnnie To shot his police procedural *Drug War* (*Du Zhan*, 2013) in China as a co-production and delivered a typically tough thriller with many of his signature touches, although the director would acknowledge that dealing with China's censorship board was one of the most difficult experiences of his career.

Xing Fei's courtroom mystery *Silent Witness* (*Quan Min Muji*, 2013) follows the trial of the daughter of a business tycoon who stands accused of her father's murder: it boasts an intricate flashback structure, but is unable to deliver the requisite sting in the tail due to ideological constraints that expect justice to be upheld and all parties that are representative of state infrastructure to emerge blemish free.

Horror films have been slow to catch on, not only due to filmmakers being prevented from suggesting that ghosts are real or showing excessive bloodletting, but also because it is perceived as a lesser genre by the mainstream audience. The low-budget shocker *Mysterious Island* (*Gu Dao Jinghun*, 2011) was a surprise hit, but the quickly produced follow-up *Mysterious Island 2* (*Gu Dao Jinghun 2*, 2012) failed to have the same impact, curtailing any chances of a franchise. As in other territories, horror is rarely the domain of the major studios in China, with most genre entries being produced by fledgling independents, and it will take a true runaway success to change its status on the production line.

The next big thing

Local films claimed six spots in China's box-office top ten for 2013 while one of the four American imports, *Iron Man 3*, had a Chinese production partner in DMG Entertainment. Audiences are currently showing a conscious preference for Chinese films, but if this market control is to be sustained, local studios must continue to improve their product across all genres rather than rely on mid-range comedies and dramas.

Following a run of slipshod animated efforts, the success of the television series spin-off *Boonie Bears: To the Rescue* (*Xiong Chumo zhi Duo Bao Xiongbing*, 2014) suggests that cartoons could prove to be the next growth sector, but more consistent quality is needed if the family audience is to choose a local product over the wonders of Blue Sky, Dreamworks or Pixar.

After consolidating the domestic market, the Chinese industry is going global again through co-productions with the Hollywood companies Legendary East and Sony Pictures Asia. It remains to be seen whether these relationships can yield blockbusters wherein elements of East and West are balanced with sufficient harmony to appeal to audiences both domestically and internationally, but if such ambitious ventures fail, China's studios can always fall back on making films for local audiences, eager to see their past and present celebrated on the big screen. ☯

11

HONG KONG: FROM THE SILENTS TO THE SECOND WAVE

BY PETER RIST

香港电影:
从无声电影到第二新浪潮

When most people think of Hong Kong cinema, they probably think of Bruce Lee and the international kung fu craze of the 1970s, or perhaps the hip films of Wong Kar Wai in the 1990s. But the former British colony's cinema has always been varied and diverse, and usually prolific – from 1959 to 1966, before Bruce Lee, Hong Kong film production exceeded even that of Hollywood.

The first films produced in Hong Kong were made by foreigners. In March 1898, seven single-shot actuality films were produced for the American Edison company. The year 1909 arguably saw the first 'drama' film productions made in Hong Kong – as many as four were made by the Shanghai-based Asia Film Co, and distributed by American Benjamin Brodsky (aka Benjamin Polaski).

However it is Lai Man-Wai (Li Minwei) who is now considered to be the 'Father of Hong Kong Cinema'. Lai played the wife and is credited as the screenplay writer of what is usually cited as the first Hong Kong multi-reel fiction film, *Zhuangzi Tests His Wife* (*Zhuangzi Shi Qi*, 1913), directed by his brother Lai Buk-Hoi (Li Beihai) for the Huanmei Film Company.

Together, the brothers founded the Minxin (China Sun) Film Company in Hong Kong in 1923. Minxin produced the feature film *Rouge* (*Yanzhi*, 1925) and a number of other films in the 1920s, but *Rouge* is the only one considered to be a Hong Kong production, because the other titles were produced by Minxin's Shanghai branch, set up by Lai Man-Wai in 1925.

In 1930, Lai Man-Wai spearheaded the merger of four Shanghai film production houses, including Minxin into the Lianhua Film Company (United Photoplay Service). Lai Buk-Hoi disagreed with his brother's total relocation to the mainland, and in 1928 he co-founded the Hong Kong Film Company with Lee Hysan (Li Haishan), for which he wrote and directed two features in 1931. In the same year, he established a Hong Kong studio for Lianhua, where four features were made over the next two years. Then in 1933 he co-founded the Zhonghua (China) Sound and Silent Film Production Company with actress Tong Sing-to, who, in producing and writing for Zhonghua, became an important female film pioneer.

The four famous Shaw brothers

However it was another group of Shanghai siblings who were the most significant for Hong Kong's emerging industry: the famous four Shaw brothers. Initially, the most influential was the oldest, Runje (Shao Zuiweng), also known as C. W. Shaw, who, in 1925 founded the Tianyi (Unique) Film Company in Shanghai. At first, Runje directed his films himself, and second brother Runde (Shao Curen) would often write them. In the mid-1920s, Runme Shaw (Shao Renmei) went to Singapore to establish a film distribution network in South-east Asia and Run Run (Shao Yifu) joined him in 1928.

After making one of the first Chinese sound-on-disc films *A Singer's Story* (*Gechang Chunse*) in 1931, Tianyi produced the first Cantonese 'talkie', *White Gold Dragon* (*Baijin Lon*, 1933). The film was a big hit in Hong Kong and other parts of South China, and its success encouraged Tianyi to build a studio in Kowloon in 1934, after which the Shaw brothers became a major force in Hong Kong Cantonese film production, with Tianyi turning out 18 films in two years.

The studio burnt down in 1936, but new premises were opened under Runde, with the company renamed the Nanyang Film Company. Production increased to approximately 15 features per year between 1937 and 1941. Just before the Japanese invasion of Shanghai in August 1937, Tianyi's film equipment was shipped to Hong Kong, enhancing the

GARDEN
HOSTEL

production facilities, but by Christmas Day 1941 Japanese forces had overwhelmed the territory and Hong Kong film production ceased.

The 1930s: the first 'Golden Age'

The 1930s was the first 'Golden Age' of Hong Kong cinema, especially of Cantonese-dialect cinema. The development of a Cantonese-dialect cinema took place in Hong Kong in the 1930s, while the influx of Shanghai filmmakers – initially in 1937 when the Sino-Japanese war closed down two of Shanghai's studios, and then during the social chaos of the 1945–48 period – enabled a Mandarin cinema industry to develop, co-exist, rival, and sometimes exceed Cantonese production in Hong Kong.

Until very recently, no Hong Kong fiction feature films seemed to have survived from the 'Golden Age', so it is difficult to know which genres became most well developed. In his book *Silver Light: A Pictorial History of Hong Kong Cinema 1920–1970*, Paul Fonoroff claims that only four of the 500 feature films made pre-war had survived, mainly because the Japanese occupational forces melted down every film print they could find for their silver component.

According to the *Hong Kong Filmography, Vol. I*, half of the 500 films are retrospectively labelled as 'melodrama', 'romance' or 'comedy,' while 66 are labelled 'national defence' films, suggesting that patriotic themes and political propaganda were popular. Fewer than 30 films are listed as 'kung fu' or 'martial arts' films, although it appears that these genres already appealed to audiences, along with Cantonese opera films.

Excitingly, among a cache of nitrate film prints donated by San Francisco theatre-owner Jack Lee Fong to the Hong Kong Film Archive in 2012, two restorations have already been completed: Tianyi's *Incident in the Pacific* (*Taipingyang Shang De Fengyun*, 1938), directed by Hou Yao, and Nanyang's *The Light of Women* (*Nüxing Zhi Guang*, 1937), directed by Ko Lei-hen.

1946-70: the 'Classical' period

Although a few films that were made before the Japanese takeover were released during the occupation, Hong Kong film production didn't begin again until 1946, when a second influx of Shanghai-based filmmakers started work. One of the results of the influx was that the Shanghai cinema's leftist tendency was continued in the colony, and a strong tradition of realism was initiated. Although some consider these films to be Shanghai, Chinese films made in Hong Kong (as a kind of temporary branch plant), they set patterns for the Hong Kong Mandarin cinema of the future.

Mostly these were the *wenyi pian*, literally translated as the film genre combining literature (*wenxue*) and art (*yishu*), and denoting films that prioritised drama, plot and character, as distinct from the *wuxia pian* action films. Popular within these were musicals starring the Shanghai-born 'sing-song girls.' Chinese-made films with songs had become very popular during the war, and so when many Shanghai personnel moved to Hong Kong, the formula was easily transported.

The genre was established in Hong Kong in 1947 and 1948 with three films starring Zhou Xuan, the actress who was forever identified with her character in Yuan Muzhi's *Street Angel* (*Malu Tianshi*, 1937). The third of these, Fang Peilin's exemplary *Song of a Songstress* (*Genü Zhi Ge*, 1948), is of particular interest, as its plot partially mirrors Zhou's own life. A more stylistically sophisticated example was *An Unfaithful Woman* (*Dang Fu Xin*, 1949), directed by Yue Feng and starring Bai Guang. While the style and the subject matter – a young country woman is sold by her father and forced by circumstances into prostitution in the city – remain

of Shanghai derivation, the overall aesthetic is more melodramatic.

It took another ten years for Hong Kong Mandarin-language film production to fully break away from its roots and achieve a 'classical' maturity, especially with films such as *June Bride* (*Liu Yue Xinniang*, 1960) and *The Wild, Wild Rose* (*Ye Meigui Zhi Lan*, 1960), both starring Ge Lan (Grace Chang) and produced by MP & GI (Motion Pictures and General Investment Film Co.) – better known as Cathay – which had become a vertically integrated company (production, distribution, and exhibition) serving the South-east Asia market.

Only ten of the 350 Cantonese-dialect Hong Kong films made from 1946–49 have survived (while almost half of the 60 Mandarin films have). But, from 1950 onwards the survival rate is much better. At the end of the decade, the Kong Ngee film company – founded by the Ho brothers Khee-Yong (Qi-Rong) and Khee-Siang (Qi-Xiang) from Singapore – came to lead the production of Cantonese-language, Hollywood-style romances, melodramas, and comedies.

But before this, another Cantonese-dialect outfit, the cooperatively formed and run Chung-Luen Film Company (Zhonglian, or Union Film Enterprise) was notable for matching the *wenyi* realism of Mandarin films. One such film is *In the Face of Demolition* (*Weilou Chunxiao*, 1953), directed by Lee Tit (Li Tie), which follows in the line of the Shanghai 'tenement' films. It is by any standards a great example of a Cantonese, left-leaning work. Closely related to director Zheng Junli's Shanghai-made, Mandarin-language *Crows and Sparrows* (*Wuya Yu Maque*, 1949) in its subject matter and realist treatment, the film is set almost entirely within one residential building. It concerns a group of people of all ages and from both working and middle class backgrounds who pull together against economic hardship and the exploitation of property owners. The frame is always filled with people and the cheapness of the sets is turned into an advantage with back walls never too far from the camera, cramping the people closer together and to the camera. *In the Face of Demolition* features many of the most distinguished Cantonese stars of the 1950s, including Cheung Ying, Mui Yee, Tsi Lo-lin, Ng Cho-fan (all of whom were founding members of Union) and a very young Bruce Lee.

Lee Tit was also one of Union's founders, as was Chun Kim, the director of another key film, *Parents' Hearts* (*Fumu Xin*, 1955). Less overtly political, *Parents' Hearts* is notable for its focus on an unglamorous, ageing couple, played by opera star Ma Si-tsang and Wong Man-lei. The film begins with Lei (Ma) performing a comic role in a Cantonese opera. With the profession in decline, he tries to pawn his opera costumes and resorts to performing crude animal roles on the streets accompanied by his younger son. His wife tries to help support their family financially by sewing and other chores, but she succumbs to illness. Intensely moving, *Parents' Hearts* is extremely well directed and arguably the peak of Chun Kim's career.

Shaw Brothers Ltd and director Li Hanxiang

In 1949, Runde renamed Nanyang as Shaw and Sons, and from 1952 to 1957, the studio's Mandarin film production increased to 12 films per year, but the competition overwhelmed Runde's low-budget model. The breakthrough came in 1957 with Run Run's acquisition of a large tract of land at Clearwater Bay in the New Territories, on which he established Shaw Brothers (Hong Kong) Ltd. Leaving the theatrical side of the business to Shaw and Sons, Run Run initially produced films in both Cantonese and Mandarin, but after 1963, when six more sound stages were scheduled for construction (to a total of 12 film

(Top)
'In the Face of Demolition' (1953), by director Lee Tit, is set almost entirely within one cramped residential building, and matched the realism of the Mandarin wenyi films.

(Above)
Chun Kum's intensely moving story of a struggling opera star and his wife, 'Parents' Hearts' (1955).

(Below)
Ge Lan (Grace Chang, left) in Cathay's Mandarin production 'The Wild, Wild Rose' (1960).

studios), no more Cantonese dialect films were made until 1973.

During this era of quality Mandarin film production, Shaw Brothers films dominated the Asian Film Awards. Many of the prize-winning films were directed by Li Hanxiang (Li Han-Hsiang), including *The Love Eterne* (*Liang Shanbo yü Zhu Yingtai*, 1963), the most successful of all films recounting the classical story of the 'Butterfly Lovers', Liang Shan Bo and Zhu Ying Tai. In 1960, Li had directed *The Enchanting Shadow* (*Qiannü Youhun*) for Shaw Brothers, perhaps the classic Hong Kong ghost story film, and an exquisite example of what could be produced inside a studio, in colour. It was also the very first Chinese-language film to be entered in competition at the Cannes International Film Festival. Li followed this up with further entries in 1962 and 1963, with *The Magnificent Concubine* (*Yang Kwei Fei*, 1962) becoming the first Chinese-language film to win a prize there.

The Love Eterne is one of Shaw Brothers's most popular films, and the one most often revived. According to Ang Lee, the film "became so popular in Taiwan that some claim to have seen it 500 times". At this time the studio specialised in historical costume films that combined Hollywood technique with classical Chinese traditions, and the genre that *The Love Eterne* fits is the *huang mei diao* opera, a hybrid of Mandarin operetta. Betty Loh Ti (Le Di) plays Zhu Yingtai, a young woman who poses as a man in order to be able to go to school and sit for the imperial exams, and the film introduced Ivy Ling Po as Liang Shanbo, the male student with whom she falls in love.

Unike traditional Beijing opera, where men played all the roles, *The Love Eterne*'s aura of romance emanates from the centrality of women. The film made a star of Ling Po, though tragically Le Di's career went downhill thereafter, and she eventually committed suicide. As in *The Enchanting Shadow*, Li Hanxiang demonstrates his penchant for replicating classical Chinese art: the sets by art director Cao Nianlong are reminiscent of Chinese paintings and the actors' deliberate movements and broad gestures during the musical sequences are clearly derived from opera. On the other hand, the fluid movements of cinematographer Nishimoto Tadashi's camera are highly cinematic. King Hu, a good friend of Li's, was credited as associate director, and he clearly contributed to the cinematic nature of the film.

The women of Hong Kong cinema

Perhaps more strongly than in any other national cinema, women have played major roles in Hong Kong film. Outside of the developing kung fu genre in the 1970s, female stars have dominated, especially in 1950s and 1960s Mandarin productions.

The first woman to direct a film in Hong Kong was the American-born Esther Eng (Ng Kam-Ha), who directed four Cantonese films in two years, beginning with *National Heroine* (*Minzu Nüyingxiong*, 1937). Another pioneering woman director was Wang Hoi-Ling, who co-directed 11 films between 1936 and 1940 with Hou Yao and Hung Chung-ho, and also directed two films on her own.

One of the most original and interesting directors in all Hong Kong cinema is Cecile Tang (Tong Shu-Shuen), whose debut feature *The Arch* (*Dong Furen*, 1970) is one of the most impressive first features in world cinema. The film is a unique combination of classical Chinese formal elements with an impressionistic, subjective cinematic style. Set in the early Qing dynasty, the film explores the inner feelings of its characters, especially the widowed Madame Tung (Lisa Lu). When a group of soldiers led by Captain Yang (Roy Chiao) is billeted in the school where she teaches, her mother-in-law (Hsiu Wen) ensures that she is kept apart from the

captain, but nonetheless their feelings for each other build in intensity.

Shot in black and white by Satyajit Ray's regular cinematographer Subrata Mitra, the pace of *The Arch* is measured, with long takes and slow lap-dissolves in consort with the soundtrack of traditional instrumentation, natural sounds and poetic voice-over. Occasionally, however, the pace is disrupted by rapid editing, dramatic camera movements and super-impositions, which reveal and heighten the characters' subjective thoughts and emotions.

Tang's next feature, *China Behind* (*Zaijian Zhongguo*, 1974), was a brave political treatise, following a group of mainland college students and intellectuals who attempt to escape the Cultural Revolution in Guangzhou by swimming across the water to Hong Kong. Tang didn't just attempt to criticise the extremes of Chinese Communism, but also sought to acknowledge the shortcomings of Hong Kong's route to capitalism – although she claimed that the film was not 'political' at all, but rather one that examines the "contradictions between the reality and idealism of young people". Nevertheless, the film was banned by the censors in Hong Kong, and was not released locally until 1987.

The 'New Wave' breaks

The Arch and *China Behind* were such a break from earlier Hong Kong-made films that they can be considered as forerunners to the 'New Wave' films. The term was applied to a group of filmmakers who emerged between 1979–81, most of whom had previously worked in television. Unlike the French *nouvelle vague* of the late 1950s and early 1960s, these filmmakers were not polemically against the mainstream of the past, but sought to refine and change it.

Some of them, notably Ann Hui and Allen Fong, sought a more realist approach to their material. In part, this came from their work in television on such shows as *Below the Lion Rock*. One of Hui's episodes, *The Boy from Vietnam* (*Lai Ke*, 1978) is now considered the first work in her 'Vietnam trilogy'. The second part is her third feature film, *The Story of Woo Viet* (*Hu Yue de Gushi*, 1981) and the third is *Boat People* (*Touben Nuhai*, 1982), which became the first Hong Kong New Wave film to be released in the West, and made Hui's name internationally.

Set in Vietnam three years after the end of the conflict, with the Communists now in control, *Boat People* follows the story of the refugee 'boat people' hoping to flee the broken nation for Hong Kong. A Japanese journalist formerly sympathetic to the Communists is invited to visit a school in the 'new economic zone', and gradually changes his mind about the regime, eventually helping a young brother and sister to escape. Unlike in Hong Kong action films, characters in *Boat People* die in ugly ways, and the violence is presented without glamour.

The 'Second Wave'

It is in what critic Stephen Teo calls the 'Second Wave', from 1984 to the early-1990s, that one finds work more closely resembling the French New Wave model, with reflexivity, allusions to other films and media, and other modernist/post-modernist tropes. The films of four of these new directors in particular introduced a new sexuality to Hong Kong cinema: Eddie Fong, director of such films as *An Amorous Woman of the Tang Dynasty* (*Tongchao Haofang Nü*, 1984); his wife, Clara Law, whose films include *Autumn Moon* (*Qiu Yue*, 1992) and *Temptation of a Monk* (*You Seng*, 1993); Stanley Kwan; and the revolutionary figure of Wong Kar Wai.

The 'Second Wave' emerged at a time when Cantonese dialect films came to completely dominate Hong Kong film production, following the commercial success of Chor Yuen's *The House of 72 Tenants* (*Qishi'er Jia Fangke*, 1973) and a series of Hui brothers' comedies including *The*

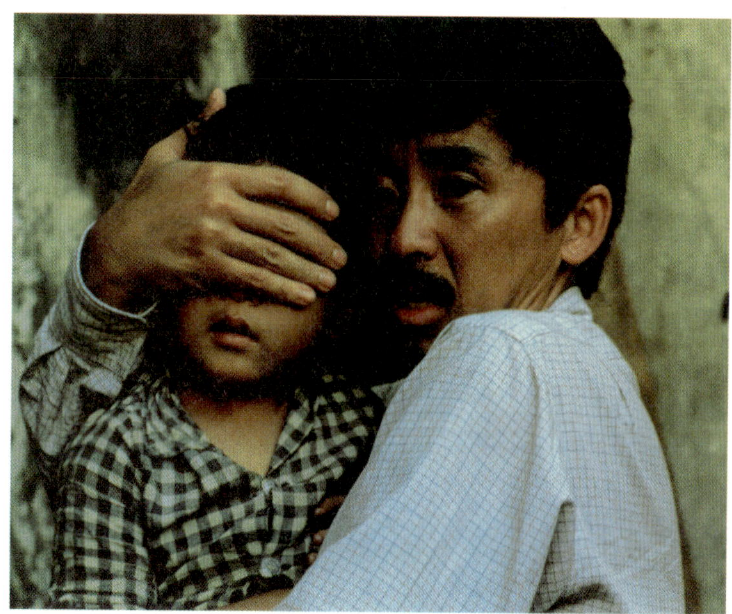

 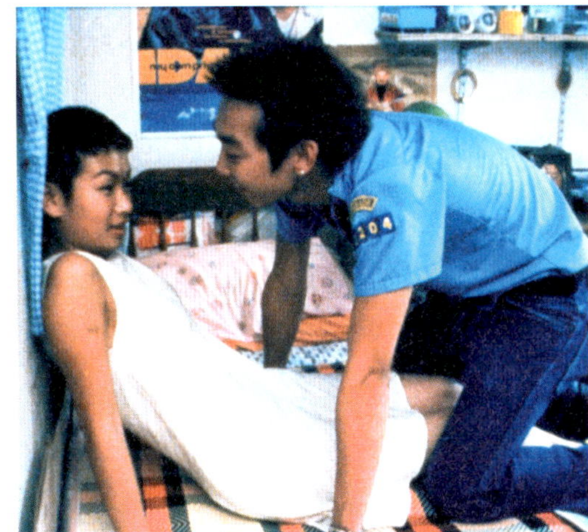

Private Eyes (*Ban Jin Ba Liang*, 1976) and *The Contract* (*Mai Shen Qi*, 1978). At the same time there was a trend towards reworking traditional genres, and one way of thinking about Stanley Kwan's films is as Cantonese variations on *wenyi pian*, with female protagonists. For example, Fleur (Anita Mui), the high-class courtesan who returns to Hong Kong as a ghost 50 years after her joint-suicide with her lover (Leslie Cheung) in Kwan's *Rouge* (*Yanzhi Kou*, 1989) is effectively a Cantonese 'sing-song' girl.

Kwan's formally innovative biopic *Centre Stage* (*Ruan Lingyu*, 1992), stars Maggie Cheung as the tragic, titular star of Shanghai silent films, and is one of the most beautiful Hong Kong films ever made. Although it is a fictional film, *Centre Stage* has a documentary veracity, incorporating black-and-white clips from Ruan Lingyu's surviving films alongside video interviews with survivors of the pre-war industry as well as newly shot 'making-of' material.

Another key figure is Peter Chan Ho-Sun, who directed his first feature in 1991 and in 1996 directed arguably the key film in relation to the 1997 handover of the territory back to China, *Comrades: Almost a Love Story* (*Tian Mimi*, 1996). Chan is a member of a Chinese family who still live in Thailand, and in making this film has said he was investigating the "rootlessness of the Chinese as a people, and of their continuing search for a new home". Maggie Cheung plays a Cantonese-speaking native of Guangzhou who migrates to Hong Kong to make money and secretly falls in love with another Chinese mainlander (Leon Lai) who, despite returning her affections, is engaged to marry someone else. Some time later they come together again in the United States, and the film ends with the playing of the Teresa Teng song 'Tian Mi Mi', the Chinese title of the film. Teng was arguably the most popular Chinese singer of all time, and when the film was released had recently died at the age of 42. The appeal of *Comrades* derives from its combination of nostalgia for the past (of popular song and romantic *wenyi* drama) and of the simultaneous excitement and apprehension about the impending handover.

As iconoclastic as Cecile Tang, Fruit Chan brought a youthful 'punk' sensibility to Hong Kong cinema and directed another key 'handover anxiety' film, *Made in Hong Kong* (*Xiang Geng Zai Zou*, 1997). Chan had directed two features before 1997, but this stylish and dynamic – albeit sordid and nihilistic – chronicle of a teenage criminal who becomes a hired killer in order to pay for his sick girlfriend's medical bills was his breakthrough success, especially with young audiences. Fruit Chan has continued to make edgy films that often combine a gritty realism with fantasy, such as *The Midnight After* (2014).

(Top, left)
'Days of Being Wild' (1990).

(Bottom, left)
'Fallen Angels' (1995).

(Top, right)
'Chungking Express' (1994).

(Bottom, right)
'Happy Together' (1997).

With their quoting of other films and their links with other media, Hong Kong 'Second Wave' films constitute the postmodern cinema *par excellence*. At the forefront of this tendency is Wong Kar Wai. Wong's first feature film, *As Tears Go By* (*Wangjiao Kamen*, 1988) remains his most conventional, mixing the Hong Kong genres of romance and the gangster film, but in its stylish pastiche of MTV music videos – including a Cantonese version of 'Take My Breath Away' – and a preoccupation with the passage of time (the love affair between the characters played by emerging stars, Andy Lau and Maggie Cheung, is late coming and doomed) it prefigures his later work.

Wong's seductively stylish second feature, the 1960s-set *Days of Being Wild* (*A Fei Zhengzhuan*, 1990), cast Leslie Cheung as a serial womaniser opposite Maggie Cheung, Andy Lau and Carina Lau, and extended his focus on characterisation rather than narrative. The film concludes with an enigmatic sequence that bears no relation to the preceding story, introducing the actor Tony Leung Chiu-Wai, who may or may not have been intended as the focus of an unmade sequel.

With *Chungking Express* (*Chongqing Senlin*, 1994) Wong had his first real international hit, and became a byword for unconventional cinematic cool. The first of the two police detectives we meet in the film, cop 223 (Kaneshiro Takeshi) is so obsessed with the date of May 1st – his birthday, and the name of his ex-girlfriend – that he buys tins of pineapple that expire on that date. Our introduction to him at the beginning of the film, chasing through Chungking Mansion, is remarkably stylised, with frames excised and others multiply printed, providing a fast/slow stutter step progression. In the film's second, virtually unconnected story, cop 663 (Tony Leung Chiu-Wai) and the 'California Dreaming'–fixated Faye (pop chanteuse Faye Wong), are filmed at the Midnight Express snack bar where she works, in what appears to be normal motion while people fly by in front of them. Wong is known to work very loosely with scripts, and to take his time finishing his films, but *Chungking Express* was shot very quickly in a break from editing his martial-arts epic, *Ashes of Time* (1994). Its follow-up *Fallen Angels* (*Duo Luo Tian Shi,* 1995) was shot with similar speed and again paired him with Christopher Doyle – a remarkable collaboration that began on *Days of Being Wild* and continued through *Happy Together* (*Chunguang Zhaxie*, 1997), a gay love story set in Argentina starring Tony Leung and Leslie Cheung, and *In the Mood for Love* (*Hua Yang Nian Hua*, 2000), before dissolving acrimoniously during the shooting of 2046 (2004).

With *In the Mood for Love* Wong made what is perhaps his most internationally celebrated film. The story is set in Hong Kong in the early 1960s, where Su Li-Zhen (Maggie Cheung) and Chow Mo-Wan (Tony Leung) are new neighbours in an apartment building. They become friends, while suspecting (correctly) that their spouses are having an affair. Much of the emotion in the film emerges from their refusal to duplicate their partners' behaviour, while the images, especially slow-motion shots following Cheung up and down staircases, are highly charged sexually.

Wong understands that much of cinema's power comes from the fact that everything we see on the screen, and hear on a soundtrack, is a recording of past occurrences. The Chinese title of *In the Mood for Love* is *Hua Yang Nian Hua*, the title of a 1946 song by Zhou Xuan, the greatest of the Shanghai 'sing-song' girls. Local audiences would have heard Zhou sing the song in *An All-Consuming Love* (*Chang Xiangsi*, 1947), a Hong Kong, Mandarin-dialect *wenyi pian*. For Hong Kong audiences at least, Wong Kar Wai in *In the Mood for Love* was making clear the enduring links between the Shanghai and Hong Kong cinema of the past and the contemporary cinema of the 'Second Wave.' ◑

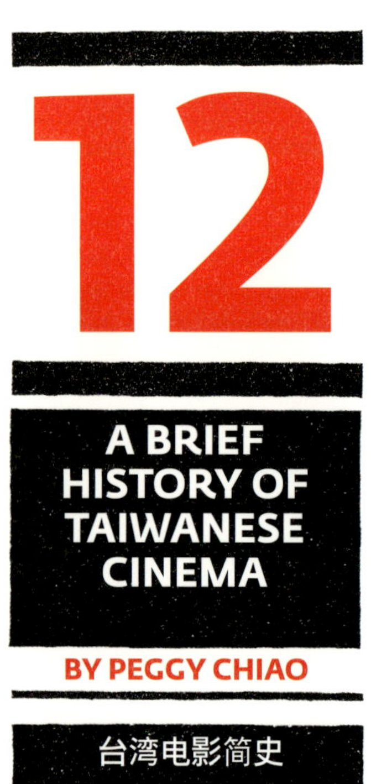

Owing to Taiwan's complex colonial history (it was ruled first by the Dutch, then briefly by the Spanish in the 16th and 17th centuries, and then by the Japanese from 1895-1945), it is difficult to define the term 'Taiwanese Cinema'. Do we count films made under Japanese occupation? And what does it mean to be Taiwanese? The question is still unresolved and a source of ongoing political turmoil.

Taiwanese films have always carried an ideological contradiction. Taiwan is a place of predominantly Chinese people, but through periods of confrontation, resolution and rejection, the political entity (the very concept?) of what is known as 'China' has been challenged. Different generations of Taiwanese filmmakers have tried to define and reflect their experiences, but always in diverse and often contradictory ways. Perhaps contradiction is the essence of Taiwanese cinema.

Cinema under Japanese colonial rule

Taiwan was ceded to Japan in 1895 in the Treaty of Shimonoseki, after the Qing Dynasty lost the first Sino-Japanese war. At the turn of the century, devices like Edison's Vitascope and the Lumières' *cinématographe* films were introduced to Taiwan and a film culture gradually established. The Japanese used films as tools to assimilate the Taiwanese people, and indigenous filmmaking was discouraged (though films from Shanghai were popular until China declared war on Japan in 1937). Many conventions of silent Japanese cinema were brought to Taiwan, for example the use of a *benshi* narrator to describe the onscreen action. Taiwanese films were treated like a colonial supplement to the Japanese cinema, in a similar way to that of Manchurian films in Japanese occupied north-east China, or Korean films during the Japanese occupation of Korea.

It was a Japanese man named Takamatsu Toyojiro (1872-1952) who was the essential driving force in initiating cinema in Taiwan. Takamatsu built theatres, set up a distribution system, and eventually shot documentaries. In 1907 he made An *Introduction to the Actual Conditions in Taiwan (Taiwan Jikkyo Shikei)*, which is considered to be the first film in Taiwan's history.

Aside from the various films made by the Japanese for the purposes of information, education and 'co-prosperity in south-east Asia', there were only 16 feature films made in Taiwan during the Japanese colonial period. Among these were films by Japanese directors, such as Shimizu Hiroshi's *Sayon's Bell (Sayon no kane, 1943)*, which served propagandistic purposes. The then-famous actress Shirley Yamaguchi, who used the Chinese name Li Xianglan (Ri Koran in Japanese), to cover her real Japanese nationality, was sent by Manchurian Films and Shochiku Company to play the lead in *Sayon's Bell*, playing an indigenous Taiwanese girl who sacrifices her life carrying her beloved Japanese teacher's luggage across a rapid in a big storm.

Only three of these 16 films were made by native Taiwanese. Two of these barely warrant a mention, though *Blood Stains (Xue Hen, 1930)*, directed by Zhang Yunhe for his own Baida Film Productions, is notable as the only successful film made by a native Taiwanese before 1949. Ultimately, 50 years of Japanese colonial rule over Taiwan left only a negligible number of films. Compared with the 140-150 films produced in Japanese-occupied Korea, the statistics reveal Japanese condescension towards Taiwan.

After 1949

The Nationalist government took over all the theatres and motion-picture equipment in Taiwan after Japan surrendered. In the years immediately after World War II, audiences in Taiwan could enjoy films

from Shanghai, pre-war Japan, Hollywood and other countries such as the USSR. In 1949, the KMT party brought two million people from China to settle in Taiwan after Chiang Kaishek was defeated by Mao. The new rulers quickly set up state-owned studios to produce films with propagandistic content: the KMT party with the Central Motion Picture Company (CMPC), the provincial government with the Taiwan Film Studio (TFS) and the military with the China Film Studio (CFS).

These state-owned studios produced newsreels and educational films, and occasionally made features with anti-Communist themes, such as *Bad Dreams* (*E Meng Chu Xing*, 1951) and *Opium Poppy* (*Ying Su Hua*, 1955). However audiences found such political films dogmatic and instead sought out the commercialised entertainments produced by Shaw Brothers and MP&GI in Hong Kong. The top ten Chinese-language films at Taiwan's box office were invariably from Hong Kong all through the 1950s and early 1960s. Li Hanxiang's (Li Han-Hsiang's) *The Love Eterne* (*Liang Shanbo yü Zhu Yingtai*, 1963) was a phenomenon, breaking all box-office records and creating a sensation akin to *The Rocky Horror Picture Show* in the US in the 1970s, with audience sing-alongs, multiple viewings, and lucrative sales of the soundtrack record.

Taiwanese-dialect films also thrived between 1955-64. There were 178 such films made between 1955-59 and 364 between 1960-64. These films were typically low-budget, quickly produced and sensational. Many of them were performed by traditional opera troupes, building upon the success of Xiamen dialect opera films that been imported from Hong Kong.

These films were lapped up by audiences who wanted to see their indigenous culture onscreen. But although there were several memorable works, most of the Taiwanese-language films of the era suffered from poor screenwriting and low production values, and finally were no competition for the more refined Mandarin-language films being produced at the same time. When television came in during the 1960s, the opera troupes went to work with the TV channels and the Taiwanese-dialect films gradually disappeared. Many of the directors and actors who had worked on them went to work for the Mandarin film industry.

The 1960s: Li Hanxiang, King Hu and 'Healthy Realism'
One of the most important figures behind the growth of Taiwanese cinema in the 1960s was Li Hanxiang. After the phenomenal success of *The Love Eterne*, Li moved to Taiwan and worked with Shaw Brothers's rival MP&GI and then collaborated with the Union distribution company to build his own Grand Motion Picture Company. Li recruited crew and actors from Hong Kong and brought a new professionalism to the Taiwanese film industry. GMPC was a privately owned mini-studio, complete with contract actors, staff, distribution departments and its own publicity fan magazine.

Li's extravagant films, with their gorgeous costumes and sets and beautifully executed *mise en scène*, made him one of the most popular filmmakers in Taiwan during the 1950s and 1960s. His first Taiwan-made opera film, *Seven Fairies* (*Qi Xiannü*, 1963), beat the Shaw Brothers film of the same title at the box office. Later, *Trouble on the Wedding Night* (*Zhuang Yuan Ji Di*, 1964), another opera film, became the highest-grossing Chinese film in 1964. Classic films like the *The Winter* (*Dong Nuan*, 1969), *At Dawn* (*Poxiao Shifen*, 1967) and *Many Enchanting Nights* (*Ji Du Xiyang Hong*, 1966), which were either produced or directed by Li, were also trendsetters.

The success of Li and GMPC was instrumental in influencing the KMT-run CMPC to reshape its output. By the mid-1960s the studio resolved to shed propaganda and began advocating 'Healthy Realism', which stated

that films should be relevant to reality – a corrective to the strident anti-Communist doctrines of earlier state productions. With the help of colour and CinemaScope, CMPC sought to make policy films in the guise of entertainments. 'Healthy Realism' films took the lives of contemporary Taiwanese as their subject matter. Their narratives were invariably about family and romance, and actors were chosen for their star qualities.

One of the pioneer filmmakers in the 'Healthy Realism' period was Li Xing (Lee Hsing). Li's *Oyster Girls* (*Ke Nü*, 1964) – Taiwan's first domestically produced colour film – and *Beautiful Ducklings* (*Yang Ya Renjia*, 1965), helped the studio's profits swell. CMPC went on to become the biggest government-owned studio and even into the 1980s was the major force behind the New Cinema movement. Li made a rare foray into period films with the powerful *Execution in Autumn* (*Qiu Jue*) in 1972, a story set in China in the Han dynasty, which observes an imprisoned murderer awaiting his execution in the coming autumn.

King Hu was another filmmaker who in the mid-1960s followed Li Hanxiang's trail to Taiwan. Hu collaborated with Union films and cashed in on the success of his *wuxia* film *Come Drink With Me* (*Da Zui Xia*, 1966) to initiate a popular new style of swordplay film. The masterful *Dragon Gate Inn* (*Longmen Kezhan*, 1966) was the first *wuxia* film Hu produced in Taiwan, and not only broke box-office records in Taiwan, but all over Korea, Hong Kong and south-east Asia.

Hu was a master, elevating a previously undervalued genre to the level of art. He was rewarded as the first filmmaker in Taiwan to win a Cannes festival prize, for *A Touch of Zen*, (*Xia Nü*, 1970). Hu's images combined traditional and modern techniques; they were imbued with the style of traditional Chinese painting and with the brush strokes of calligraphy, and his use of music was influenced by traditional Peking opera.

From Qiong Yao melodramas to anti-Japanese films

By the mid-1960s, Taiwan was changing. The country was transforming from an agricultural society into a largely urban one, and political tensions with China were easing. It was in this atmosphere that a new generation of young audiences – chiefly schoolgirls and young female labourers – devoured the romance novels of Qiong Yao (Chiung Yao). Qiong's stories invariably involved a strong female protagonist suppressed by a patriarchal society. She was extremely popular not only in Taiwan, but throughout south-east Asia – even though her plots dealt in exalted pathos and her lurid dialogue struck some as overly sentimental.

Romantic melodramas based on Qiong Yao books dominated Taiwanese cinema throughout the 1960s and 70s, in films like *Where the Seagull Flies* (*Hai'ou Fei Chu*, 1974) and *Outside the Window* (*Chuang Wai*, 1973). Such films provided a *bona fide* escapist cinema, with female stars of astonishing beauty and wholly unrealistic settings (the films were often mocked as the 'three-room movie' genre, since the actors are always in one of a living room, a coffee shop or a restaurant). By the late-1970s, audiences finally began to tire of her fairytales and looked to a more realistic New Wave cinema. Qiong Yao accordingly withdrew to television – where she enjoys a second spring in China even to this day.

But Qiong Yao films are only part of the story of 1970s Taiwanese cinema. In the 1970s, a series of diplomatic setbacks pushed Taiwan into international isolation. It started in 1971, when Taiwan was expelled from the United Nations. A year later, Japan pulled out its embassy and severed diplomatic relations. Increasing numbers of countries recognised the Communist Mainland as the legitimate representative

of China. Taiwan was suffering from a new identity crisis.

It was in this atmosphere that an anti-Japanese genre appeared. Films were typically set during the Sino-Japanese war, their style an amalgamation of the war and spy genres and melodrama. The overtly mawkish plots of films like *Everlasting Glory* (*Ying Lie Qian Qiu*, 1976) and *Eight Hundred Heroes* (*Babai Zhuangshi*, 1978), with their patriotic, sacrificing heroes, were a response to the national sentiment of patriotism.

As the 1970s progressed, Qiong Yao-style *ingénues* were transformed into war heroines. Japanese films were banned. Taiwanese film production was at an apogee, with 250 films produced in 1972.

The 1980s and the emergence of the New Wave

By the early 1980s, Taiwan was reaping the fruits of the economic reform policies instituted by President Chiang Ching-kuo. Taiwan's economic miracle won it the status of one of the 'Four Little Dragons of Asia'. Its GDP per capita rose from US$360 in 1970 to a miraculous US$2,155 in 1980 (it would rise still further to US$7,285 by 1990).

With this relative social prosperity, people turned increasingly to art and culture. A solid film culture was forming, with active film criticism, a newly established film library, and the founding of international film festivals. This newly enlightened audience, which grew along with the revived literary Nativism Movement (*Xiangtu Wenxue*, which advocated for the depiction of a realist fiction centred on local people and concerns), clamoured for realistic images on their cinema screens.

CMPC was the first to respond, when it initiated two portmanteau films, *In Our Time* (*Guangyin de Gushi*, 1982) and *The Sandwich Man* (*Erzi de Da Wan'ou*, 1983), which between them presented seven young directors, among them Edward Yang, Hou Hsiao-Hsien and Wan Jen, most of whom were making their directorial debuts. In the following years, at least 20 Taiwanese directors made their first film; some of them were trained in the old system, but many learned their craft in film schools abroad. This new generation supported one another's projects in ways that were not so different from the early days of the French New Wave.

Weary of the escapist cinema of Taiwan's past, these young filmmakers (mostly in their 30s) told stories about real life. Many drew from their childhood experiences or adapted novels from the Nativism Movement. Their style involved long takes, static camera positions, natural light, actual locations and sync sound, and they also used non-professional actors in preference to stars.

Two directors stood out as particular talents. One was Hou Hsiao-Hsien, a commercial director who had started out making romantic comedies in the Qiong Yao style. Hou's films *The Boys from Fengkuei* (*Fenggui Lai de Ren*, 1983), *A Summer at Grandpa's* (*Dongdong de Jiaqi*, 1984), *The Time to Live and the Time to Die* (*Tongnian Wangshi*, 1985) and *Dust in the Wind* (*Lian Lian Feng Chen*, 1986) were based on the memories of screenwriters Wu Nien-Jen, Chu Tien-Wen (one of Taiwan's most distinguished novelists) and Hou himself.

Hou's works were a hybrid of Japanese film aesthetics (especially that of Ozu Yasujiro), Italian neo-realism and Western modernism – witness his use of ellipsis and off-screen sound in *A City of Sadness* (*Beiqing Chengshi*, 1989), *The Puppetmaster* (*Xi Meng Rensheng*, 1993) and *Good Men, Good Women* (*Hao Nan Hao Nü*, 1995). Where his earlier films had been concerned with small, personal stories and were often overtly autobiographical, from *A City of Sadness* onwards Hou became a self-appointed historian of Taiwan in the 20th century. *A City of Sadness* charts the lives of one family between 1945 and 1947, and broke a national taboo in discussing the

(Above)
Jonathan Chang as Yang Yang in
Edward Yang's masterful family
drama 'A One and a Two' (2000).

February 28th Incident, in which the Kuomintang massacred protestors in Taipei in 1947. The film confirmed Hou's status as the leader of the pack when it won the Golden Lion prize at the Venice Film Festival.

The other major Taiwanese film director of this era, Edward Yang, also won international recognition. Yang was a former computer engineer who was inspired by the likes of Werner Herzog to become a filmmaker. He enrolled and then dropped out of film school, and his directorial career began with his contribution to the portmanteau film *In Our Time*. His great films include *That Day, on the Beach (Haitan de Yitian, 1983)*, *Taipei Story (Qing Mei Zhu Ma, 1985)*, *The Terrorizers (Kongbu Fenzi, 1986)*, the epic 1960s-set *A Brighter Summer Day (Guling Jie Shaonian Sharen Shijian, 1991)* and the brilliantly observed family drama *A One and a Two (Yi Yi, 2000)*, for which Yang won the Best Director prize at Cannes in 2000. In contrast to his colleagues, Yang's works demonstrated a strong introspective style, influenced by Ingmar Bergman and Michelangelo Antonioni. Yang was the most intellectual of the New Wave – his sharp and analytic views on modernisation and the global economic system, and his disdain for the hypocrisy of a Confucian society, made him a true philosopher of the late 20th century. He could also be cynical and disillusioned with the world, as revealed in *A Confucian Confusion (Duli Shidai, 1994)* and *Mahjong (Majiang, 1996)*, and he remained a loner who was in conflict

The Time to Live and the Time to Die

Hou Hsiao-Hsien, 1985

The Time to Live and the Time to Die **is my all-time favourite. During the past 20 years I have watched the film over 20 times with new discoveries each time. It is almost organic with its seamless merge of form and content: the form so experimental and unique but not calling attention to itself. The content: revelatory at different viewings at different stages of my life**

with the authorities and the press until his tragic death in LA in 2007.

There were also other, less well-known figures in this New Cinema era: directors such as Chang Yi, Wang Jen, Ko I-Chen and Roy Tsang; novelists turned screenwriters such as Chu Tian-Wen, Hsiao Ye, Huang Chun-Ming and Wu Nien-Jen (who as well as being a prolific screenwriter, acted in Edward Yang's *Yi Yi*, *Taipei Story* and *Mahjong*, and also directed films himself, including *A Borrowed Life* [*Duo-sang*, 1994]); critics like Edmond Wong, Jan Hong-Chi and this author; and technical people like Liao Ching-Sung, Mark Lee, Tu Duu-Chih. All were instrumental in consolidating the movement.

The 1990s: the 'Second Wave'

In the 1990s, a 'Second Wave' emerged, even as the market for Taiwanese films dwindled. If the first 'New Wave' filmmakers expressed collective memories and consciously worked to assert a Taiwanese identity, those of the 'Second Wave' were more individualistic and postmodern.

The most successful of them has been Ang Lee (Li An), whose work has reflected Taiwanese approaches to Confucianism and patriarchy. Lee's films, in whatever genre he has worked, are characterised by their attempts to elucidate binary contrasts, whether between man and woman, East and West, parents and children, gay and straight, mainstream and marginal, tradition and modernity. Lee made his feature debut with *Pushing Hands* (*Tui Shou*, 1991), the first film in his so-called 'father trilogy', which also includes *The Wedding Banquet* (*Xi Yan*, 1993), and *Eat Drink Man Woman* (*Yin Shi Nan Nü*, 1994). These three films focus on an individual renegotiating traditional values in a modern society.

Lee first worked with the American producer and writer James Shamus on *Pushing Hands*, and together they went on to achieve great critical and financial success, with Lee travelling back and forth from Hollywood to Taiwan. Following *The Wedding Banquet* and *Eat Drink Man Woman*, Lee's success abroad continued through such films as *The Ice Storm* (1997), *Brokeback Mountain* (2005) and *Life of Pi* (2012). *Crouching Tiger, Hidden Dragon* (*Wo Hu Cang Long*, 2000) was another milestone, becoming the all-time box-office champion for foreign films in North America.

Tsai Mingliang is another prominent figure of the 'Second Wave'. The world in Tsai's films is filled with despair, frustration, alienation, nihilism and an inability to communicate with others. Critics have cited Brecht and Fassbinder to describe his minimalist aesthetic style. Perhaps because of his background in theatre, Tsai's work reveals a certain obsession with confined and segmented space. His protagonists invariably suffer from humiliation and maladjustment in an all-too-depressing postmodern environment. *Rebels of the Neon God* (*Qing Shaonian Nezha*, 1992), *Vive L'amour* (*Aiqing Wansui*, 1993) and *The River* (*Heliu*, 1997) mark the trajectory of his characters' descent into self-exile and isolation. In Tsai's cinema, family is a burden and the individual is reduced to a sex organ or a machine to indulge his personal desires/libido. Be it an allegory or a fancy, Tsai's later films mix absurdity and illusion as a profound critique of the banality of existence in a fatalistic society, as in *The Hole* (*Dong* 1998) and *What Time is it There?* (*Ni Na Bian Ji Dian*, 2001). Tsai's *Goodbye, Dragon Inn* (*Bu San*, 2003) takes place at the Fu-Ho Grand cinema in Taipei on the night of its final-ever screening – of King Hu's *Dragon Gate Inn*. The film makes a link to the Taiwanese cinema of the past, while also a commenting on how the great communal experience of watching a film in a cinema is being lost.

Into the new millennium

The 1990s saw difficult and anxious times return to Taiwan. Earthquakes,

SARS, the transference of political power from the KMT to the rival party DPP, further economic recession, the constant threat of missiles from China... At the same time, Taiwanese films struggled in the international and domestic market, as US trade representatives pressured the KMT government to lift Taiwan's foreign film screen quota system. Taiwanese-produced films barely managed to hold on to a market share of 1 per cent in these years. All the state-owned studios folded, and there was little financial investment in films. Interesting new directors like Stan Lai, Chen Kuo-Fu, Chang Tso-Chi (Zhang Zuoqi), Yee Chih-Yan, Ho Ping, and Wu Nian-Jen emerged, but could not save the industry.

Both Hou and Tsai eventually lost their domestic audience as their films become more recondite. International critics called them 'transnational auteurs' as they received money from Japan, France and other European countries – *Café Lumiere* (*Kohi Jikou*, 2003), *Three Times* (*Zhi Hao de Shiguang*, 2005) and *Flight of the Red Balloon* (2007) in Hou's case, and *I Don't Want to Sleep Alone* (*Hei Yanqan*, 2006), *Face* (*Lian*, 2009) and *Stray Dogs* (*Jiao You*, 2013) in Tsai's.

Then in 2008 a small film shocked everyone in Taiwan. *Cape No. 7* (*Hai Jiao Qihao*), an effervescent comedy about a group of quirky losers in southern Taiwan who put together a band to play at a concert, has become the second highest-grossing film in Taiwan's history after *Avatar* (2009), taking US$17 million.

Cape No. 7 embraced ordinary people from diverse ethnic and class backgrounds and (temporarily, at least) healed the wounds of a society scarred by political splits. Director Wei Te-Sheng has gone on to become the symbolic leader of a new film culture that emphasises Taiwanese national pride. Films of this new movement typically use the Taiwanese dialect, highlight local customs and honour local values. They tend to be market-oriented and share a subtle antagonism towards the centre of mainstream culture in the north, Taipei – instead finding a new sense of identity defined by southern and rural Taiwan.

Recent years have seen a diverse range of genre films find a youthful audience in Taiwan, such as the gangster film *Monga* (*Meng Jia*, 2010), the rowdy comedy *Night Market Hero* (*Jipai Yingxiong*, 2011), the cop thriller *Black and White: Episode One, Dawn of Assault* (*Yingxiong Shoubuqu: Quanmian Kaizhan*, 2011), the romantic comedy *Love* (*Ai*, 2012) and the melodrama *Din Tao: Leader of the Parade* (*Din Tao*, 2012). In 2011 the medium-budget comedy *You Are the Apple of My Eye* (*Naxienian, Women Yiqi de Nuhai*) became the highest-grossing Taiwanese film of all time at the Hong Kong, Singapore and China box offices. Some films have clandestinely carried a nostalgic yearning for the colonial past; Wei Te-Sheng, with *Warriors of the Rainbow: Seediq Bale* (*Sai De Ke Ba Lai*, 2012), depicted the 1930 Wushe indigenous rebellion against the Japanese. At the same time, documentary filmmaking is thriving in Taiwan, and even if the films are often mawkishly sentimental, all typically offer signifiers of Taiwanese national pride.

It's as if Taiwan has come full circle, back to the problem of national identity. The reality remains: can the Taiwanese market sustain its local film industry? Do Taiwanese films need China as a primary or secondary market? Chen Kuo-fu, Leste Chen, Stan Lai and Tom Lin have all moved to China for various projects. Doze Niu, director of *Monga* and *Love*, has signed with the Huayi Brothers in China, as has Tsai Yueh Hsun of *Black and White: Episode One, Dawn of Assault*; even Hou Hsiao-Hsien's forthcoming swordplay film, *The Assassin*, secured half its budget from China.

To China or not to China – that remains the essential dilemma for Taiwanese cinema. ☉

FILM STARS AND STARDOM IN CHINA

By Yingjin Zhang

To Western viewers, the mention of Chinese film stars may prompt images of Gong Li and Zhang Ziyi, two female stars brought into the international spotlight in the 1990s. For those who have tracked Chinese cinema for longer, the America-born, Chinese-American actress Anna May Wong from the 1920s may come to mind, and Bruce Lee's image has, of course, been ubiquitous since the 1970s. The roles made famous by these two ethnically Chinese stars – the evil, scheming 'Oriental' slave-girl and the fierce, bare-chested martial artist — helped to define a spectrum for the international reception of Chinese film stars. It is against such an entrenched overseas Orientalism that Chinese cinema has developed its own system of stardom over the past century.

Emergence: 1920s-40s

The Chinese star system emerged in the early 1920s when feature-length films began to be made in Shanghai. The first stars to attract audiences were female. In the early 1930s, roles depicting traditional, virtuous women, who endured miseries with resilience on screen, helped bring fame to actresses like Hu Die – crowned the movie queen by popular vote in 1933, and best known for her dual roles in *Twin Sisters* (*Zimei Hua*, 1933) – and Ruan Lingyu, the luminous lead in such films as *The Goddess* (*Shennü*, 1934), whose career ended prematurely in a tragic suicide.

By the mid-1930s, however, a new group of female actresses such as Li Lili and Wang Renmei began to project refreshing new personas; they embodied, on and off screen, the fashionable image of the sporty 'modern girl', with their athletic physiques and professional training in song and dance. A comparison between *The Goddess* and *Queen of Sports* (*Tiyu Huanghou*, 1934) nicely illustrates the change. In the former, Ruan Lingyu portrays a self-sacrificing streetwalker determined to give her son a proper education, while in the latter Li Lili plays an athlete whose attractive body is frequently displayed in public.

By contrast, male stars of the 1930s, such as the Korean-Chinese Jin Yan, whose roles include *The Highway* (*Da Lu*, 1934), were not as prominent in the Shanghai industry. The ensuing war with Japan, however, gave spoken dialogue a new lease of life as part of patriotic war mobilisation efforts during the late 1930s and early 1940s, and it became increasingly important to an actor's success. Male stars like Zhao Dan and female stars like Bai Yang, both featured in *Crossroads* (*Shizi Jietou*, 1937), became key figures in these spoken dramas. Meanwhile, a few actresses, such as Chen Yunshang, found stardom in occupied

Ruan Lingyu

Hu Die

Li Lili (left) in 'Queen of Sports' (1934)

Shanghai, in such films as *Mulan Joins the Army* (*Mulan Cong Jun*, 1939).

The brief pre-1949 postwar phase saw the maturation of the early period of Chinese stardom, as both male and female leads such as Shi Hui and Li Lihua delivered outstanding performances in films like *Phoney Phoenixes* (*Jia Feng Xu Huang*, 1947), especially in genres like melodrama and comedy.

Divergence: 1950s-70s

After 1949, in its effort to eradicate the influence of Hollywood, the PRC immediately promoted a series of new stars – even though very the term 'star' was frequently avoided for its connection to bourgeois lifestyles and capitalist culture. The term 'film workers' was preferred, suggesting as it did that film stars were the equal of workers in other fronts of socialist construction — factory workers, rural farmers and army soldiers, the officially designated three principal audiences for arts and literature.
The lead performers from the pre-1949 era were quickly removed in the 1950s to pave the way for a new line-up. Among them were Tian Hua and Zhang Ruifang, whose facial features and strong physiques were meant to embody revolutionary heroism and the socialist spirit. In films such as *The White-Haired Girl* (*Baimao Nü*, 1950) and *Li Shuangshuang* (1962), they provided onscreen models for the audience to emulate and thus promoted communist ideals. As an exception to his pre-1949 fellow stars who had seen their careers ended, Zhao Dan continued to build on his screen persona, transforming himself into historical heroes with his titular roles in *Nie Er* and *Lin Zexu* (both 1959). But even he was incarcerated during the Cultural Revolution, and deprived of any chance of screen acting.

As a neutral zone during the Cold War, Hong Kong cinema rapidly developed into a regional powerhouse, where both the 'left-wing' (pro-the PRC) and the 'right-wing' (pro-Taiwan) studios actively promoted their own line-ups of stars in the 1950s and 60s: the former introducing Wu Chufang (*Spring* [*Chun*, 1953]) and Xia Meng (*New Widow* [*Xingua*, 1956]), and the latter Lin Dai (*The Kingdom and the Beauty* [*Jiangshan Meiren*, 1959]) and Zhong Qin (*Peach Blossom River* [*Taohua Jiang*, 1956]). From the mid-1950s to the mid-1960s, female stars like Ge Lan (*Mambo Girl* [*Manbo Nülang*, 1957]) and Ling Bo (*The Love Eterne* [*Liang Shanbo yü Zhu Yingtai*, 1963]) dominated the Hong Kong screen in both Cantonese and Mandarin cinema, especially in such genres as the ancient costume drama, the musical and the melodrama – variously promoting delicate femininity, youth culture and urban modernity. Indeed, two major Mandarin studios, Shaw Brothers and Cathay, engaged in fierce competition to lure leading stars from each other, with many stars moving back and forth between them. Likewise, Cantonese cinema produced its own female stars in the 1960s, such as Feng Baobao and

Zhao Dan in 'Nie Er' (1959)

Josephine Siao, the stars of such films as *Seven Princesses* (*Qi Gongzhu*, 1967).

But the pendulum swung to the other extreme when the martial-arts genre took over the market from the late 1960s to the late 1970s, and male stars like 'Jimmy' Wang Yu performed the sadomasochistic stunts of the one-armed swordsmen. Before his premature death in 1973, Bruce Lee brought this kind of tough masculinity to international prominence in films such as *Fist of Fury* (*Jingwu Men*, 1972) and the Hong Kong-USA co-production *Enter the Dragon* (1973).

Taiwan relied on Hong Kong to develop its film industry, and Hong Kong stars saturated the Taiwanese market during the 1950s and 60s. In the 1970s, however, Taiwan found its own niche in the genre of the tear-jerking romance, which became the foundation of its own star system, one that featured two female Lins (Lin Fengjiao and Brigitte Lin Ching Hsia) and two male Qins (Qin Han and Qin Xianglin) as appealing screen lovers. By the late 1970s, the migration of Taiwanese stars like Brigitte Lin and Sylvia Chang to Hong Kong constituted a reverse cross-border flow.

Convergence: 1980s-present

In the contemporary period, an unprecedented convergence of film talents in all three geopolitical territories of China has gradually taken place. In mainland China, male stars have transformed from handsome young men like Tang Guoqiang — the screen equivalent to the stage *xiaosheng* — in such films as *Peacock Princess* (*Kongque Gongzhu*, 1981), to rough masculinity, as embodied by Jiang Wen in *Red Sorghum* (*Hong Gaoliang*, 1987) and *Devils on the Doorstep* (*Guizi Lai Le*, 2000). Many different types of masculinity have been projected by male stars, most noticeably Ge You, who embodies the everyday man in films such as *Big Shot's Funeral* (*Da Wan*, 2001), and is beloved for his verbal humour.

Female stars have also seen their screen personas change – from suffering women (as embodied by Liu Xiaoqing in *Hibiscus Town* [*Furong Zhen*, 1986]) to fashionable youth idols (as personified

Zhang Ziyi and Kaneshiro Takeshi in 'House of Flying Daggers' (2004)

by such figures as Xu Jinglei in films such as *Go Lala Go!* [*Du Lala Shengzhi Ji*, 2010]), while international stardom has been attained by the likes of Gong Li and Zhang Ziyi, two figures of exotic but resilient 'Oriental' femininity.

In Hong Kong, after the Cantonese and the Mandarin industries merged into one in the late 1980s, an eminent group of film stars emerged, often in connection with the 'Canto-pop' scene – figures like Leslie Cheung, Andy Lau and Anita Mui. The Hong Kong New Wave directors and their commercial counterparts further pushed these new stars to international prominence — Jackie Chan and Michelle Yeoh for their daredevil action stunts, Jet Li for his marvellous martial-arts skills, Chow Yun-Fat for his cool gangster persona, Maggie Cheung for her graceful femininity, and Tony Leung Chiu Wai for his irresistible romantic charm. Since the late 1990s, a younger group of stars,

among them Kaneshiro Takeshi and Leo Lai, have become active in Hong Kong, but their star power still pales in comparison with their predecessors.

New Taiwan Cinema, meanwhile, emphasised non-professional acting and did not produce major stars, except for Chang Chen, who made his debut in Edward Yang's *A Brighter Summer Day* (*Guling Jie Shaonian Sha Ren Shijian*, 1991). However, the new century has seen increasing collaborations between Hong Kong, Taiwan and mainland stars in such blockbusters as Zhang Yimou's *Hero* (*Yingxiong*, 2002), whose cast includes Jet Li, Chen Daoming and Zhang Ziyi from the mainland, and Tony Leung Chiu Wai and Maggie Cheung from Hong Kong, and John Woo's *Red Cliff I-II* (*Chibi*, 2008, 2009), starring Tony Leung Chiu Wai alongside Chang Chen from Taiwan and Zhao Wei from the mainland.

Typically, the formula for domestic success now is an all-star gala, which has transformed star appeal from nuanced performance to visual spectacle. Regardless, in the international scene, Chinese film stars still vacillate between belligerent masculinity and oppressed femininity, as once defined by the personas of Anna May Wong and Bruce Lee, and as recently evident in *Memoirs of a Geisha* (2005), starring Zhang Ziyi and Gong Li, and *The Forbidden Kingdom* (2008), starring Jet Li and Jackie Chan. ⊙

Jet Li in 'Hero' (2002)

FILM INDEX

Edward Anderson is a curator of non-fiction at the BFI National Archive and specialises in amateur film. He is currently curating a programme of archive films of China made between 1901-49 for exhibition at BFI Southbank and on the BFI Player.

Robin Baker is head curator at the BFI National Archive.

John Berra is a lecturer in film and language studies at Tsinghua University. He is the co-editor of *World Film Locations: Beijing* and *World Film Locations: Shanghai*.

Chris Berry is professor of film studies at King's College London. In the 1980s, he worked for China Film Import and Export Corporation in Beijing, and his academic research is grounded in work on Chinese cinema. His most recent BFI book is *Chinese Films in Focus II*.

Michael Berry is professor of contemporary chinese cultural studies and director of the East Asia Center at the University of California, Santa Barbara. He is the author of *Speaking in Images: Interviews with Contemporary Chinese Filmmakers, A History of Pain: Trauma in Modern Chinese Literature and Film*, the BFI Film Classic on Jia Zhangke's *The Hometown Trilogy* and *Boiling the Sea: Hou Hsiao-hsien's Memories of Shadows and Light*. He is also the translator of several novels, including *The Song of Everlasting Sorrow* (with Susan Chan Egan), *To Live, Nanjing 1937: A Love Story* and *Wild Kids: Two Novels About Growing Up*.

Peggy Chiao is a film producer, writer and professor. She is considered one of the most important figures in shaping New Taiwan Cinema in the 1980s and 90s. She has produced over 22 features, seven documentaries and three television series. Her filmography includes *Beijing Bicycle, Betelnut Beauty, The Hole, A Portrait of Hou Hsiao Hsien* and, most recently, *The Lord of Shanghai*. She was the founder of the China Express Film Award, which became the Taipei International Film Festival.

Victor Fan is lecturer at the department of film studies, King's College London, specialising in Chinese cinemas and contemporary Hollywood. He was assistant professor at the department of East Asian studies, McGill University, and graduated with a PhD. from the film studies program and the comparative literature department of Yale University. His book *Cinema Approaching Reality: Locating Chinese Film Theory* will be published in 2015 by the University of Minnesota Press.

Grady Hendrix is one of the founders of the New York Asian Film Festival and was the guest editor of *Film Comment's* May/June 2014 special issue on Hong Kong cinema.

Kevin B. Lee is a filmmaker, critic and video essayist. He is founding editor and chief video essayist of *Fandor Keyframe* and founding partner of dGenerate Films, a distribution company for independent Chinese cinema. In 2013 he co-curated the film series 'Chinese Realities / Documentary Visions' at the Museum of Modern Art in New York. He has written on Chinese cinema for *Cineaste, Moving Image Source* and *Senses of Cinema*, and has also written for *The New York Times, Sight & Sound, Slate* and *Indiewire*.

Li Zhen is a film historian at the China Film Archive.

Tony Rayns is a London-based critic, filmmaker and festival programmer. He has been a frequent visitor to Hong Kong, China and Taiwan since 1977. He co-organised the world's first historical retrospective of Chinese cinema at London's National Film Theatre in 1980 (and a larger follow-up event in 1985), and visited Beijing Film Academy for a semester as a guest lecturer in 1987. He has made four documentaries about Chinese cinema for Channel 4 TV, and has helped many Chinese film-makers (including Jia Zhangke, Hou Hsiao-Hsien and Wong Kar Wai) with the English subtitles for their films..

Bérénice Reynaud is the author of *Nouvelles Chines, nouveaux cinémas* (Cahiers du cinéma,1999) and the BFI Modern Classic on Hou Hsiao Hsien's *A City of Sadness*. Her writing has been published in *Sight & Sound, Film Comment, CinemaScope, Senses of Cinema, Cahiers du cinéma, Le Monde diplomatique* and *Libération*, among others.

Peter Rist is a professor of film studies in the Mel Hoppenheim School of Cinema at Concordia University in Montreal, Canada, and has served as chair of the school (formerly the Department of Cinema) for eight years. His most recent book, *Historical Dictionary of South American Cinema*, has just been published by Rownam and Littelfield, and he has written extensively on East Asian films and filmmakers.

Yuqian Yan is a PhD student in cinema and media studies and East Asian literature and civilisation at the University of Chicago.

Yingjin Zhang is professor of Chinese literature at University of California, San Diego. His recent books include *Screening China* (2002), *Chinese National Cinema* (2004), *From Underground to Independent* (2006), *Cinema, Space, and Polylocality in a Globalizing China* (2010), *Chinese Film Stars* (2010), *A Companion to Chinese Cinema* (2012), and *New Chinese-Language Documentaries* (Routledge, 2014)

SUGGESTIONS FOR FURTHER READING

The History of the Development of Chinese Cinema Chen Jihua (Chinese Film Press, 1965)

Dianying: An Account of Films and the Film Audience in China Jay Leyda (MIT Press, 1972)

Chinese Cinema: Culture and Politics Since 1949 Paul Clark (Cambridge University Press, 1987)

Hong Kong Cinema: The Extra Dimensions Stephen Teo (BFI, 1997)

Planet Hong Kong: Popular Cinema and the Art of Entertainment David Bordwell (Harvard University Press, 2000)

'Labyrinth of Chances' (on Shanghai cinema of the 1930s) Tony Rayns (*Sight & Sound* magazine, July 2001 issue)

A City of Sadness Bérénice Reynaud (BFI Modern Classic, 2002)

Chinese Films in Focus: 25 New Takes edited by Chris Berry (BFI, 2003)

Kung Fu Cult Masters: From Bruce Lee to Crouching Tiger Leon Hunt (Wallflower, 2003)

Chinese National Cinema Yingjin Zhang (Routledge, 2004)

An Amorous History of the Silver Screen: Shanghai Cinema, 1896-1937 Zhang Zhen (University of Chicago Press, 2006)

China on Screen: Cinema and Nation Chris Berry and Mary Farquhar (Columbia University Press, 2006)

Speaking in Images: Interviews with Contemporary Chinese Filmmakers Michael Berry (Columbia University Press, 2006)

Chinese Films in Focus II edited by Chris Berry (BFI, 2008)

Chinese Martial Arts Cinema: The Wuxia Tradition Stephen Teo (Edinburgh University Press, 2009)

Jia Zhangke's 'Hometown Trilogy' (Xiao Wu, Platorm, Unknown Pleasures) Michael Berry (BFI Film Classic, 2009)

The Chinese Cinema Book edited by Song Hwee Lim and Julian Ward (BFI/Palgrave Macmillan, 2011)

A Companion to Chinese Cinema edited by Yingjin Zhang (Wiley-Blackwell, 2012)

PICTURE CREDITS

All images courtesy of BFI National Archive/Special Collections or the China Film Archive except: p115 (top & middle), p116 (both images), p125 (top and middle) courtesy of the Hong Kong Film Archive; p37 photograph by Zhang Yaxin courtesy of +see gallery in Beijing; inside cover, p5, p47, p67, p71 (top) courtesy of the Kobal Collection; p51, p81 (top left) courtesy of the Ronald Grant Archive; p114 (bottom) © Kong Chiao Film Company, courtesy of the Hong Kong Film Archive; p115 © Cathay-Keris Films Pte. Ltd, courtesy of the Hong Kong Film Archive; p89 gallery of images from *West of the Tracks* courtesy Documentary Educational Resources; p17, p18 (top & bottom), p20 (top & bottom), p21 (top & middle), p22, p26, p57, p58 (top and bottom), p59, p60 (top left & top right), p61, p63 (top & bottom), p96 (bottom), p97 (top & bottom), p103 courtesy of Tony Rayns.

ACKNOWLEDGEMENTS

Thank you to all of the contributors. Thanks for their advice and assistance to Edward Anderson, Robin Baker, Jack Bell and Jen Davies at Park Circus, Chris Berry, Lorraine Caldwell at TIFF, Noah Cowan, Rhidian Davis, David Edgar, Jane Giles, Satwant Gill, Wendy Hau at the Hong Kong Film Archive, Nick James, David Jenkins, Kevin B. Lee, Robert Lundberg at China Lion Film Distribution, Pippa Selby, Heather Stewart, Hsi-Wen Yang at the Taipei Representative Office in the UK, Jacky Xing, Rob Winter and Juliane Zenke. Special thanks to Lisa Kerrigan, Jamie McLeish, Lan Zhang at the China Film Archive, Chanel Kong for her invaluable help, and to Christopher Brawn, this book's designer. Particular thanks to Tony Rayns for his encouragement and expert advice, and for the generous loan of many rare stills and DVDs.

A CENTURY OF CHINESE CINEMA SEASON

Main Sponsor

Season Sponsors

With special thanks to Cathay Pacific Airways

1896

The Lumière brothers' *cinématographe* is shown for the first time in China, on 11 August in Xu Garden, Shanghai

1905

The Battle of Dingjunshan becomes the first film made in China by a Chinese filmmaker

1909

Benjamin Brodsky founds the Hong Kong-based film company Yaxiya (Asia), and also establishes the Xinmin Film Company. Lai Man-Wai produces *Stealing a Roast Duck*

1911

The Xinhai revolution overthrows the Qing dynasty

1912

The Republic of China is founded

1913

Lai Man-Wai makes *Zhuangzi Tests His Wife*, the first Hong Kong film

1916

Lai Man-Wai establishes the Huanxian Motion Picture Company. Huanxian makes what is probably the first multi-reel film in China, *Lost Souls on the Black [Opium] Register*

1919

The May Fourth Movement begins

1920

Gu Kenfu founds the magazine *Yingxi Zazhi (Motion Picture Review)*

1921

Yan Ruisheng, the first Chinese feature film, based on a real criminal case about the murder of a prostitute, is made in Shanghai

1922

Lai Man-Wai and Lai Buk-Hoi establish the Minxin (China Sun) Motion Picture Company. Zhang Shichuan and Zheng Zhengqiu buy Brodsky's Xinmin and turn it into the Mingxing (Star) Motion Picture Co. Zhang Shichuan makes *Love's Labours*. It is the oldest surviving Chinese fiction film

1925

Runje Shaw (Shao Zuiweng) establishes the Tianyi (Unique)

Spring in a Small Town (1948)

Film Company in Shanghai

1926

Film director Hou Yao publishes the screenwriting manual *Yingxi Juben Zuofa (Methods of Writing a Shadow Play)*

1927

Hou Yao makes *Romance of the Western Chamber* at China Sun in Shanghai. Dan Duyu makes *Cave of the Silken Web*

1928

Star's *wuxia* film *Burning of the Red Lotus Temple* is a huge hit, and becomes an ongoing series, with 18 parts made by 1931

1930

Luo Mingyou (Lo Ming-yau) and Lai Man-Wai establish the Lianhua Film Company (United Photoplay Service) in Shanghai

1931

Zhang Shichuan makes the first Chinese sound film *Sing-Song Girl Red Peony*, starring Cantonese actress Hu Die (Butterfly Wu), using sound-on-disc technology

1933

Cheng Bugao directs the social realist *Spring Silkworms*. Sun Yu makes *Daybreak*, starring Li Lili, at United Photoplay Service

1934

Sun Yu's *The Highway* is released. Lily Yuen (Ruan Lingyu) stars in Wu Yonggang's *The Goddess* and Cai Chusheng's *New Women*. The Denton (Diantong) production company is founded in Shanghai, and it produces China's first sound-on-film 'talkie': *Plunder of Peach and Plum*

1935

Ruan Lingyu commits suicide at the age of 24. Yuan Muzhi makes *Scenes of City Life*

1937

Shen Xiling makes the social comedy *Crossroads*. Yuan Muzhi makes *Street Angel*. Ma-Xu Weibang directs *Song at Midnight*, the first Chinese horror film. Shanghai's Chinese city falls to the Japanese

1939

In the 'Orphan Island' period in Shanghai, Richard Poh makes *Mulan Joins the Army* for the Hwa Cheng Studio

1940

The Wan brothers make *Princess Iron-Fan*, the first Chinese animated feature film

1942

Kawakita Nagamasa is appointed by the Japanese government to head the remaining Chinese film industry in Shanghai

1947

The Peak Film Industries Corporation produces the two-part *Spring River Flows East*. In the former Manchuria, Jin Shan directs *Along the Sungzri River*

1948

Fei Mu's masterpiece *Spring in a Small Town* is released. In Hong Kong, Zhou Xuan stars in Fang Peilin's *wenyi pian* 'sing-song girl' musical *Song of a Songstress*

1949

The People's Republic of China is founded. The ruling Communist Party is led by Chairman Mao Zedong. Wang Bin's *The Bridge* is the first feature made in the PRC. Zheng Junli's *Crows and Sparrows* is released by The Peak. The first kung fu film, *Wong Fei-hung: The Whip That Smacks the Candle*, is released in Hong Kong

1950

Shui Hua and Wang Bin's *The White Haired Girl* helps establish the new national model for storytelling and character portrayal. Shi Hui makes *This Whole Life of Mine*

1951

An anonymous editorial published in the *People's Daily* national newspaper accuses Sun Yu's *The Life of Wu Xun* (1950) of being politically incorrect in praising philanthropy over revolution. This unsigned work of film criticism was in fact written by Chairman Mao, and has a major influence over future film production

1953

Lee Tit's Cantonese film *In the Face of Demolition* is released in Hong Kong

1954

Sang Hu and Huang Sha's filmed version of the classic Shaoxing opera *Liang Shanbo and Zhu Yingtai* becomes the PRC's first colour production

1956

Sang Hu makes *New Year Sacrifice*. Lü Ban directs the bold satire *Before the New Director Arrives*

1958

Run Run Shaw founds Shaw Brothers in Hong Kong

1961

Xie Jin's *The Red Detachment of Women* is released. It marries the spirit of pre-war leftist films with the Maoist model

1962

Lu Ren's *Li Shuangshuang* is released

1963

Li Hanxiang's *The Love Eterne* becomes a huge box-office hit in Hong Kong and Taiwan. The Communist Party's official history of Chinese cinema, edited by Cheng Jihua, is published

1964

The Shanghai Animation Film Studio makes *Uproar in Heaven*. Li Xing's 'Healthy Realism' film *Oyster Girls* is made in Taiwan

1965

Xie Jin's *Two Stage Sisters* is completed but not released until after the Cultural Revolution. King Hu makes the influential *wuxia* film *Come Drink With Me* in Hong Kong

1966

The Cultural Revolution begins

1967

Shaw Brothers release Chang Cheh's *The One-Armed Swordsman*. Lung Kong makes *The Story of a Discharged Prisoner*

1969

King Hu's *A Touch of Zen* is released in Taiwan

1970

The film version of *The Red Detachment of Women*, a 'revisioning' of the story of Xie Jin's 1961 film, first presented on stage, is released. It is one of the 'model operas' of the Cultural Revolution period. Cecile Tang makes her debut film *The Arch*

1972

Jay Leyda publishes his pioneering English-language account of Chinese film history, *Dianying – Electric Shadows*

1973

Bruce Lee dies aged 32

1978

The 36th Chamber of Shaolin is released. Jackie Chan stars in *Drunken Master*

1979

Ann Hui, Tsui Hark and other film school-trained directors move from TV to filmmaking in Hong Kong

1982

The 'Fifth Generation' filmmakers graduate from the Beijing Film Academy. Ann Hui's *Boat People* is released. Central Motion Picture Corp (the KMT-owned production company in Taiwan) starts to produce portmanteau films with episodes by such new directors as Edward Yang and Hou Hsiao-Hsien

1983

Hou Hsiao-Hsien makes *The Boys from Fengkuei*, his first independently produced film. Tsui Hark's *Zu: Warriors from the Magic Mountain* is released

1984

Johnny Mak makes the influential crime film *Long Arm of the Law*. Chen Kaige makes the seminal *Yellow Earth*, with cinematography by Zhang Yimou. It is first shown in 1985

1986

Xie Jin's *Hibiscus Town* is released. Tian Zhuangzhuang makes *The Horse Thief*. John Woo's *A Better Tomorrow* is released, sparking the 'Heroic Bloodshed' trend, and making a star of Chow Yun-Fat

1987

Zhang Yimou makes *Red Sorghum*, his first film as director. It makes a star of its lead actress, Gong Li. Their collaboration continues through such international successes as *Ju Dou* (1990), *Raise the Red Lantern* (1991) and *The Story of Qui Ju* (1992). Chen Kaige makes *King of the Children*

1989

The Tiananmen Square protests in Beijing. Hou Hsiao-Hsien's *A City of Sadness* wins the Golden Lion prize at the Venice Film Festival

1990

Wu Wenguang's *The Last Dreamers: Bumming in Beijing* is completed. It is the first authentically independent film made in China since 1949. Wong Kar Wai makes *Days of Being Wild*

1991

Zhang Yuan's *Mama* kick-starts the first wave of independent fiction filmmaking. Edward Yang's *A Brighter*

Still Life (2006)

Summer Day is released. Tsui Hark casts Jet Li in *Once Upon a Time in China*

1992

Stanley Kwan makes *Centre Stage*, starring Maggie Cheung as Ruan Lingyu, winning her the Best Actress prize in Venice

1993

Chen Kaige's *Farewell My Concubine* is released. It shares the Palme d'Or at Cannes with Jane Campion's *The Piano*. Wang Xiaoshuai makes his debut feature, *The Days*. Zhang Yuan makes *Beijing Bastards*. Ang Lee's *The Wedding Banquet* is released

1994

Wong Kar Wai's *Chungking Express* becomes an international hit

1996

The Film Bureau outlaws independent, unauthorised productions. Zhang Yuan makes *East Palace, West Palace*. Peter Chan's *Comrades: Almost a Love Story* is released

1997

Jia Zhangke's *Xiao Wu* is completed. Over the next couple of years it becomes the foundation stone for a second wave of independent filmmaking. Zhang Yang's *Spicy Love Soup* is released, as is Feng Xiaogang's *The Dream Factory*

1998

Jia Zhangke publishes his influential essay 'The Era of Amateur Cinema is Near'

2000

Ang Lee's *Crouching Tiger, Hidden Dragon* becomes an international hit. Jia Zhangke makes *Platform*. Jiang Wen makes *Devils on the Doorstep*. Wong Kar Wai's *In the Mood for Love* is released

2002

Zhang Yimou makes the *wuxia* epic *Hero*. The first part of Andrew Lau and Alan Mak's *Infernal Affairs* trilogy is released

2003

Wang Bing's nine-hour documentary *West of the Tracks* is shown at festivals around the world

2005

Johnnie To releases *Election,* the first film in what will become a two-part crime epic

2006

Ning Hao's *Crazy Stone* becomes a huge box-office hit in China. Jia Zhangke's *Still Life* wins the Golden Lion award at the Venice Film Festival

2010

Xu Jinglei directs and stars in *Go Lala Go!*

2012

The comedy *Lost in Thailand*, directed by actor Xu Zheng, becomes a box-office sensation in China

2013

Jia Zhangke's *A Touch of Sin* is released

2014

Diao Yinan's *Black Coal, Thin Ice* wins the Golden Bear award at the Berlin Film Festival. Run Run Shaw dies at the age of 106

Election (2005)